PhilanthropyRoundtable

Agenda Setting

A Wise Giver's Guide to Influencing Public Policy

John J. Miller and Karl Zinsmeister

with Ashley May

Current Wise Giver's Guides from The Philanthropy Roundtable

Karl Zinsmeister, *series editor*
For all current and future titles, visit PhilanthropyRoundtable.org/guidebook

TABLE OF CONTENTS

There are many ways to reform public policy. Meet donors

who are trying to build models that sidestep partisan conflict.
- Policy Player Profile Tom Carroll
- Policy Player Profile Fred Klipsch

If the group you seek doesn't exist, you need to create it.
- Policy Player Profile Dick Weekley
- Policy Player Profile Paul Brest

Not all public-policy philanthropy involves politics; more
donors are turning to litigation.
- Policy Player Profile Clint Bolick
- Policy Player Profile Seamus Hasson & Bill Mumma

Sometimes the ideas and leadership that philanthropists
contribute are as important as their money.
- Policy Player Profile Art Pope

Spot a problem in your own community, fix it in an
innovative way, and you might be surprised how your
work echoes on the national stage.
- Policy Player Profile Betsy DeVos

Serendipity is not a strategy, but some of the great
achievements in public-policy philanthropy were unexpected.

PREFACE

What is Public-Policy Philanthropy?
And Why Is It so Hard?

The traditional categories of philanthropy are familiar and broadly accepted: faith and religious works, medicine and health, scientific research and the advancement of knowledge, the education of young people, almsgiving and economic uplift, disaster relief, environmental conservation and stewardship, culture and the arts, and so on. It may not be self-evident that trying to reshape public policy is an equally worthy cause. Yet donating money to change public thinking and government policy has now taken its place next to service-centered giving as a constructive branch of philanthropy.

In its highest-octane version, policy philanthropy is sometimes combined with political contributions. Political giving, of course, is not tax-deductible, and must be done separately from charitable giving. But many of the leading-edge donors quoted in this book have found that charity is often more effective and lasting if supplemented by an intelligent mix of policy giving and political giving.

Education reformers, for instance, have learned that in addition to planting better schools, they need to hold policy and political umbrellas over the new seedlings to prevent them from being dashed in storms. Mind you, nearly all donors give away far more money on the charitable side than they do on the policy or politics sides. For instance, a *Chronicle of Philanthropy* analysis of the last Presidential cycle found that among America's top philanthropists, the ten who donated most to political campaigns—people like Sheldon Adelson and George Soros—gave many times more to charitable causes than to political causes.

Grants that aim to reform society's rules are sometimes controversial, but less so than in times past. Professor Stanley Katz has traced changing views on this matter:

> The early foundations mostly danced around public policy and denied that they sought policy influence. That remained characteristic until the mid-twentieth century, when the overtly policy-oriented behavior of the Ford Foundation, under the

leadership of McGeorge Bundy, evoked the congressional backlash of the Tax Reform Act of 1969. After that episode, the major
foundations were once again ostentatiously careful about taking
strong positions on matters of political contention. All that has
changed in the twenty-first century.

Today, many donors view public-policy reform as a necessary
adjunct to their efforts to improve lives directly. From charter schooling to creation of think tanks of all stripes, from tort reform to gay
advocacy, donors have become involved in many efforts to shape
opinion and law. This is perhaps inevitable given the mushrooming
presence of government in our lives. In 1930, just 12 percent of U.S.
GDP was consumed by government; by 2012 that had tripled to 36
percent. Unless and until that expansion of the state reverses, it is
unrealistic to expect the philanthropic sector to stop trying to have a
say in public policies.

Sometimes it's not enough to build a house of worship; one must
create policies that make it possible for people to practice their faith
freely within society. Sometimes it is not enough to pay for a scholarship;
one must change laws so that high-quality schools exist for scholarship
recipients to take advantage of. Sometimes it is not enough to fund cancer research; one must press for more sensible regulations that allow labs
and pharmaceutical companies to explore nature and follow economic
incentives that stoke innovation.

This is harder than it sounds. In public-policy reform, the choice
of goals will often involve fundamental questions about individual
freedom and responsibility, the scope of the state and social control,
and interpretations of human nature. Public-policy philanthropists
routinely confront not just rivals in tactics who share mutual goals,
but bitter opponents and even outright enemies who operate from
different principles entirely.

The final third of this book is a detailed list of the major projects
in public policy philanthropy undertaken in the U.S. over the last
182 years. Because one man's good deed is another man's calamity
when it comes to giving with political implications, we have included
policy advocacy of all sorts. We're not categorizing these as desirable
projects, just listing them because they are socially consequential (or
seem likely to be, in cases where they haven't yet run their course).
These are efforts that must be considered significant, whether you

admire or mourn the effect. Even those that don't succeed sometimes offer important lessons.

Public-policy philanthropy has special ways of mystifying and frustrating its practitioners. Investments in other types of philanthropy more often deliver clear results: scholarships lead to college degrees, research points to cures, and construction projects build symphony halls. Attempting to draw straight lines between acts of philanthropy and particular policy outcomes can be a maddening chore, however. Moreover, public-policy struggles never seem to end. Victories one year become defeats the next, then turn into comebacks, and setbacks, and on and on. A sense of philanthropic satisfaction often requires zen-like patience.

Perhaps nothing is easier than giving away money poorly. Dwight Macdonald once described the Ford Foundation (an aggressive practitioner of public-policy philanthropy) as "a large body of money completely surrounded by people who want some." There are endless ways to fail as a patron, particularly when you are trying to encourage public-policy solutions.

Where can philanthropists turn for honest, disinterested appraisals? A lesson from many walks of life—picking stocks, judging job applicants, scouting baseball players—shows a reliable way to predict future performance is to study past results. And so modern-day philanthropists in public policy would be wise to look at the examples of the donors who came before them. This book starts with the first stirrings of public-policy philanthropy in our pre-Civil War era, and runs through the explosion of activity in the latest two generations. By examining what their forerunners did and why, today's benefactors will improve their chances of meeting their goals and making a difference.

So this guidebook is a collection of case studies in applied philanthropy. Learn from them and you can dramatically improve your own efforts to alter the direction of American governance. To make this evidence easy and sometimes even enjoyable to absorb, we present it mostly in human stories. We hope they give both pleasure and new power to your philanthropy.

Adam Meyerson
President, The Philanthropy Roundtable

Karl Zinsmeister
Vice president, publications, The Philanthropy Roundtable

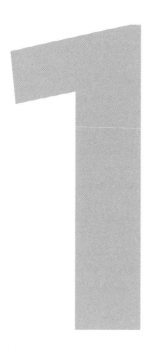

A Modern Home Run

Throughout the past generation, the Lynde and Harry Bradley Foundation has had as many successes in influencing public policy as any philanthropy in America. The foundation arguably made its greatest achievement in welfare reform. It did so by starting on the local level, creating a smashing triumph in its home state of Wisconsin, and then using potent ideas, savvy strategy, and patient funding to lead the way to a national transformation of the way our governments aid poor people.

By the mid-1980s, Wisconsin was more than ready for a fresh approach to welfare. Its benefits were generous, abuses were common, and the public was becoming fed up with the social dysfunction encouraged by having whole generations grow up dependent upon the "mailbox economy" of government checks. Wisconsin's low-income population was swelling rather than shrinking, as the state's generous welfare payments drew residents out of the work force, and made it a magnet for applicants from other places.

So the Bradley Foundation began a multiyear effort to uncover a better way. By the time Tommy Thompson was inaugurated as governor in 1987, Bradley had begun blazing a whole network of paths toward a new system. With practical, intellectual, and financial assistance for welfare reform from Bradley, Wisconsin's new chief executive committed his state to bold transformation. Though the social-work establishment resisted vehemently, insisting starvation and social disorder would result, Wisconsin's welfare rolls began to plummet.

Between 1989 and 1999, the fraction of families in the state relying on welfare shrank from over 7 percent to less than 2 percent. In Milwaukee, home to some of the hardest cases, the rate dropped from more than 15 percent to under 5 percent. People weren't simply kicked off welfare, they were required (and helped) to find jobs as a condition of receiving any public benefits. Contrary to gloomy predictions, most participants embraced that tradeoff. Other recipients decided they didn't need aid after all on those terms. As the work-for-welfare trade progressed, family and child poverty declined sharply, and indicators of well-being turned upward.

To lay the intellectual foundations for this triumph, Bradley both practiced its own brilliant public-policy philanthropy and built on successful public-policy philanthropy by other foundations. In 1982, social scientist Charles Murray had published a long article on welfare dependency in the *Public Interest*, an influential donor-supported journal co-edited by Irving Kristol. Special grants from the John M. Olin Foundation and the Smith Richardson Foundation allowed Murray to expand his essay into a pathbreaking book. *Losing Ground* added a persuasive polemic to the detailed social science that had been Murray's professional specialty up to that point, and it changed the national conversation about welfare when it was published in 1984.

This work came under fierce attack from defenders of the status quo. The *New York Times* editorial page blasted it as "unlikely to survive scrutiny," and "troubled by some big holes." A dozen years later, however, the *Times* confessed that Murray had written the "book that many people believe begat welfare reform."

The Bradley Foundation built upon what Murray, Olin, and Smith Richardson started with *Losing Ground*. One of its initial grants, for $300,000 in 1986, supported a yearlong seminar that brought together some of the country's top scholars on welfare, including both conservatives like Murray, Lawrence Mead, and Michael Novak, and liberals such as Franklin Raines, Robert Reischauer, and Alice Rivlin. Called the Working Seminar on Family and American Welfare Policy, it produced months of cooperative investigation, a series of research papers, and a final book-length highly readable report.

The seminar report, which Michael Novak drafted and shepherded to unanimous approval, sketched a remarkable new consensus. The conservatives in the group allowed that "a good society is judged by how well it cares for its most vulnerable members." The liberals acknowledged that "no able adult should be allowed voluntarily to take from the common good without also contributing to it."

Published as *The New Consensus on Family and Welfare Policy*, the book laid out many specific points of agreement. It described a pernicious form of poverty created by behavioral dependency rather than simple low income, and urged new policies that would emphasize work and family integrity. Its 1987 recommendations, observed economist Ron Haskins in 2006, "uncannily anticipated several major provisions of the 1996 reform legislation" that would transform the federal government's welfare policies. Additional intellectual contributions to the welfare debate flowed from the Bradley Foundation's support of Marvin Olasky, a University of Texas professor selected to investigate social policy in 1989 as a Bradley Fellow at the Heritage Foundation. In the stacks of the Library of Congress, Olasky later wrote, "I found some dusty old records from the nineteenth century. They weren't in the card catalogue, and it was obvious that nobody had looked at them in a long time." They described a dense network of grassroots organizations, none of them governmental, many of them religious, that had attacked poverty and social breakdown a hundred years prior—when disease, drink, overcrowded housing, lack of language and cultural skills among millions of immigrants, and other threats had been dealt with energetically.

Olasky had discovered the social-healing power of civil society in an earlier America. His eventual book, *The Tragedy of American Compassion*, suggested the effective nineteenth-century models of faith-based charity could be revived, and succeed today where the secular welfare state was failing. Local action, personal involvement, religious compassion, and private charity could fix many problems that cannot be touched by impersonal welfare bureaucracies. One welfare expert who heard this presented by Olasky was Jason Turner. Turner would go on to head Tommy Thompson's welfare-reform efforts in Wisconsin.

Another scholar who would advise the state of Wisconsin on its policies with support from the Bradley Foundation was Lawrence Mead of New York University. He had served on the Working Seminar on Family and American Welfare Policy. He also wrote two carefully researched books of his own showing that welfare recipients would have better lives if they were required to work and participate in the wider economy.

Politicians need more than enticing proposals before they take action, however. They need political comfort and cover. The Wisconsin Policy

> To lay the intellectual foundations for this triumph, Bradley both practiced its own brilliant public-policy philanthropy and built on successful public-policy philanthropy by other foundations.

Research Institute had been established with Bradley funding to help with important public debates exactly like this one. It joined the debate over welfare reform, putting out research papers and commissioning a series of opinion polls that became important to leaders in the state capital of Madison. Its survey research showed that voters wanted lawmakers to tackle welfare. "All of a sudden, everybody was reading WPRI's polls. The newspapers were printing stories on them," said Allen Taylor, who served as chairman of the Bradley Foundation. Both Republicans and Democrats paid attention when it became clear that welfare reform was popular on both sides of the public-opinion aisle.

The Thompson administration enacted a flurry of reforms at the county level and to some extent state level. They quickly showed striking results. In the early 1990s, a minor recession caused welfare rolls across America to expand—but in Wisconsin they actually shrank, as beneficiaries were converted into workers rather than recipients. That garnered attention.

Although many Democrats in the legislature had supported Thompson's initial agenda, by 1993 they thought the reforms had gone far enough. To press the brakes without getting blamed by the public for obstruction, they tried a risky political maneuver: They voted to abolish Wisconsin's welfare system entirely. They expected that Thompson would veto such a dramatic move, blurring perceptions about which party backed real change. Thompson decided to call their bluff and signed the bill.

This gave the governor a blank slate and chance to build an entirely new system. His state could apply new insights discovered by the various investigators backed by Bradley and other public-policy philanthropists. But he would have to do this under strict deadline, risking chaos if a substitute program couldn't be designed quickly to replace the old regime.

> Politicians need more than enticing proposals before they take action. They need political comfort and cover.

The administration needed lots of help to engineer the nuts and bolts of a new welfare structure that would be unlike anything in existence elsewhere. Traditionally, political leaders in the Badger State looked to professors at the University of Wisconsin for policy assistance of this sort. There was even a name for the tradition: the "Wisconsin Idea" was the notion that state-employed professors wouldn't just teach students in classrooms, but also serve taxpayers via policy recommendations.

The University of Wisconsin, however, had become a hotbed for radical politics. Professors in its social-welfare departments were for the most part doctrinaire leftists who hated the welfare-reform ideas that interested Bradley and Thompson and their allies. The Wisconsin welfare establishment had no intention of helping anyone replace the existing system.

So Thompson, relying heavily on the Bradley Foundation for rapid funding, turned to the Hudson Institute, a Midwestern think tank then based in Indianapolis. Hudson agreed to do much of the detailed research and design work needed to transform Wisconsin's system from its old focus on income maintenance to a new emphasis on supporting work by poor individuals. Bradley ponied up around $2 million, starting in 1994, to contribute to this crucial work.

"It was a terrific opportunity for us to look at welfare and say, 'Knowing what we now know about dependency, how can we build a new and improved system from scratch? And that's basically what we did," said Andrew Bush. He ran the special office that the Hudson Institute set up in Madison, with Bradley's support, to coordinate this work.

Bradley made non-financial contributions to the effort as well. After Jason Turner joined the Thompson administration, he and a group of colleagues visited the Milwaukee foundation and asked for introductions to community activists who received Bradley grants to address social ills, such as a church that ran a job-training program, a public-housing activist who encouraged marriage among inner-city girls, and innovative school and child-care programs. "The experience gave us the idea that we should get government out of the business of running welfare," said Turner. "This was an important insight for us."

In his memoir, *Power to the People*, Governor Thompson described the core principle that animated the Wisconsin reform: "Everyone would have to work, and only work would pay." The state agreed to provide basic services such as child care and health insurance, but only for a limited time while recipients became self-supporting. Welfare recipients would have to agree to seek and find work, and make sure their children attended school.

The ultimate results were striking. When Thompson took office in 1987, Wisconsin had 98,000 people on its welfare rolls. The numbers dropped every year after the workfare reform—to just 11,000 by 1998, an astonishing 89 percent reduction. And recipients, families, and children ended up with better quality of life.

It was this brilliant real-life success in Wisconsin, powered by timely philanthropy, that provided welfare reformers elsewhere across the country with the confidence to change their own approaches to welfare. In the early 1990s, as the depth of Wisconsin's success became clear, and various examples of philanthropy-supported research on positive alternatives accumulated, a spirited welfare-reform debate broke out at the federal level. As Congress weighed various measures, though, hysterical voices began to scream in resistance.

The *Nation* wrote that "the welfare bill will destroy our state of grace. In its place will come massive and deadly poverty, sickness, and all manner of violence. People will die, businesses will close, infant mortality will soar, everyone who can will move. Working- and middle-class communities all over America will become scary, violent wastelands created by a government that decided it has no obligations to its neediest citizens. In such a landscape, each of us becomes either predator or prey."

Thanks to years of diligent research and experimentation supported by donors like the Bradley Foundation, however, there was an answer to such emotion-fueled alarmism. "That's not what happened in Wisconsin," reformers could calmly answer. A bustling state, working with private organs of civil society, had built a laboratory where theories were tested and proven desirable.

In 1996, a new Republican Congress created a landmark federal welfare-reform statute, modeled on Wisconsin's example. After much effort, President Clinton was finally convinced to sign the measure into law. It ended the Depression-era program called Aid to Families with Dependent Children, which had fed welfare dependency, and replaced it with Temporary Assistance for Needy Families. The new system offered extensive child, medical, and job help, but ended any long-term entitlement to an annual income. Recipients had to work, and families were limited to five years of assistance. Wisconsin was the lodestar.

Rather than plunging America into mayhem, as opponents insisted, the law catalyzed many brilliant improvements. Between 1997 and 2011, the national welfare caseload dropped in half. Former recipients went to work. Child poverty rates fell dramatically—reaching all-time lows. Crime tumbled. Family deterioration leveled off.

In public policy, no victories are permanent. In 2012, the Obama administration announced that it would allow states to use waivers to skirt the work requirements that are the core of the Bradley-researched reforms. Future trends in welfare, and many other sectors of society, will obviously depend upon the will of the men and women Americans elect to run our government.

But a crucial corner was turned in U.S. social policy. If politicians lose ground in this area in the future they will have their records compared to the hard, sparkling results of the last two decades. Welfare reform was the most successful public-policy innovation of its time. And it was an achievement driven unambiguously by public-policy philanthropists.

MICHAEL GREBE

Mike Grebe grew up in a small town near Peoria, Illinois. "My father was a football coach and my mother was an English teacher," he explains. After attending West Point, Grebe fought in Vietnam (earning two bronze stars), then enrolled in law school at the University of Michigan, graduating near the top of his class. Instead of moving to Chicago or New York, he chose to settle in Milwaukee. "I liked the city," he says. "I liked the people more than the people in other places."

Grebe built a thriving legal career at Foley & Lardner. He rose to chairman and CEO, and helped turn the law firm into one of the largest in the country. He also chaired the Board of Regents of the University of Wisconsin and the Board of Visitors of the U.S. Military Academy. He had no idea that he would eventually take up a second career in public-policy philanthropy. But, in 1996, Grebe was invited to join the board of Milwaukee's Lynde and Harry Bradley Foundation, one of the wealthiest and savviest funders of conservative public-policy creation. Six years later, Grebe retired from his legal practice to run Bradley full time.

Grebe thinks of himself as a steward. "My job is to honor the philanthropic legacy of our founders." The Bradley Foundation took its modern shape in 1985, when Rockwell purchased the Allen-Bradley manufacturing company, pumping several hundred million dollars into the foundation established by the company's founding brothers. By the 1990s, the Bradley Foundation had become a potent force in local and national philanthropy, best known for its pioneering efforts to promote school choice and welfare reform.

Today, the Bradley Foundation gives away nearly $45 million per year. Its 2013 annual report characterized its mission as "defending the tradition of free representative government and private enterprise that has enabled the American nation and, in a larger sense, the entire Western world to flourish intellectually and economically." About a third of its donations go to Milwaukee organizations to improve the foundation's home city. The remainder is channeled to groups like Americans for Tax Reform, the American Enterprise Institute, and the Federalist Society, with the goal of refining public policies. "Bradley Foundation-funded ideas, as well as political leaders who turn those ideas into action, have helped drive America's conservative revolution over the past quarter-century," summarized the *Milwaukee Journal-Sentinel* in 2011.

The foundation's success, says Grebe, comes from its particular method of making grants. "We tend to approach public-policy funding as venture capitalists," he says. "We don't approach problems from the top down, where we come up with ideas and find people who can execute them. Instead, we come up with the subject areas we'd like to address and invite people to approach us."

Patience and humility are important. "We're not looking for quick, short-term solutions," says Grebe. "In many cases, we're trying to solve long-term problems." He cites *Politics, Markets, and America's Schools*, a 1990 book by John Chubb and Terry Moe outlining the potential of school choice. "We didn't really know how good that book was until years later, when legislators had picked up on it and began to make school choice a reality in so many places," says Grebe. "This can take a long time." And not every grant will work out. "We expect a certain amount of failure," he says. "That's what happens when you're willing to take chances."

When the foundation wants to explore a new subject, it convenes a group of experts, and both the foundation's directors and its staff engage in intense discussions aimed at finding philanthropic opportunities.

For instance, "several years ago, we recognized that America's image in the world had slipped," says Grebe. "So we established a working group on how private philanthropies might enhance the effectiveness of public diplomacy and statecraft." Participants from government agencies, the military, and research organizations offered ideas. Several grants emerged from this, including support for the American Islamic Congress and the Institute for Foreign Policy Analysis.

Judging the success of grants is a special challenge. "This is one area in which public-policy philanthropy is different from other areas of philanthropy—it's less susceptible to the measurement of outcomes," he says. "We try to measure effectiveness, but this is difficult, especially in the early stages. When you fund a book, what do you ask? How many times was it cited in the press or in academic journals? That tells you something, but what it tells you may not be very helpful. You may not see the impact for years. Then there's another problem: The people who conceive ideas are usually not the same people responsible for their implementation. When scholars come to us for support, we ask them to have a strategy for public discourse. How will they disseminate their ideas?"

As with so many people involved in public-policy philanthropy, Grebe is active in politics. In 2014, he chaired the re-election campaign of Wisconsin Governor Scott Walker. He has also served as general counsel to the Republican National Committee. "I'm very careful about this," says Grebe. "I keep everything separate. I don't make political calls from the foundation office. I do that from home or from campaign offices. I won't let the foundation get mixed up in partisan politics."

At the same time, it's impossible for public-policy philanthropy to proceed without an awareness of political context. In 2010, the Bradley Foundation supported *Refocus Wisconsin*, a monograph from the Wisconsin Policy Research Institute, a free-market think tank it helped establish. "We saw how much the Reagan administration relied on the Heritage Foundation, and how much Mayor Rudy Giuliani relied on the Manhattan Institute in New York City," says Grebe. "We wanted to support a project that provided a similar level of policy assistance to our own governor and lawmakers." The 154-page publication provided information and policy recommendations on the major features of state government, from budgets and taxes to public pensions and economic opportunity. Scott Walker became a national leader at reining in runaway state spending (more on this in Chapter 6).

In the 1990s, Bradley enjoyed great success at uncovering new strategies for serving the poor via school choice and welfare reform, partly because then-governor Tommy Thompson was receptive to trying the fresh approaches Bradley and its nonprofit partners pioneered. "You do have to keep the political environment in mind," says Grebe.

"At the same time, we've been longtime supporters of school choice and other policies no matter who has been in power, in Wisconsin or anywhere." He points out that in school-choice debates, urban Democrats have been some of the foundation's best allies. And a few years ago, when Milwaukee was searching for a new police chief, the Bradley Foundation provided financial support for the Fire and Police Commission to retain George Kelling, who helped create Rudy Giuliani's anti-crime strategy, as a consultant. "We did that with a Democratic mayor," says Grebe.

Since 2004, the foundation has awarded four $250,000 Bradley Prizes each year to the likes of economist Thomas Sowell, Constitutional scholar Robert George, school-choice activist Clint Bolick, and commentators Charles Krauthammer and George Will. The goal is to recognize individuals who have encouraged useful public reforms, and publicize their work. "We've been more successful at the honoring part," concludes Grebe, "and less successful at creating broad awareness of what they've done."

MELISSA BERMAN

Melissa Berman is the president of Rockefeller Philanthropy Advisors, a nonprofit that started out advising members of the Rockefeller family then broadened into a service providing guidance to more than 160 different donors—families, foundations, and corporations—on how they might best steer their giving. "The donors we work with represent a very broad range of interests and positions. It's our job to help them achieve their goals."

Philanthropy aimed at influencing public policies appeals to only some clients. "Sometimes a donor has not run across policy work in her life before, or she has a deep-seated conviction that the political system and public opinion are too big to change. For many people, policy and advocacy work isn't tactile and concrete enough. You can't always be sure you're making progress. For people who are relatively new to philanthropy, it can seem like you're going to graduate school when you still haven't fulfilled the requirements for the undergrad major."

Public-policy philanthropy can create special concerns for individuals. "If you're from a very prominent family and you want to take a strong position on policy in a certain area, one thing you need to understand is how that might impact other members of your family who either disagree with you or hate the limelight."

There are clients, however, who after thinking through these issues do want to work on public policies. For these, Berman first distinguishes between trying to change law (policy), and changing the groundswell support around a law (advocacy). "They are slightly different things to me. For example, take the campaign that made drunk driving unacceptable. It was already illegal, but through efforts like Mothers Against Drunk Driving, people began to feel more comfortable saying, 'No, you can't get behind the wheel of a car.'"

"We have worked over the years with Laurie Tisch in New York, who was a big supporter of a project called Green Carts. This created a set of licenses for street-cart vendors to sell fresh produce at a very reasonable cost in low-income areas of New York that didn't have access to fresh fruits and vegetables. Some of the project was policy focused—they needed to change the city regulations on who could vend where. But a bigger piece of the effort involved advocacy rather than pure policy. The nonprofit built a base of support for this idea, and helped people understand why it was important for these neighborhoods to have access to healthy food at a reasonable cost. They communicated that these carts were not depriving local merchants of their livelihood."

"It ended up being a combination of grant-funding and interesting communications. She funded a beautiful photo exhibit in Grand Central Station, an exhibit and programming at the Children's Museum, and a documentary film which showed nationally. These efforts are spurring a national movement to put policies in place to allow these kinds of innovations in other cities. I think of that project as pretty successful. But it was not a narrow effort to get legislators to pass something. It was more around the enabling environment that makes a policy succeed."

"As a donor, you have to understand how change happens. What are the best levers to pull? Where do you see yourself as an actor? Your answers to those questions may or may not lead you to policy work. Policy and advocacy work is just a tool. The question is, what is your end goal, and how do you want to get there?"

Sometimes philanthropists must take calculated risks to advance public policies. "The city of San Francisco was interested in the question of whether they could get a cheap source of electricity from tidal power, the power of the tides going in and out of San Francisco Bay. The engineering was very unclear. In many cities, running an experiment that might not work can be politically poisonous. Headlines immediately blare: 'City Wastes Millions of Taxpayers' Dollars.'"

"This can be a great opportunity for philanthropy. We helped a foundation fund basic research to see whether this idea would work. Once local tidal power had been shown to be workable, the foundation was able to step back. A local utility company and other sources of funding came forward. So what philanthropy was able to do was put in the highest-risk capital and demonstrate the concept."

"One common mistake in investing to change public policies is thinking that just putting facts in front of people creates action. Everybody wants to believe that the truth will set us free, but that's not how it happens. There's a classic mantra that describes three stages: Awareness. Agreement. Action. It's important to understand that often you have to create all three."

"We've been in situations where a donor has said to us, 'Why don't you put on a symposium, and invite people that you know and we know, and that will result in action.' And we say, 'No, it won't.' People have to go through a process get to awareness, agreement, and then action."

"Donors need to think through what other resources besides their financial capacity they can bring to bear. Do you have knowledge? Networks? Reputational capacity? Technical skills? The chasm from funding to doing is one that you need to understand."

"And it's important that you plan ahead how you're going to assess results. If you wait until balls are in the air, it may be too late. If it's a long-term public awareness campaign, are you going to track earned media, are you going to track the number of people who sign up via social media, or send a message to a Congressperson, are you going to track where a piece of legislation is?"

"You have to figure out what your indicators are for progress. And that varies depending on the campaign. 'I want the city council to make parking on the left side of the street illegal on Thursdays,' is a very different assignment from, 'I want there to be a complete change in how we think about crimes against children.'"

"The key to being an effective donor in this space is patience. And respect for other people's points of view is important. Someone who believes that anybody who doesn't agree with him is stupid is not likely to change many minds. Understanding how to create a coalition in which everybody can see some of their own success is really helpful."

The Very First—and
Still Biggest—Triumph

The most consequential change of public policy in American history was the abolition of slavery. It took a terrible war and generations of suasion to make that transformation of opinion and law complete. But it was philanthropists who launched and sustained this revolution in human freedom and racial equality—and later donors like George Peabody, John Rockefeller, Julius Rosenwald, and George Eastman who continued the process through Reconstruction and beyond. The abolition movement showed that there is no cause too big for philanthropy, if backers possess adequate courage, determination, and patience.

Decades of private charity by givers large and small sustained the campaign to end slavery. Individuals and private associations purchased slaves in order to free them. Volunteers served as guides and stationmasters along the Underground Railroad. Donors built schools and colleges where white children could be taught to disdain bondage, and black children could be offered literacy and practical instruction for the first time. Hundreds of privately funded publications, meetings, and conventions built arguments against human chattel, drawing on everything from Christian morality to economic self-interest. Philanthropic efforts to fulfill the promise of our Declaration of Independence that all men are created equal were backed by the time and treasure of many thousands of Americans.

Even the individuals who funded the radical activities of John Brown and sent guns to Kansas and raiders to Harper's Ferry were public-policy philanthropists in their own peculiar ways. Central New Yorker Gerrit Smith is a prime example. The family fur-trading fortune made him the largest landowner in New York, but he lived simply so he could donate the modern equivalent of a billion dollars to undo slavery and heal its wounds. His spending ranged from buying enslaved families and giving them their freedom, to funding Frederick Douglass's newspapers, to organizing civil disobedience and rescues in response to the Fugitive Slave Law, to gun-running with John Brown, to paying the bail to free Jefferson Davis after the Civil War as an act of reconciliation.

Wealthy businessmen Arthur and Lewis Tappan were among the most devoted and successful philanthropic campaigners for abolition. Brothers born in Northampton, Massachusetts, the Tappans made their fortunes in Boston and New York. Arthur, who was two years older, was particularly famous for hard work and frugality. He worked from a cubicle, and did not provide chairs for visitors to prevent lingering meetings and preserve more time for productive work. Lewis partnered with his brother on some ventures, and eventually founded the Dun & Bradstreet Company, an institution for identifying and rewarding companies for rectitude and honest finance, which continues as an important American financial-information agency today.

Raised in an evangelical home, both Tappans were deeply committed to Christian giving. Their initial philanthropic forays were mostly conventional donations to assist the indigent, but they soon became quite inventive. When Lewis heard that British philanthropists had opened savings banks for the working class so their earnings might accumulate interest, he started his own version in Boston. More and more, religious enthusiasm began to dominate the Tappans' giving, and by the 1820s Arthur was the most generous philanthropist in Boston. "Money was his passion; to give it away his security," wrote historian Bertram Wyatt-Brown.

The Tappans supported a wide range of organizations that shared similar goals, supplying them with money as well as administrative advice. Arthur underwrote the American Bible Society (which aimed to provide the Good Book to every family in the U.S.), the American Sunday School Union (offering religious education in the frontier towns of the Mississippi valley), and the American Tract Society (which published religious sermons). He also helped launch Oberlin College, which

> Although they were not afraid to court controversy, much of the Tappans' abolitionist philanthropy was done in secret, partly for reasons of modesty, partly out of necessity.

today has a Tappan Hall and a Tappan Square. "This is enjoying riches in a high degree," Lewis once wrote of the family giving.

By the 1830s, the Tappans had turned deliberately to philanthropy that aimed to modify public policy. They first became involved with government practices in a push to end postal deliveries on Sunday. This was part of the effort known as Sabbatarianism, which aspired to clear a day for rest and spiritual reflection by workers and families.

As with other evangelicals of their time, the Tappans were soon swept deeply into the cause of eliminating slavery. Arthur's first major action took place in 1830, when he learned that a libel conviction had put William Lloyd Garrison behind bars. Garrison would eventually become a household name but at this time he was an obscure journalist whose crime was to have exposed the slave profiteering of a Massachusetts businessman. Tappan paid his fine, even though Garrison was a stranger to him.

Later, Arthur helped Garrison launch the *Liberator*, a weekly newspaper that would become a major voice of radical abolitionism. "I might have died within those prison walls, if your sympathizing and philanthropic heart had not prompted you, unsolicited, to send the needed sum for my redemption," wrote Garrison in an 1863 letter to Arthur.

The Tappans tried anything that seemed to have a chance of advancing the cause of manumission. In 1834, for instance, Arthur gave $5,000 to the American Bible Society to distribute Bibles to slaves in the South—a controversial gift, and perhaps a quixotic one given the general illiteracy of slaves. Arthur and Lewis started the American Anti-Slavery Society, which would become an important organ of abolitionism. One of its main achievements was to help bring escaped slave Frederick Douglass to prominence as a public speaker.

Although they were not afraid to court controversy, much of the Tappans' abolitionist philanthropy was done in secret, partly for reasons of modesty, partly out of necessity. They were early supporters of the Underground Railroad, for instance, which would have exposed them to legal recourse if done openly. "He was always ready to help the flying fugitive on his way to Canada, or elsewhere, and was active in this benevolent work," observed Lewis of his brother.

As Arthur stepped away from public action in the later 1830s, Lewis became the dominant brother in philanthropy to change slave laws and practices. His great success came in 1839, when the human cargo aboard a slave transport called the *Amistad* took up arms against their captors. They gained control of the ship and intended to sail for Africa, but their navigators—hostages from the crew—tricked them into making for the United States. The mutineers wound up in New Haven, Connecticut, where authorities imprisoned them for piracy and murder. The decision to treat the Africans as criminals for trying to free themselves outraged Lewis, who formed a committee to aid them.

First Lewis had to solve the language barrier. He eventually discovered from the wharves of New York City a cabin-boy named James Covey who, from his wanderings at sea, knew the Mendi tribal dialect spoken in what is now Nigeria. Lewis hired Covey as a translator, and paid Yale students to tutor the jailed Africans in English and American social practice. Lewis then arranged and paid for top-flight legal counsel, and even recruited former President John Quincy Adams to represent the Africans before the Supreme Court, which ultimately ordered the release of the prisoners in 1841.

Lewis realized that the *Amistad* trial was a vivid teachable-moment for the American public. It brought the moral arguments around slavery onto the nation's front pages for many months, and highlighted the horrors of the slave trade. It became a public-relations coup for aboli-tionists, and built emotional support for their claims of justice. It also gave the famously fractious abolitionist movement a cause behind which it could come together.

After the favorable decision, Lewis helped fund transportation of the captives back to their native land. One of his hopes was that they would serve as Christian missionaries in Africa. With this experience as a springboard, Lewis also created and oversaw the American Missionary Association, which aimed to spread the message of abolition around the world. In the U.S., the association also founded colleges for freed slaves, including Howard University in Washington, D.C., and Fisk University in Nashville.

Arthur and Lewis Tappan gave deeply of both their talents and their money in the effort to change slavery policies. For their troubles they endured savage attacks from opponents, including burnings of their homes and personal possessions, murder attempts, and regular vilifica-tion. Both brothers lived to see the end of the Civil War, though, and enjoyed the satisfaction of knowing that slavery, at long last, had been banished from American society.

THE KOCH BROTHERS

Charles and David Koch—variously celebrated or vilified as "the Koch brothers"—are a bookish pair who have made it their central philanthropic mission to expose people to the ideas of liberty. In their lives as titans of capitalism, they head Koch Industries, the Kansas-based company founded by their father that is now the second-largest privately held firm in the U.S. But wide reading and strong philosophical bents have also led them, through their family foundations, to become highly visible champions of economic and cultural liberty. They have channeled large amounts of their own time and money into efforts to motivate others to value freedom as they do. "If we want to restore a free society and create greater well-being and opportunity for all Americans, we have no choice but to fight for those principles," concludes Charles.

The Kochs fight this philosophical battle through philanthropy—and in recent years their efforts have attracted enormous attention and scrutiny. "On the Left, 'the Koch brothers' became a political meme, a crude caricature of corporate fat cats subverting democracy and science as they secretly advanced their plutocratic agenda," wrote Daniel Schulman in his 2014 biography, *Sons of Wichita*.

In 2010, Jane Mayer of the *New Yorker* devoted nearly 10,000 words to arguing that the Kochs were more than just "the primary underwriters of hard-line libertarian politics in America"—their giving was a selfish effort to increase their personal wealth. This was an odd allegation to level at men who have given away hundreds of millions of dollars in areas ranging from medical research to education to the arts. Just as strange was the article's headline: "Covert Operations." As David commented in the *Daily Beast*: "If what I and my brother believe in, and advocate for, is secret, it's the worst covert operation in history."

The Kochs have used philanthropy to encourage liberty-oriented policies in many ways. Back in the 1970s, for instance, they pursued a fairly simple "build a think tank" strategy to create the Cato Institute. Today Cato is the most prominent and influential libertarian policy-research group in the nation's capital. Over the years, the brothers have adopted many additional causes and organizations—and increasingly complex philanthropic mechanisms—as levers for encouraging liberty-oriented public policies.

In 2006, Charles suggested to Brian Doherty, author of the 2007 book on the American libertarian movement *Radicals for Capitalism*, that libertarians "need an integrated strategy, vertically and horizontally integrated, to bring about social change, from idea creation to policy development to education to grassroots organizations to lobbying to litigation to political action."

This all-of-the-above approach is not the result of indecision, but rather of careful planning and accretion of additional strategies through years of experience. Richard Fink, a former academic who is a longtime executive with the Kochs, described their philanthropic strategy in the pages of *Philanthropy* magazine in 1996. "Universities, think tanks, and citizen activist groups all present competing claims for being the best place to invest resources," he wrote. "While they may compete with one another for funding and often belittle each other's roles, we at the Koch Foundation view them as complementary institutions, each critical for social transformation."

Koch giving, wrote Fink, takes an insight from Friedrich Hayek on the three stages of production in a market economy: Businesses generate raw materials, convert them into products, and finally deliver them into the hands of consumers. Successful public-policy philanthropy works much the same way, supporting intellectuals who generate ideas, think tanks that propose specific policies, and advocacy groups that shape the hearts and minds of voters and political leaders. There is a need for all three kinds of work.

"At the higher stages we have the investment in the intellectual raw materials...exploration of abstract concepts and theories," wrote Fink. This means financial support for scholars, research, and conferences. In the latest five years examined by Schulman (2007-2011), the Kochs donated $31 million to endow professorships, sponsor academic forums, and underwrite scholarships. Academic centers and professors at some 200 colleges and universities have received financial support from the brothers, including Nobel Prize-winning economists James Buchanan and Vernon Smith.

The problem with academics, of course, is that they often speak only to each other—the ideas they generate must be packaged into a "usable form," as Fink puts it. "This is the work of think tanks and policy institutions." The Kochs have played indispensable roles in founding the Cato Institute and the Mercatus Center at George Mason University, and have been important supporters of other think tanks as well. They have reinforced many public-policy nonprofits by funding internships and fellowships for college students and young professionals, placing them at the disposal of such organizations for four days of the week while offering them instruction in economics and political philosophy on the fifth day.

Finally, the Kochs have sought to involve everyday people in political advocacy. In the 1980s, they established Citizens for a Sound Economy, which later evolved into Americans for Prosperity and claims more than 2 million activists at present. "What we needed was a sales force that participated in political campaigns or town hall meetings, in rallies, to communicate to the public at large much of the information that these think tanks were creating," said David Koch, in an interview with the *Weekly Standard* in 2011.

It all played into the plan Fink described 15 years earlier: "Citizen activist or implementation groups are needed in the final stage to take the policy ideas from the think tanks and translate them into proposals that citizens can understand and act upon. These groups are also able to build diverse coalitions of individual citizens and special-interest groups needed to press for the implementation of social change."

From Nobel winners to leading think tanks to some of the country's most active grassroots organizations, this is quite a legacy. But the inexorable growth of government supervision of private life from the 1970s to the first decade of the new millennium left the Kochs wholly unsatisfied with policy trends. "It was obvious we were headed for disaster," Charles told the *Weekly Standard*. So they decided to go beyond just their own giving, to reach out for allies among other philanthropists, hoping to achieve a multiplier effect. The result was the Koch Seminars, which seek to expose major conservative and libertarian donors to opportunities in public-policy philanthropy.

The first of these twice-yearly meetings took place in Chicago in 2003. It started small, attracting fewer than 20 participants. "Back then, these invitation-only confabs, where presenters bored attendees senseless with marathon economics lectures, held little mystique," wrote Schulman. As the conferences became more polished they gathered in size and strength. Within a decade they were attracting hundreds of business and philanthropic leaders. Participants networked with each other, and learned about groups they could support to promote freedom, prosperity, and enterprise.

One of the big differences between the early Koch Seminars and the later ones involves the role of politicians. The Kochs have long been much more interested in ideas and policies than in politics and campaigning. "It was only in the past decade that I realized the need to also engage in the political process," wrote Charles in the *Wall Street Journal* in 2014. The more recent seminars have featured forums with elected officials and candidates.

In their philanthropy, the Kochs believe in holding beneficiaries accountable for success or failure at meeting expressed goals. The Kochs generally also resist major, ongoing support. A 2011 profile of Charles Koch in *Philanthropy* magazine noted that he "is willing to play a key role in the founding of institutions.... He can be a leading supporter in an organization's early years. But a key element of the experimental discovery process involves the deliberate decision to step back. If a group is creating real value in the marketplace of ideas, other funders will step forward to support it." Too much reliance on a single donor, Koch believes, can cause a nonprofit group to see a major philanthropist as a customer rather than an investor.

The Kochs encourage fellow philanthropists to take risks. "In business there will be more failures than successes," says Charles. Likewise, in philanthropy, "we don't mind failures. It's just that when you have something that's not working, you have to cut your losses."

The Kochs urge donors to take an active role in their philanthropy. Invest your own time, they urge, and write out not just mission statements but concrete examples of what you hope to achieve, so when you are not around there will something to keep your investments focused on the efforts you truly believe in. Charles has expressed optimism that his foundation will continue to represent his principles well past the end of his life. "There are no sunset provisions," he told *Philanthropy*. "The main thing is to have the right board, and I have people on the board who are very dedicated to these ideas."

Like the Tappan brothers, the Koch brothers have been demonized by some for diving into national policy arguments. In a 2014 *Wall Street Journal* essay entitled "I'm Fighting to Restore a Free Society," Charles warned that "Instead of encouraging free and open debate, collectivists strive to discredit and intimidate opponents. They engage in character assassination. I should know, as the almost daily target of their attacks." (Other leading donors have likewise had to weather the excoriation that sometimes comes with policy activism. See John Arnold's experience on page 87.)

Koch announced, however, that he would not be driven away. Principled participation in battles over the vision and direction of our nation, he wrote, is essential to national success. And worth fighting for as a philanthropist.

CHESTER E. FINN, JR.

Chester Finn entered the policy arena in the late 1960s as a liberal who was optimistic about ending poverty through education. He evolved into a conservative attentive to the unintended side-effects of social engineering. He remains an advocate of energetic public-policy reform, a proponent of private giving as an alternative to bureaucratic social programs, and one of the nation's leading experts on excellent education.

"I was drawn into education by a desire to improve the world. Lyndon Johnson persuaded me that the path to ending poverty ran through education. So I went to a school of education and became a social studies teacher, then later realized I wanted to work on a larger canvas, in public policy. But donors in those days were mostly just paying for programs that would benefit people directly." Few philanthropists were involved in efforts to change public policy in education. Except for the Ford Foundation.

"The most famous policy intervention by a donor at that time was the Ford Foundation's effort to bring local control to the schools in New York City. This was a pet project of McGeorge Bundy, who had been the White House national security adviser before becoming president of Ford. They decided that the New York City school system should be turned over to the people of New York at the neighborhood level. That unexpectedly led to all sorts of awful stuff: racism, anti-Semitism, and the first major teacher strike in the country's history."

"That scared donors away from governance change in education. Funders generally opted for safer and simpler solutions. 'Let's build a library.' 'Let's give scholarships to 87 kids to go to private school.' 'Let's donate computers.'"

But a gradual push toward more fundamental governance reform began to simmer in the donor community. Three approaches emerged beginning in the 1980s. "One was focused on curricular standards and school accountability. Another promoted school choice. A third emphasized teacher quality."

"Each strand had its own dedicated philanthropic funders. And for the most part, donors concentrated on one particular strand. Walton from the beginning was about school choice. Gates emphasized standards. Carnegie and others pushed for teacher professionalism."

"As fresh ideas for reform began to bubble up, more and more reformers started to seek private funding. To launch their new mechanism for change, many sought out private donors, not government. Whether they were providing direct services, research, or policy advocacy, the venture capital for educational experimentation often came from philanthropy."

And funders became more and more devoted to hands-on philanthropy. There remained practitioners of the old style, who would just write checks to worthy organizations. But many of the most generous and active foundations developed their own strategies for breaking the decades-long gridlock of declining schools, and actively managed giving to advance policy agendas.

To improve the chances of real and lasting change, "a lot of philanthropists added political engagement to their foundation work. Outside of their tax-exempt, charitable work they made donations to 501(c)(4) advocacy groups and to political action committees that supported political campaigns, as well as to 501(c)(3) advocacy organizations that 'educate' and nudge policymakers. Now donors are very mindful of groups like StudentsFirst (founded by Michelle Rhee), 50CAN, and the Policy Innovation in Education (PIE) Network that are pushing for dramatic school reforms. Donors like the Fishers, Eli Broad, the Waltons, the Gates Foundation, and others strategize together and even coordinate their work to counteract political and policy sclerosis."

"My own Fordham Institute is an example of this. Our roots are in Ohio, and recently it became one of our top priorities to get Ohio's messed-up charter-school law rewritten. Toward that end, we undertook what the IRS calls a 501(h) election, so that our institute can legally engage in part-time lobbying, even though we're a 501(c)(3) nonprofit. We are cultivating a policy strategy that includes working with other groups whose legal status allows them to engage in political reform even more directly. We're doing this because the Ohio charter law is so bad and truly needs to be changed."

"In other places, we're engaged in public policy as a kind of defense. We at Fordham have, for example, turned into significant defenders of the Common Core academic standards, which are under political assault in some states."

"The foundation side of Fordham also continues to fund projects that provide good services directly to needy people. That will always be the heart of philanthropy. But there are so many bad policies in education that beg for change. The bad policies get in the way of good works, and can swamp any benefit you do."

Before it entered combat in Ohio, Fordham built a base of facts. "We're starting with two research studies that are both philanthropically funded. One is an evaluation of charter-school performance that documents how much these schools vary depending on how they are structured, and how mediocre our Ohio schools are. The other study is a forensic analysis of current charter laws in Ohio. We are identifying the many statutory elements that get in the way of good charter schools in Ohio."

This is classic nonprofit research pursued in the public interest. It provides the public with useful information. It allows the foundation to set an accurate and useful agenda. It helps Fordham set smart priorities in its push against counterproductive policies.

"We're also quietly rallying allies to join a coalition that will inform and encourage legislators to support changes. We won't quarterback a change team. It needs to be a grassroots, local, popular coalition. But we are helping to recruit players, and carrying water to the people on the field."

"And then there's a public case we need to make. We have to persuade John Q. Public and members of the media that there's a problem. That we have viable solutions. And that there's a moment of opportunity to act."

While Fordham's effort to rewrite the Ohio charter law is a state effort, the foundation's work to help defend the Common Core standards is both local and national. "Donors are giving money to coalitions of organizations in states where Common Core standards are in jeopardy. On the ground, people are developing materials and public information. They are networking. They are visiting legislators and testifying at their hearings."

"My organization is making intellectual and advocacy contributions to Common Core defense. Across the country we're contributing op-eds, and testimony to legislators. We're brainstorming with state-based advocacy groups, and with leading national organizations. Our work is not political—a 501(c)(3) organization can't do that—but it's got elements that are hard to distinguish. For example, I flew to Michigan recently to testify before their House Special Committee on Academic Standards on why I think the Common Core is better than what Michigan has been using."

As a former Senate and Cabinet-department staffer, Finn knows that measuring impact is tricky in this kind of work. "Every policy change has opponents, and even if they lose they will do their best to undo the change as soon as they can. Things don't stay done. So it requires constant vigilance in order to keep improvement on track. And the payoff can be very slow in coming. Funders always want evidence of impact. But kids take years to demonstrate what they learn."

"Meanwhile, defenders of the status quo are usually more deeply invested than those who want change. Beneficiaries of an existing system know exactly what they will lose if change occurs. They're fighting for their present benefits and advantages—and sometimes their jobs."

"In comparison, the benefits of change are just a future abstraction, until and unless they actually take place. They're only something promised, not a real thing. A parent hears, 'Your kid's odds of getting a good teacher will rise if this law passes.' But a teachers thinks, 'I will lose my job if this law passes.' Guess who fights harder?" That's one of the reasons donors are so important. They can help balance the incentives. They can promote long-term promise over short-term expediency. They can risk the ire of politically powerful interests.

Planting Seeds
for the Long Run

Rather than press the government and the public directly for changed policies, some philanthropists have chosen to have their effect by transforming aspects of intellectual life. Creating a new movement of thought usually requires long and steady investment, a canny strategy, great patience, and an ability to exploit opportunities when they arise. Those who succeed will often eventually see this new line of thinking transform people, institutions, laws, and culture. The changes may not be direct or immediate, but a new cadre of leaders with seeds of revised thinking planted in their breasts can sometimes have wide long-term influence.

Though it labors under a dull name, the "law and economics" movement is one of the more creative and influential departures in public thinking of the last half century. Over the course of a generation, it revolutionized legal culture, inspiring judges, lawyers, and law professors to rethink many of their basic assumptions about the consequences of laws and court decisions. The central premise of law and economics is simple: The lessons and tools of modern economics should be applied to legal rules and procedures. In addition to traditional factors like truth and fairness, legal rulings should consider economic outcomes and incentives in the dispensing of justice. The movement has been described by Yale professor Bruce Ackerman as "the most important thing in legal education since the birth of Harvard Law School."

> This movement, described as the most important development in legal education since the birth of Harvard Law School, was largely the work of one insightful donor.

This new approach to jurisprudence was largely the work of one insightful donor: the John M. Olin Foundation. When Ronald Coase of the University of Chicago Law School won the Nobel Prize in economics in 1991, the president of the Olin Foundation, William E. Simon, sent him a note of congratulations. Coase replied in a handwritten letter: "You should not forget that without all the work in law and economics, a great part of which has been supported by the John M. Olin Foundation, it is doubtful whether the importance of my work would have been recognized. So I give you special thanks."

The Olin Foundation birthed a variety of important intellectual movements during its existence. (The organization's grantmaking essentially ceased in 2005, after the foundation deliberately depleted its endowment.) Olin invested more of its resources in law and economics than any other single area, though, with the total value of its grants there topping $68 million. Its support of this subject was especially determined, especially long-lived, and sharply focused on elite institutions, with a gimlet eye for unexpected opportunities.

The intellectual roots of law and economics stretch back to David Hume and Adam Smith. The modern movement, though, began to take shape at the University of Chicago in the 1950s. Aaron Director, whose sister, Rose, married Milton Friedman, was an economist on the faculty of the law school, hired to help law students understand economics. In his day, however, legal economics confined itself to a few narrow fields, such as antitrust regulation. Director and his students, who included future prominent judges like Robert Bork and Richard Posner, introduced economic thinking into entirely new areas. After Ronald Coase (the Nobel laureate) succeeded Director on Chicago's law-school faculty, he quipped that "I regarded my role as that of Saint Paul to Aaron Director's Christ."

The gospel of law and economics began to spread to other institutions after it came to the attention of the Olin Foundation in 1973. Frank O'Connell, who then ran the foundation, became acquainted with another disciple of Director, Henry Manne, who was trying to start a new law school that would make economic education a centerpiece of its instruction. When O'Connell first presented the concept to John Olin himself, the industrialist snapped skeptically: "What the hell is a lawyer doing teaching economics?" Olin changed his mind, however, after looking over materials O'Connell left with him. He sensed the real-world discipline that economic logic could bring to law, and decided to become the great patron of the effort.

His foundation's first grant in this area, worth $100,000, supported Manne in 1974 as he established the Law and Economics Center at the University of Miami. Its mission was to provide law-school fellowships for students with advanced degrees in economics. In what would become perhaps its most important activity, it also hosted economics seminars for judges. Over time, Manne's LEC moved from Miami to Emory University in Atlanta, and then finally to George Mason University, just outside Washington, D.C., in northern Virginia.

In parallel, the Olin Foundation made special efforts to introduce law and economics scholars into the nation's very top tier of law schools. It took aim at places where "faculties, alumni, and students tend to influence the climate of opinion." One of its savviest interventions came at Harvard Law School, which in the 1980s had become torn by internal strife.

Harvard Law had experienced an influx of scholars associated with a trendy field called critical legal studies, which viewed the law as an oppressive tool of the ruling class. These scholars were so aggressive they made it impossible for several years for the school to hire anybody out-side of their claque for a tenured job. Relations between new and older professors turned hostile, and frostiness enveloped the faculty.

"It was ludicrous," recalled Stephen Shavell of this time at the law school. "Students would hiss in the classroom. The climate was simply unbelievable."

Matters boiled over when one of the professors who specialized in critical legal studies urged young law-school graduates to act as subver-sives within corporate law firms. "Young associates should think of it as a requirement of moral hygiene that they defy the people they work for, and do it at regular intervals," wrote Duncan Kennedy, giving alumni and potential employers great concern.

Sensing an opportunity, Olin stepped into the breach. The foundation offered to fund a new program in law and economics with a multiyear grant. This would introduce a fresh intellectual spark into the school, and help balance the perception that it had become a one-party-line mono-lith run by Marxists. Harvard president Derek Bok leaped at the offer. The John M. Olin Center for Law, Economics, and Business eventually received more than $18 million from the Olin Foundation, and it was a smashing success. By 2005, the number of Harvard faculty whose central interests could be defined within the sphere of law and economics had jumped to 23. More than four dozen alumni of the program had been hired as faculty at other law schools, bringing law and economics insights to top schools like University of California-Berkeley and Michigan. The John M. Olin Fellowships for students have turned into springboards to prominent clerkships.

Similar programs were established by Olin at the law schools of Stanford and Yale, and they experienced equivalent successes. The Olin Foundation had a small number of misfires—a law and economics center at Duke flopped—but these were the exception. The foundation also helped create the American Law and Economics Association, which linked scholars at all schools and helped them collaborate through con-ferences and publications.

Very soon the fresh insights and activism of the law and economics movement began to produce victories in courtrooms and legislatures. *Takings*, a 1985 book by law and economics pioneer Richard Epstein of the University of Chicago, focused new attention on the clause of the Fifth Amendment to the Constitution that asserted: "…nor shall private property be taken for public use without just compensation." Epstein argued that government should reimburse property owners not only when it takes full possession of their holdings but also if it imposes new regulations that dramatically degrade the use or value of private property. This legal logic bolstered an emerging property-rights movement, and formed the basis of a Supreme Court decision that ordered South Carolina to compensate a beachfront landowner after a new law forbade him from building homes as he had planned under prior regulations.

Although law and economics is often viewed as a force for conservative politics and policy, it is in fact better understood as utilitarian. It strives to obtain the greatest good for the greatest number of people. It puts its faith in people's preferences as expressed by their market behavior. It prefers evolved voluntary solutions to government directives.

Because it becomes a powerful analytical tool for decentralized decision-making rather than dictates by a mandarin class, and substitutes rational logic for sentimental visions of justice and resource allocation, law and economics has, however, been welcomed by many conservative intellectuals and donors. Lots of subfields within the law continue to be dominated by the Left—labor law, family law, constitutional law, civil-rights law, etc. Thanks to John Olin's determined backing, however, the law and economics movement has introduced a measure of balance to American legal education and practice.

GARA LAMARCHE

Gara LaMarche leads America's savviest network of large-scale liberal policy and politics donors—the Democracy Alliance. Roughly 100 of the country's wealthiest left-leaning philanthropists, like George and Jonathan Soros, Tom Steyer, Chris Hughes, Weston Milliken, and others participate. They collectively channel around $70 million per year of donations to nonprofits anointed by the Alliance as carriers of the progressive torch.

"Democracy Alliance was organized around the idea that there were institutions on the progressive side of the spectrum that needed to be created or built up," LaMarche explains. "To a great extent we were inspired by people on the right who had invested over a period of 30 or 40 years in key institutions that were policy focused. The Bradley Foundation or the Olin Foundation, for instance. We saw donors giving multiyear support to organizations like the Federalist Society and the Heritage Foundation. The Right really understood the need for infrastructure building."

"On the progressive side we saw gaps in think tanks, media work, and leadership development. So the Democracy Alliance looks for investments that can build policy and politics infrastructure. Our donors agree to be advised by us on key investments and give hundreds of thousands of dollars to causes and institutions that we identify. We are like a venture-capital organization for progressive institutions. And we also work with recipient groups on their business plans, funding needs, and metrics."

"The organizations we recommend for donors are a mix of 501(c) (3) charities and 501(c)(4) advocacy groups. For instance, the progressive counterpart to the Federalist Society is the American Constitution Society. It's a (c)(3) operation that runs campus chapters for students very similar to the Federalist Society's. The Center on Budget and Policy Priorities and the Brennan Center for Justice are likewise 501(c)(3) charities. Organizations like Center for American Progress and the Center for Community Change, on the other hand, have both a (c)(3) and a (c)4 arm."

Prior to becoming president of the Democracy Alliance, LaMarche was a top executive at two of the largest left-wing foundations: Chuck Feeney's Atlantic Philanthropies and George Soros's Open Society Foundations. "Soros's early philanthropy was to promote democracy and independent media in Eastern Europe and the former Soviet Union, so he had many conservative allies circa 1993-1994. Then he began to be involved in the United States." Soros took up issues like euthanasia and drug legalization, "commissioned papers, studies, and public fora, and tried to shake up debate."

On drugs, Soros felt that "the harm caused by the war on drugs and the costs associated with the war on drugs were arguably more harmful than the drug problem itself. For many, many years, we faced a lot of criticism and opposition from all parts of the political spectrum, because it was a toxic issue. We funded a social movement to enable communities of color and families of people incarcerated to agitate for change. We supported organizations like Families Against Mandatory Minimums and the Drug Policy Alliance. Now we have a bill, the REDEEM Act, sponsored by Rand Paul and Cory Booker together."

"The general lesson in any significant social change is that it is a long-term proposition. Immigration reform has slipped from our grasp for the moment and probably awaits at least a new Congress if not a new administration. People have been at it for 15 years. The last significant immigration reform was almost 30 years ago. It's a long-haul proposition which involves steady investment."

"When Atlantic Philanthropies put $27 million into advocacy for health-care reform while I was there, we were following the failed efforts of the Clinton administration. But a lot of the policy groundwork was laid by previous investments by foundations concerned with health care. Atlantic came in to fund a certain kind of activism to push Obamacare over the line."

"We made a grant to launch Health Care for America Now, a coalition of labor, civil rights, and religious groups backing what became the Affordable Care Act. We were holding town hall meetings, and advertising, and meeting with legislators. A member of Congress might be greeted at the airport by people congratulating his vote on health care. There was polling. There were all the elements of a modern campaign." (Because Atlantic Philanthropies is based in Bermuda, it was able to fund direct lobbying and other activities that U.S. foundations are forbidden from being directly involved in.)

"Sometimes you have to create the opportunity if the opportunity does not exist.

And once you pass a major piece of social legislation, you can't just go away. You have to focus on the implementation of it. Obamacare shows that very clearly. We stayed involved for a couple of years afterward in defense of the bill."

"Atlantic put a lot of money into health care, and a lot of people would say that we made a critical difference to getting Obamacare passed. I hope that's true. But it's hard to know. It passed by one vote and could just as easily have failed."

"Our tendency with big issues has been to fund collaborative campaigns which bring a number of people together. So HCAN was a coalition for the period of time when the health-care fight was on. It doesn't exist anymore. Our similar immigration campaign, the Alliance for Citizenship, stayed together even though the prospects are dim at the moment."

"One of the diseases of philanthropy is people are so afraid of being partisan that they end up splitting the difference and funding a lot of conflicting strategies. It helps to have an actual point of view."

"I think one of the reasons the Right has been successful is because they have a world view, they have a coherent ideology, and they are willing to lose rather than compromise sometimes. Often, change is incremental, but I think you start out with a point of view and try to see what you can get. See what gets you closest to your goal and does not violate your core principles."

LaMarche has watched donors debate the merits of investing in policy ideas and infrastructure versus investing in politicians. "In 2003, Soros thought that Bush was an obstacle to his work. If only he could get rid of Bush. So he spent tens of millions of dollars on politics in 2004—all from his personal funds, not from the foundation. Yet Bush won. It was a calculation."

In the war of ideas, LaMarche is somewhat skeptical of shortcuts. "One of the things those of us on the left admire about conservative policy philanthropy was that it took a long view. It was very ideas-focused, and it didn't expect change to happen tomorrow. It was understood that you lay the groundwork for change over a period of time with ideas first. In my view, that was the hallmark of philanthropy on the right. More recently, though, there has been a lot of focus on givers who are very, very focused on elections."

"Of course we worry about the Kochs, because they're a challenge for us on the Left. But I also hear disquiet from intellectual parts of conservative philanthropy, where some feel the shift from long-term infrastructure and idea-building to a more short-term electoral strategy is ill-considered."

"We have these tensions too among my donors at the Democracy Alliance. We all want to be politically active. But we also believe we need to invest in infrastructure and ideas over a period of time. So my job is to say it's a false dichotomy—that if you're interested in politics of course you need to be electorally engaged, but that electing the right people is only a predicate for change, and not sufficient. Politicians always disappoint and need to be held accountable or pushed. You're trying to build a movement that will hold someone accountable. The idea that you can short circuit movement-building and idea-building and just elect the right person and go home doesn't really work."

Policy Player Profile

KIM DENNIS

When Kim Dennis started as a staffer at the Olin Foundation back in 1980, the body of funders and nonprofits trying to nudge public policy from the right "was a very small universe. The Bradley Foundation didn't exist back then. It was Olin, Smith Richardson, Scaife, and JM. The Institute for Educational Affairs was making some grants. The American Enterprise Institute was around, and the Heritage Foundation was small. They were working on economic policies, but it wasn't fine-grained down-in-the-weeds empirical studies. It was much more about the broad principles of free-market economics. The principles weren't practiced in policy at that time, and people were rediscovering them. So the research and the activities going on were basic, about the advantages of free markets as opposed to socialism."

"By the end of the '80s, we won that argument. People came to understand that free markets were much more efficient and produced more prosperity and freedom than redistributed socialistic ways of organizing. The disappointment for a lot of us now is that in 2014 society seems to have forgotten much of what it learned." Questions about the morality of a free-market economy and frettings about income inequality haven't died down, but rather intensified.

The data are much richer today, however, and there are many more actors and voices. "When I started there were a lot more general support grants to think tanks, and the universe of think tanks was much, much smaller. I've seen a huge proliferation of research groups. We have a lot more niche players focused on specific issues."

"Olin invested broadly in people and institutions where it saw potential. The foundation was never a micromanager of the groups or individuals it funded. It was trying to build a movement, and succeeded in doing so. It was a broad-brush effort to expand and strengthen conservative ideas across a wide range of cultural and economic issues."

Now Dennis leads a foundation herself—the Searle Freedom Trust, endowed by the late Dan Searle with proceeds from the sale of the G. D. Searle pharmaceutical company. Like Olin, the Searle Freedom Trust focuses heavily on academic research. "Our grants are focused on certain people and projects, and we avoid academic bureaucracies. We deal directly with the faculty we want to work with. It's rare for us to communicate with university presidents or deans unless the deans are the drivers of the project. A lot of donors think that you need to go through the university foundation, but that's not true."

"We have a policy that says we don't pay university overhead. We will pay operating costs associated with the program we run, if that requires administrative assistance or office space, but we don't pay the approximately 50 percent overhead that government grants do. Donors often think they have to cover that, but when we say we don't according to our bylaws, universities understand."

"Another problem of funding academe is that there can be pushback if it's known that a conservative foundation or donor is giving to a university. The Kochs, for example, get a lot of grief. Their opponents portray it as an academic-freedom issue."

When working directly with faculty it's crucial to choose the professor wisely. "Academics have a trail of work and research, so it's pretty easy to read the papers they've done and know what you're dealing with. We also get a lot of information from talking to other academics we trust, or people in the policy world who are good judges of their work. A lot of our knowledge comes from that kind of networking."

"Perhaps the hardest thing about working with academics is that you don't find many who are entrepreneurial. These are people who have jobs for life. The big thing for them is getting an article in some academic journal; you know how many people read those. It's very hard to find academics who want their work to be read by more than 100 specialists, who really want to make a difference in the world. When we find ones with motivation, we work with them."

Agreeing on research agendas can be tricky. "There's a bit of push and pull. We're always looking for where we can make a difference right now. For example, at this current time there's not much going on in tax policy—one of our big economic interests—just because of the political stalemate. But regulation is also an interest, so that's an area we're focused more on right now. These things shift as political opportunities come along."

"Even when we don't see a lot of potential for policy movement on certain issues, it's not like we can drop the priority. If you stop supporting all the tax economists, where will we be when there's an opportunity? So you tread water on some issues while you're pushing others."

"We also respond to what's out there. We've done a lot of work on how people admitted to college under preferences don't thrive because they've been mismatched to a level where they can't compete. That's not an issue we had any special interest in, but we found some academics really keen to pursue it, so it's become a front burner issue because of that. Often we just seize opportunities. We see someone talented who is driven, who wants to work on a subject, and we say, 'Let's support it and see what comes of it.'"

"It's often impossible to track progress in policy work. We support litigation efforts, and those are easy to track—how far does the case proceed through the courts? Do you win? Do you lose? Social-service grants can be problematic, but if you're trying to get homeless people off the streets there's at least something you can see and count. Policy is a lot more nebulous."

"We do look at things like the number of citations of a study, and how many times it was downloaded off a website. But how does attention translate to enacted policy? That's much harder. And even when policies that have been promoted in studies get enacted, who gets credit? When cap-and-trade legislation was defeated in Congress, every single group and researcher we funded on that topic claimed credit for it. And a lot of them played some role."

"The policy process is very serendipitous. Often the best studies we fund don't get much traction with their objective, high-quality assessments, while some lesser study catches a wave at the right time and makes a difference. A lot of it is timing that you can't predict."

"One frustration for lots of new donors, especially accomplished businesspeople, is how slow, indirect, and fuzzy policy change can be. They think they can apply their business talents to charitable giving and get quick results. It's a much more complicated sector, though, so they get frustrated."

"Dan Searle did this at the start. He just wanted to leave the country a freer place. When I began working for him, he would fund what he thought was a great study on, say, Social Security reform. It would be released, and he would say, "This makes such sense. Why don't we have reform? Why hasn't it happened?"

"For donors who go into this area, it helps a lot if they understand from the outset that it's going to be a long, meandering process, that it's very hard to track what your investments produced. Never mind that major reforms rarely flow in direct linear fashion out of any particular intervention."

"To balance the sometimes glacial pace of policy change, we added grants in other areas where we hoped to encourage social change: New media was an area we got into recently. To my surprise, we're one of the few center-right foundations doing much in media and new media. It's a fun area to work in."

"Also litigation. We've put more and more resources into lawsuits in recent years because we can see progress. Our biggest victories lately have come in the legal arena."

"There have been numerous Supreme Court decisions that we helped to fund. These produced decisions in policy arenas as diverse as voting rights, environmental regulation, education, and health care."

"Of course these things can all be changed by one heart attack on the Supreme Court. But there are also state courts. There's a lot you can do in litigation."

"In terms of other policy outcomes, there have been precious few recently. The fact that cap-and-trade didn't happen was a good thing. We've been very pleased with the work that we've supported on the college-mismatch issue, which has changed the debate over the use of preferences in admissions."

"We're focusing on the same kind of talent development in academe that Olin was doing a couple of decades ago. We know it's an arena dominated by the Left, and will continue to be unless we support talented thinkers willing to step outside the prevailing orthodoxies. It's a very long process. We're investing in someone who is 20-something years old, and it could be 30 more years before they hit their stride in their profession. They also might go nowhere."

"Another thing center-right donors could invest in is online higher education. It's not at all clear where online learning is going to go, but I think online education is one way we could gain more market share at the college level. We are way outgunned in the old-line academy, though thanks to Olin and the Institute for Humane Studies and so forth we do have a solid core of market-thinking people on campuses. Perhaps we can make up for our smaller numbers by reaching more people through online vehicles. I don't think anyone knows how to do it. But we're trying to fund in the area. It's hit and miss, but we ignore it at our peril."

Betting on People

The Olin Foundation's support for law and economics was part of a larger success in public-policy
philanthropy. The foundation wanted to build up
an alternative intellectual infrastructure that could
compete with entrenched academic and media
elites at generating new ideas for the governance
of American society. "What we desperately need in
America today is a powerful counterintelligentsia,"
wrote longtime Olin president William Simon in his
1978 bestselling book, *A Time for Truth*. He wanted

to bolster thinkers dedicated to "individual liberty...meritocracy...and the free market.... Such an intelligentsia exists, and an audience awaits its views."

Just about every aspect of the Olin Foundation's philanthropy involved meeting that long-term goal. It was a monumental challenge. Though much of the funder's grantmaking focused on scholars at colleges and universities, today left-wing orthodoxies are even more dominant on campuses than when the foundation first started to address this problem in the 1970s. Can we consider Olin to have succeeded in fostering fresh thinking that translates into altered public policies?

First, it's important to note that Olin had a few savvy allies in its cause. The earliest efforts in this area were made by the William Volker Fund way back in the 1940s. In 1947, the Volker Fund agreed to help a group of 17 economists fly from the United States to Switzerland for the first meeting of the Mont Pelerin Society, an organization of libertarian economists founded by Friedrich Hayek to promote free markets and refute socialism. Hayek was the author of *The Road to Serfdom*, published in 1944 and never out of print since. It is an enduringly convincing and popular account of why government control of the economy leads to tyranny.

The University of Chicago professor who helped create the law and economics movement, Aaron Director, helped Hayek secure a contract for publication of *The Road to Serfdom* by the University of Chicago Press. Then in April 1945 *Reader's Digest* ran a condensed version of the work, touting it as "one of the most important books of our generation" and giving it a massive audience. Hayek's little volume made a deep impression in the United States, especially among business owners like William Volker of Kansas City, Missouri. When Hayek's efforts to organize the Mont Pelerin Society came to the attention of Volker's nephew and partner, Harold Luhnow, the Volker Fund offered up a check that allowed figures such as Director, Milton Friedman, Henry Hazlett, Leonard Reed, George Stigler, and Ludwig von Mises to make the trip to Europe.

The Mont Pelerin Society went on to become a hub of free-market ideas. Eight of its members won the Nobel Prize in economics. Others served in government. Many more became professors at colleges and universities around the world.

Under the influence of Luhnow, the Volker Fund played a crucial role in the emergence of free-market ideas after the Second World War. It supported groups that worked to influence economic teaching, such as the Foundation for Economic Education, the Institute for Humane Studies, and the Intercollegiate Studies Institute. In 1956, it sponsored a series of lectures at Wabash College by Milton Friedman, which evolved into *Capitalism and Freedom*, one of Friedman's most significant works. ("This series of conferences stands out as among the most stimulating intellectual experiences of my life," wrote Friedman in the preface.) The Volker Fund also underwrote the fellowship that allowed Hayek to teach at the University of Chicago for many years, and the grants that supported von Mises at New York University. "Ideas do not originate in monuments but in the minds of creative individuals," said the Volker Fund's statement of policy, explaining why it chose to underwrite people rather than things like university buildings.

The Volker Fund was active at a time when few other philanthropists showed an interest in supporting the ideas behind free enterprise, so it had an outsized influence. It aided an important platoon of intellectuals as they wrote books and articles, trained graduate students, and otherwise prepared a powerful vision of economics that differed radically from the centrally planned welfare states that swept Europe and much of the rest of the world during the socialist and modernist wave of the 1930s-1960s. Eventually, the market model would emphatically surpass socialism, but that day was in the future.

Many of the individuals supported by Volker saw themselves as a "remnant" (a term coined by Albert Jay Nock in 1936) who kept ancient, time-tested ideas alive. "They are obscure, unorganized...each one rubbing along as best he can," wrote Nock. "They need to be encouraged and braced up, because when everything has gone completely to the dogs, they are the ones who will come back and build a new society." In the 1940s and 1950s, the philanthropy of the Volker Fund did much of this encouraging and bracing up. In doing so, the skeleton of a true conservative counterintelligentsia was created, for fleshing out later on.

In time, about a score of foundations of varying size would become involved in funding this movement. The largest contributors were the Lynde and Harry Bradley Foundation, the Sarah Scaife Foundation, the Smith Richardson Foundation, and Olin. Others included Volker, the Carthage, Earhart, W. H. Brady, Charles Koch, David Koch, and Claude Lambe foundations, the Searle Freedom Trust, and the Philip McKenna, JM, Samuel Roberts Noble, Randolph, and Henry Salvatori foundations.

The combined assets of these funders favoring conservative or libertarian public policies did not approach the massive endowments of their liberal counterparts. Left-wing foundations have wildly outspent right-wing foundations for more than a half century. In their book *The New Leviathan*, David Horowitz and Jacob Laksin calculated that, "as of 2009, the financial assets of the 115 major tax-exempt foundations of the Left identified by our researchers added up to $104.6 billion," while "the financial assets of the 75 foundations of the Right" cumulated to a collective $10.3 billion. The rightward foundations spent a total of $0.8 billion on conservative causes, while the leftward foundations provided $8.8 billion for liberal causes.

In other words, public-policy philanthropy that aims left gets about eleven times as much foundation money as that which aims right. (Individual donors are more evenly split, though there are still more on the left.) The *Washington Post* once observed that the Ford Foundation alone has given more to liberal causes in one year than donor Richard Mellon

> The powerful influence of the Olin Foundation was less a matter of its wealth (quite modest in fact) than of the perspicacity and persistence with which it invested.

Scaife (sometimes called the Daddy Warbucks of the Right during the 1990s) gave to conservative causes in 40 years.

Despite their size disadvantage, the right-leaning donors have had many successes. The powerful influence of the Olin Foundation was less a matter of its wealth (quite modest in fact) than of the perspicacity and persistence with which it invested. Through the 1950s and into the 1960s, most of Olin's giving had taken the form of quite traditional charity, like support for Cornell University, his alma mater, and Washington University, in St. Louis, where he lived. In the 1960s, however, as the political and social trends of the day worried the industrialist, his philanthropy turned in the direction of public policy.

In 1969, black militants at Cornell occupied the student union, brandished rifles, threatened certain professors, and issued a list of demands that included full pardons for their vandalism and threats. Olin was appalled when the administration capitulated within a day and a half, allowing the gun-toting radicals to march out in triumph. By 1973 he had decided to reorient his philanthropy. "I would like to use this fortune to help to preserve the system which made its accumulation possible," he told Frank O'Connell, who managed Olin's giving. With those words, the John M. Olin Foundation turned into an investment fund for persons and groups defending individual liberty, economic freedom, and Western traditions.

The foundation sustained many of the people and organizations that led the conservative intellectual revival. It became a generous supporter of think tanks, giving more than $9 million to the American Enterprise Institute and over $6 million to the Hoover Institution. Olin was willing to back brand-new institutions as well as established ones. In 1975, it offered $10,000 to the recently formed Heritage Foundation. Another $10 million would follow over the next quarter century.

Olin helped finance *Free to Choose*, the popular public-television series on free-market economics hosted by Milton Friedman. It financed the creation of journals such as the *New Criterion*, which focused on arts and culture, and the *National Interest*, which concentrated on foreign policy. The foundation gave only small grants to the *Public Interest*, the influential social-issues quarterly edited by Irving Kristol, but it underwrote Kristol's positions at New York University and the American Enterprise Institute.

For the most part, these were off-campus investments. Yet the Olin Foundation, as we've seen, also pursued a special interest in the academy, knowing that if new philosophical paradigms were really going to thrive, proponents would have to find perches at colleges and universities. Its support for campus law and economics centers reflected this belief, and so did a number of other projects.

The National Association of Scholars, which received more than $2 million from the foundation, worked to mobilize professors and graduate students in support of classic education, through conferences and publications. The NAS recruited thousands of members, and a foundation memo once described the group as "one of the best organizations we support." The California Association of Scholars, a chapter of the national organization, performed the initial work behind Proposition 209, a ballot initiative approved by voters in 1996 to ban the use of racial preferences in the state government, including admissions and hiring at public universities.

The foundation also supported the rise of a network of right-of-center student newspapers, such as the *Dartmouth Review*, the *Michigan Review*, the *Princeton Sentinel*, the *Stanford Review*, and the *Virginia*

Advocate. These publications launched many successful journalists, like Pulitzer-winner Joseph Rago (*Dartmouth Review*), ABC News correspondent Jonathan Karl (*Vassar Spectator*), *New York Times* columnist Ross Douthat (*Harvard Salient*), commentator Ann Coulter (*Cornell Review*), *National Review* editor Rich Lowry (*Virginia Advocate*), blogger Michelle Malkin (*Oberlin Forum*), author and Silicon Valley investor Peter Thiel (*Stanford Review*), author Dinesh D'Souza and radio host Laura Ingraham (both *Dartmouth Review*), and many others. "If everything we have done since was stripped away, leaving only the Collegiate Network as our legacy," said longtime Olin Foundation head James Pierson of these newspapers in 2004, "we would still proudly say our work yielded enormous success."

Another major initiative was the John M. Olin Faculty Fellowships program. It aimed to help promising young scholars by making it possible for them to take a year off from teaching in order to write a book or journal articles—thus gaining the credentials, in the "publish or perish" world of the academy, to secure a career at a top school. The fellowships started in 1985 and eventually boosted more than a hundred scholars, mostly political scientists, historians, legal scholars, and philosophers. The typical recipient was an assistant professor who had accumulated a bit of experience but remained a couple of years away from a tenure decision. Over the years, the foundation spent more than $8 million on the fellowships. Prominent recipients included Peter Berkowitz, a Hoover Institution fellow and a prominent critic of modern liberalism; John DiIulio, an expert on crime, religion, and public policy at the University of Pennsylvania; Aaron Friedberg, a Princeton University professor and national-security analyst; Caroline Hoxby, Stanford University economist and education authority; Frederick Kagan, an American Enterprise Institute scholar who helped develop warfighting strategy in Iraq; Mark McClellan, the Brookings Institution scholar who served as chief administrator of Medicare and Medicaid and as a commissioner of the Food and Drug Administration; Jennifer Roback Morse of the Ruth Institute, which promotes traditional marriage; Jeremy Rabkin, law professor at George Mason University; Paul Rahe, Hillsdale College classicist; C. Bradley Thompson, Clemson University economist; Eugene Volokh, UCLA law professor and popular blogger on legal issues; and John Yoo, law professor at the University of California at Berkeley and a high official at the Department of Justice early in the war on terror.

Many Olin programs depended heavily on the foundation to meet their budgets, but some managed to migrate to other sources of funding. The James Madison Program in American Ideals and Institutions, created at Princeton University with a mission to promote "teaching and scholarship in constitutional law and political thought," was one. It aimed to provide the traditional civics education that so many colleges now forego, as well as to balance the left-of-center political orthodoxies at Princeton. The Madison Program offers courses, lectures, and conferences, and sponsors fellowships for visiting professors and post-doctoral students.

The initial backers of the Madison Program were the Olin and Bradley foundations, but contributions from individuals surpassed foundation grants within two years. "Fine museums and hospitals are important," stated investment banker Peter Flanigan in explaining his support, "but only in a society with sound fundamental principles." Flanigan

> If new philosophical paradigms were really going to thrive, proponents would have to find perches at colleges and universities.

and other backers were graduates of Princeton who saw the Madison Program as a way to invest in their alma mater without handing philanthropic dollars to administrators who would very possibly put them to work for objectionable causes. Many Princeton alumni, for instance, were turned off by the school's decision to have Peter Singer, a philosopher who has defended the practice of infanticide and other extreme causes, run Princeton's University Center for Human Values.

Donations to the Madison Program go straight to its programs, without any portion being redirected by the university to other purposes. To protect its freedom to determine its own activities, the center foregoes funding from Princeton. And apart from a pair of small gifts that have established a prize for a senior thesis and an annual lecture, the center has refused to create its own endowment, because donors "have fears about what will be done with the money down the line. They would rather give us more money now to do good with, while people they trust are doing the spending."

Similar programs exist at other schools, such as the Ashbrook Center at Ashland University in Ohio, and the Political Theory Project at Brown

University. For many years, prominent philosopher Allan Bloom organized influential lectures and seminars at the University of Chicago under the auspices of the John M. Olin Center for Inquiry into the Theory and Practice of Democracy. In 1987, Bloom stormed onto the national stage with his book *The Closing of the American Mind*, an indictment of the moral relativism that had become so pervasive at colleges and universities. It became one of the unlikeliest success stories in the history of book publishing, spending ten weeks at No. 1 on the *New York Times* bestseller list and eventually selling more than a million copies. That accomplishment would have delighted Stephen King or James Patterson; for a book whose chapters have titles like "From Socrates' *Apology* to Heidegger's *Rektoratsrede*" it was a remarkable achievement. The book drove a national conversation about the purpose of higher education, and for many readers introduced the idea that something was amiss in modern education. Bloom became an important member of the conservative counterintelligentsia.

The book had a modest beginning: it started out as an essay for *National Review* in 1982. A grant of $50,000 from the Olin Foundation allowed Bloom to devote time to expanding that germ into a fuller argument. Five years later, Olin's vote of confidence had yielded the runaway bestseller. By 2001, when Bloom's center in Chicago received its final grant, the John M. Olin Foundation had committed more than $9 million in backing to his efforts.

If conservative philanthropists thought they were going to transform the political climate on campus, they failed. American colleges and universities are more left-wing now than they were a generation ago. Voter registration records and survey results show that nine out of ten professors at elite schools place themselves on the Left. (See "The Shame of America's One-party Campuses," the *American Enterprise,* September 2002.)

If, however, donors can find satisfaction in cultivating a fertile class of dissenters from liberal orthodoxy, whose knowledge can be valuable in creating wise and balanced national policies, then there is reason to be pleased. The monopoly of the liberal academy in guiding public-policy creation has been broken compared to the way it existed circa 1960. There is now a conservative intelligentsia with many obvious accomplishments.

This modest but crucial success required philanthropists with an ability to identify first-rate talents and a willingness to back them over long periods of time, recognizing that some bets will come through spectacularly while others will flop. The best public-policy donors of the last generation had the confidence to identify promising recipients, and then stick with them without expecting obvious and immediate "achievements." These donors understood that intellectual tides are not predictable, can shift rapidly, and often cannot be measured in simple ways, but that it *is* possible to nurture new ideas into public prominence if you have strong partners—and that fortune favors the brave, the well-prepared, and the patient.

ROGER HERTOG

When Roger Hertog retired as a leader of one of the world's top investment firms in 2000, he launched a second career as a philanthropist. Some of his donations have been generous but conventional—like funding a large expansion of the Bronx Library Center—but most have been highly idiosyncratic investments in ideas. "Can you really invest in ideas?" Hertog asks. "The answer, broadly speaking, is yes."

Hertog has supported think tanks, newspapers, magazines, scholars, and students. By the end of 2014 he had given away roughly $200 million to various intellectual causes and institutions, ranging from the free-market Manhattan Institute to the *Jewish Review of Books* to his own Hertog Political Studies Program seminars that unite promising students with outstanding teachers and great documents.

At some level, all philanthropy is about ideas, maintains Hertog: "You can invest in bricks and mortar, but really that's about ideas too. Brain science, cancer research, museums of history and art—they all end up being about ideas. People who love modern art as opposed to the impressionists or the great masters are engaged in a great debate about the idea of art."

Even Hertog's $5 million donation to the Bronx Library Center was a kind of homage to the power of ideas. He grew up just a couple of miles from the glistening new library, in a one-bedroom apartment with a single mother. The first book he recalls reading at a predecessor library was *The Autobiography of Benjamin Franklin*. He also has early memories of searching for titles about Franklin Delano Roosevelt—he wanted to know why the wartime President had not done more to prevent the Holocaust, which claimed the lives of many of Hertog's relatives. (Hertog's parents left Germany in 1938 and he was born three years later in the United States.)

Nowadays, Hertog aims to fuel good ideas by investing in the people who generate them and the institutions that promote them. "It's a lot like investing in a business," he says. "Sometimes you see returns right away. But it can also take years before the investment pays off. If you invest in a magazine or a think tank, you quickly get a sense of the scholars—how good they are, the quality of their work, and so on. You have to have quality before you can have impact. You may not see the impact right away, but you know you want to continue to invest."

Having impact in the philanthropy of ideas and public policy is tricky, says Hertog. "I think there are three or four big rules that apply to idea-driven philanthropy in particular. First, you have to know what you believe in. Can you put it in writing? You have to have a strategic vision, and you need the clarity of mind to describe what it is. Aristotle said that a small mistake at the beginning of a journey is a large error at the end. You need to think about this early."

Next comes people. "At the organizations you support, you need the best people in leadership, and you must broadly agree with their worldview. In this way, think tanks are no different from businesses: If you pick the wrong people, you'll suffer irreversible problems." He offers a cautionary note: "Don't be too impressed by intellectual pedigrees. That can be a good place to start, but often what matters more is what's in the heart and soul and mind of an individual."

Then there's the board. "You have to have a good board, and this is about good people too," he says. "They don't need to be area experts. They should have common sense and life experiences. Sometimes that can lead to an argument. That's good. You need to stay sharp, and competitive discussions can help." Too much collegiality can actually pose a threat to excellent philanthropy. "When you're giving away money, everyone thinks you're smart and right. People will agree with you even when you're making a mistake. On the board, you want people who are principled and who will warn you when you're wrong about something."

And Hertog thinks about philanthropy very broadly, without over-focusing on mechanisms. "Anything that furthers intellectual debate can be a part of the philanthropic package," he says. "Often that means giving to a nonprofit group, but on some occasions it makes sense to invest in a venture organized instead as a business. Even if it will lose money, when the people are strong and the vision is consistent with your own, that can be an excellent donation." In his own career, Hertog has put cash into nominally for-profit organizations like *The New Republic* (a political magazine) and the *New York Sun* (a New York City daily newspaper) recognizing that they were unlikely to make any returns, but could still be considered successes as philanthropy. Of course, "you have to use private funds. You can't do this through your foundation."

In 2010, Hertog created the Hertog Political Studies Program. "We're trying to build a new generation of leaders," he says. The way to do this, he believes, is through teaching. "Most of us have felt the influence of great teachers. Somewhere along the way, we've had great teachers—in high school or college, while pursuing advanced degrees, or even in books that exposed us to great thinkers, even if they were written hundreds of years ago."

Many students are discouraged from non-utilitarian study by the high cost of tuition. The Hertog Political Studies Program actually pays some of America's best college students to attend its courses, which can vary in length from a few days to a few weeks. It seeks the best and brightest, and puts those it accepts into classrooms with first-rate teachers who lead them in lectures and conversations about great books, political theory, and the good life.

"We began with the observation that the academy is increasingly politicized and narrow and miniaturized," says Hertog. "Political science keeps dealing with smaller and smaller questions. Our idea is to take a different approach, bringing together theory and practice." Students read the texts of Machiavelli, Tocqueville, and others, then hear from practitioners such as Supreme Court Justice Antonin Scalia, columnist Charles Krauthammer, or Harvard professor Harvey Mansfield. "Our idea is to catch students at the start of their careers and prepare them for writing, advanced degrees, the diplomatic corps, and so on."

Hertog won't live to see the full return on this investment—a complete measure of the impact of these programs won't be possible until the students have finished their own careers. Did any of them become great American statesmen? Did they develop policies that met new challenges? Did they become teachers themselves, shaping the minds of a generation not yet born?

These things will mostly happen after the Hertog Foundation has itself slipped into history. "I'm broadly supportive of sunsetting foundations," says Hertog, referring to the practice of spending assets until they're gone rather than trying to preserve a trust in perpetuity. "One can never know with any great certainty that future trustees will follow donor intent. And maybe they shouldn't. As time moves on, new problems and solutions emerge. Things change. A point of view that's relevant today may not matter later. This is especially true in the philanthropy that's oriented to ideas."

CHRISTOPHER DEMUTH

From 1986 to 2008, Chris DeMuth presided over the blossoming of the American Enterprise Institute into one of Washington's most influential think tanks. From that work, and his other experience in government, academe, and corporate life, he has become an expert in how good national policy is made—and thwarted—and the vital role that private donors play in nudging debates toward productive ends.

"Think tanks produce different kinds of work than universities," he notes, work "that is more applied than theoretical, and highly focused. The first think tanks were concerned with problems in government, and wanted to improve the world. They weren't just seeking abstract truth. They were seeking a better here and now in public policy."

This mission created its own funding strategies. "Universities will go after donors by implying, 'this school made you everything you are, and now you should help the next wave succeed.' Historically, think tanks went after people who had a concern with politics, people who thought America was in trouble and needed a policy revolution. Think tanks tend to have a point of view, and seek donors who share that point of view. Brookings mostly went after liberals. They got a lot of money from the Ford Foundation, for example. AEI and Heritage went after successful entrepreneurs and businessmen worried about the fate of the private-enterprise system."

"There are many areas where the contributions of think tanks have been distinct from anything in university research, and dramatically influential. For instance, the antitrust revolution of the late 1970s and '80s, the movement abolishing regulation of airlines and trucking, and the reform and deregulation of financial markets. Those programs were essentially researched out of Brookings and the American Enterprise Institute, and donors like Smith Richardson and Searle were staunch supporters, even when we were doing things that were controversial. Their support of scholars like Robert Bork and others working in these areas made a difference."

"Now that the established think tanks have become successful and flush with funds, there is the risk that they will begin to look and operate like universities, with more bureaucracy and internal politics, and with output that is more flaccid and less fecund, in the style of university research. I think that the institutional character of the successful think tanks is pretty strong, and that they are mostly continuing to be productive and creative. But there are risks in being big, established organizations. A large endowment can actually be a problem, because everybody knows you're rich so it's hard to raise new money, and the scholars become more demanding."

"There are important entrants that keep coming in, like the state think tanks. The Goldwater Institute, for example, has been doing terrific work. I'm happy that the restrictions on entry into this world are very low, and that it's easy for people with distinctive ideas to hang up a shingle and go to work on strategies for government reform."

The donors willing to write checks to think tanks have changed over time, according to DeMuth. "When I first came to AEI we did not have any endowment to speak of, but we did have regular annual support from many corporations. Many of the Fortune 500 made a significant annual grant. That was something my predecessors had cultivated over a long period of time. When I left AEI, corporate support was a smaller component of our budget because corporate donations had become more difficult and I had turned to individual and foundation support. Big corporations have become increasingly cowed by the growth of government and their growing entanglement with and reliance upon large government bureaucracies. Many do not wish to be perceived as oppositional to anything."

"If you look up the speeches on government policy made by the presidents of big corporations in the '50s and '60s, you'll be amazed. They were fierce, unabashed champions of the private-enterprise system. Today, CEOs are likelier to be apologetic about their work and the harmful effects of corporations, and submissive to the government agencies that regulate them, tax them, and tell them how and where to operate."

One person who spotted the political domestication of big companies early on, and spent much of his life pushing businesspeople to play a bolder role in public discussions, was Irving Kristol. "Irving was a strong free-market man who believed that cultural and social issues were paramount. He spent a good deal of his life preaching to businesspeople who didn't want to hear that."

"Irving found some allies, the most important one being Bill Simon Sr., who was head of the Olin Foundation for many years. Bill, too, was a staunch social conservative as well as an articulate defender of free markets. He was a full-spectrum conservative, and like Irving thought that our cultural and social problems were the most urgent—because economic success depends as much on sound cultural and social mores as on sensible tax and regulatory policies."

"During the decades when Irving was a leader of our movement, it became much easier and more respectable for businesses to make large contributions to public-policy organizations. He published trenchant columns in the *Wall Street Journal.* He founded a group called the Institute for Educational Affairs whose board was half academics and half businesspeople; it raised money from business firms and channeled it into sensible political and policy research."

"Today, large corporations have been neutered and scared out of assertive public-policy philanthropy. Fortunately, strong leaders and advocates for refreshed public policies are emerging from other sectors. We now have a very strong entrepreneurial culture that produces people of great energy and strong principle. That's relatively new."

"Finance has changed also. In the past, finance was heavily concentrated in the big money centers and a couple of investment banks. Today we have a highly variegated system of financial intermediation that includes money market funds, hedge funds, and widely scattered investment vehicles of one kind or another. A lot of people in finance have done well and have strong political views—on the left as well as on the right."

"So today's sharpest critiques of dysfunctional public policies are much more likely to come from entrepreneurial commerce and entrepreneurial finance than from the large established firms. That's quite different than it was 40 years ago."

DeMuth still admires the early donors who backed the rise of a new conservative intelligentsia in the middle of the last century, when American governance was dominated by a homogeneous liberalism. "It is easy to point to important policy changes where the support of the old philanthropists like Olin, Smith Richardson, Scaife, and Bradley was absolutely crucial. Take, for example, Bradley's longstanding support of school choice and voucher programs. It's not an exaggeration to say the foundation almost single-handedly put that new policy mechanism on the table."

"John Olin and the Olin Foundation supported Michael Novak, who was not so much a policy person as a philosopher of the private-enterprise system. When Michael Novak began working on the idea of democratic capitalism almost everybody, including its defenders, viewed capitalism as useful for fueling progress and high levels of material welfare, but essentially amoral and selfish at its root. Nobody did more to uncover the ethical attributes of the free-market system than Michael Novak, and he did this entirely on year-to-year philanthropic support."

"Olin was an early supporter and stuck with him year after year—a theologian from Syracuse University whose only background in politics had been working for people like Bobby Kennedy and Sargent Shriver. That was a pretty high-risk investment. We look back on it and can see that it was a brilliant bet, but I'm sure there were some blunt conversations around the table at Olin and at the American Enterprise Institute."

DeMuth sees many opportunities for donors to guide public policy in innovative ways today—especially the nimble entrepreneurial givers. "They're spending their own money. They're not bureaucratic. And they are successful businesspeople who understand real-world problems."

DeMuth hopes that these financially successful Americans won't shy from the difficult work of keeping our governance on track. "I think a very large challenge for public-spirited citizens today—liberals as well as conservatives—is to design institutions that protect the traditional values of limited constitutional government within the modern welfare state. In all of the advanced democracies, the old constitutional traditions have been giving way."

As our federal government takes on a kind of nurturing role, it suffocates as many citizens as it succors. "Preserving a large sphere for civil society and private institutions—be they voluntary organizations, or churches, or the family—is important to keeping us free and self-reliant. We need to relieve government of this populist tendency to want to solve every problem immediately, to convert every micro-group into clients, and every policy issue into an electoral strategy."

"Contriving new institutions that preserve limited government and prevent the bureaucratic state from encroaching further and further on private life is imperative. Politicians and corporate executives aren't going to lead that crusade. Private donors might."

Winning Now

Some public-policy problems can't wait a generation. They require fast action, with time horizons
measured in months, years, or election cycles rather
than decades. Can philanthropy contribute to these
sorts of issues?

Back in 1955, Dwight Macdonald argued that
most public-policy philanthropy was too sluggish to
be consequential in pressing cases. "A philanthropoid
would deal with the problem of a man trapped in a
burning house by subsidizing a study of combustion,"

he wrote. In 2015, though, there are many philanthropists who are itchy to send in firefighters. They have little interest in funding long-term studies or nurturing slow-growing careers. These donors are looking for fast-moving action organizations who know how to turn on a hose.

In 1993, Bill Kristol (Irving's son) founded an action organization that defeated President Clinton's national health-care plan, a signal accomplishment of the decade. Kristol's work was not an Olin-style culture-changing marathon, but rather a current-events sprint. There are times, when stakes are high and timetables short, where that is the only way to proceed. Public-policy success or failure must come in months or weeks.

This is tricky work. It requires clever strategies, strong messages, and slick communications. But it can pay off in very consequential ways: blocking or creating legislation, birthing a new social movement, nudging an entire state into a different political position, reviving a downtrodden interest or forgotten issue.

In 1992, Democrat Bill Clinton had won a three-way Presidential race with 43 percent of the vote. Perhaps overestimating his mandate, he launched in his first year a mammoth effort to create a new federal health-care regimen. The venture was led by First Lady Hillary Clinton, and the health-care plan she helped construct came to be known as "HillaryCare." It was a massive government intervention that critics skewered as a federal takeover of one seventh of the U.S. economy.

Bill Kristol had been hired by the Bradley Foundation in the early 1990s to think through the future of conservative politics and policy, in the wake of electoral defeat and intellectual exhaustion. It was a task straight from the philanthropic playbook for long-term cultural transformation. But after the Clintons signaled their ambition to remake health care, Kristol set up a 501(c)(4) advocacy nonprofit called the Project for the Republican Future. His new goal was to help the GOP develop a reform agenda on a briefer timeline.

"The name 'Project' was purposeful," said Kristol. "We wanted to signal to donors that we weren't starting an institution. We were short term." The initial board included Michael Joyce of the Bradley Foundation and New York financiers Virginia James and Thomas Rhodes. "I made clear to everyone that this was a moment of opportunity, and supporting us was like placing a bet," said Kristol. "Everything was speculative."

As HillaryCare gained momentum and importance, the group zeroed in on stopping the legislation. Their main weapon was the fax machine—

then a leading technology. Every day or so, as the debate grew hotter, they dispatched to journalists, politicians, and interested parties a steady stream of inside-the-Beltway memos deconstructing the Clinton effort. The first memo was dated December 3, 1993.

At a time when many Republicans were dispirited and ready to capitulate, the Project encouraged them to stiffen their spines. It was pointed out that a large majority of Americans were satisfied with their own health-care coverage. Readers were urged to reject the President's assertion that weaknesses in the existing system required a wholesale reinvention of U.S. health care, overseen by bureaucrats in Washington. The slogan was simple: "There is no health-care crisis."

Within months, the debate over health-care reform shifted dramatically, as conservatives began to adopt the rhetoric of Kristol and company. Organizations such as the National Association of Manufacturers and the Christian Coalition launched efforts to defeat HillaryCare. The Health

> Through their combination of public-policy philanthropy and traditional campaign contributions, the Gang of Four built a well-oiled machine whose central purpose was to persuade voters not to vote for conservative candidates.

Insurance Association of America ran a multimillion-dollar television ad campaign featuring a middle-class couple worried by the implications of national health care.

In the end HillaryCare flopped, and set the stage for the elections of 1994, where Republicans captured not just the Senate but also the House of Representatives for the first time in decades. "Nearly a full year before Republicans would unite behind the 'Contract with America,' Kristol provided the rationale and the steel for them to achieve their aims of winning control of Congress and becoming America's majority party," wrote *Washington Post* reporters Haynes Johnson and David Broder.

All of this grew out of a $1.3 million investment in the Project for the Republican Future, made at a time when that future seemed grim. Irving Kristol had advised the Olin Foundation on a long-term strategy to build a counterintelligentsia. Now his son, Bill, was acting as a member of this very counterintelligentsia, and winning a near-term political victory.

The prospect of nationalized health care was pushed off for almost two decades. And Kristol and his associates, as promised, closed shop. The project was a short-lived, single-purpose enterprise. "When we dissolved in 1995, we returned what was left in our bank account to donors, on a prorated basis," said Kristol.

The reason conservatives found themselves needing to defeat a proposal for nationalized health care was because several years earlier Bill Clinton had benefited from a different creative application of philanthropy to public policy. In 1985, in the wake of Ronald Reagan's landslide re-election, moderate Democrats decided that their party needed to move away from doctrinaire liberalism and toward the center. Democrat fundraisers like William Crotty, Peter Kelly, and Charles Manatt helped former Congressional staffer Al From launch a new 501(c)(4) called the Democratic Leadership Council. Soon, the DLC was hosting private retreats for donors and politicians seeking to refresh the party of FDR.

Just as Kristol's Project for the Republican Future initially met with skepticism from a GOP establishment worried about a possible rival to the national party, the DLC was seen by some as a competitor to the Democratic National Committee. In 1988, though, Democrats lost their third Presidential election in a row, and a growing number of activists saw the DLC as an effective ally in an urgent revival mission. One admirer was Bill Clinton, the governor of Arkansas. He tied himself tightly to the group that promised to create a generation of "New Democrats."

In 1989, the DLC formed the Progressive Policy Institute, a 501(c)(3) think tank charged with developing new policies that the Leadership Council could organize people around. The goal, according to From and his collaborator Will Marshall, was to design "an intellectual counterforce that can fashion progressive alternatives" to right-of-center policies.

Wall Street magnate Michael Steinhardt served as PPI's board chairman, and pledged hundreds of thousands of dollars to the cause. As a nonpartisan group, PPI developed and promoted policy ideas that any public official could adopt—though the idea, of course, was to push ones that would help the DLC and its New Democrats become a governing majority. By 1992, this "pint-sized think tank" with a budget of just

$700,000 had "become a wing of Clinton's campaign" for President, reported the *National Journal*.

Once in the White House, Clinton filled positions in his administration with officials plucked from the DLC/PPI orbit. They organized many of the Clinton Presidency's genuine accomplishments, such as trade liberalization and welfare reform. The debacle over HillaryCare, by contrast, never was associated in a significant way with the DLC or PPI.

Through the 1990s, New Democrats grabbed the reins away from many of the liberals in their own party. They did not hold on permanently, however. During the Presidency of George W. Bush, liberals roared back to life, culminating in the election of Barack Obama. By 2011, the DLC had dissolved, donating its archive to the Clinton Foundation. The Progressive Policy Institute survives as a small group far from the limelight.

Just as the rise of the New Democrats depended heavily on philanthropy to engineer their achievements in public policy, so did the liberal resurgence. Nowhere was this more apparent than in Colorado. In 2004, Colorado was a solidly Republican state, with the governor, both U.S. senators, and five of its seven members of the House belonging to the GOP. That same year, Colorado gave its electoral votes in the Presidential election to Bush.

By the time of the 2008 elections, however, the politics of the state had been turned upside-down. After all the ballots had been counted, the governor, both U.S. senators, and five of seven House members were Democrats, plus Obama carried the state. It was a full-fledged flip.

National political trends explained some of this movement, as the whole country had shifted in a liberal direction. The largest part of this dramatic shift, however, could be ascribed to a group of liberal philanthropists who set out to remake Colorado politics through a mix of public-policy giving and campaign donations. The so-called Gang of Four consisted of Rutt Bridges, a venture capitalist; Tim Gill, founder of the software firm Quark; Jared Polis, an Internet businessman who would win election to Congress as a Democrat in 2008; and Pat Stryker, the heiress of a medical-equipment company.

All were motivated to some degree by gay rights. "Nothing can compare to the psychological trauma of realizing that more than half the people in your state believe that you don't deserve equal rights," Gill told the *Chronicle of Philanthropy* after Colorado voters amended the state constitution to prohibit the government from granting

Charity, Advocacy, Politics—
Where Are the Boundaries?

As this book makes clear, American donors have exhibited a new willingness and desire over the last decade to take up policy reform, and even direct advocacy and politics. It is now common for savvy philanthropists to supplement their charitable giving with some correlated donations that aim to adjust the law and rules of governance, to inform public opinion, or to influence or change occupants of public offices.

The federal rules circumscribing what tax-protected foundations and charitable organizations can do in the areas of governance and elections are extensive and detailed, so care is required in this area. In most cases, only charitable and other qualified nonprofit work can be supported with foundation money. So donors fund direct advocacy and campaign assistance out of their personal checkbooks.

Individuals and foundations that would like to be active in public policy should consult their attorneys, as this book is not written as a legal guide. However: to give a basic picture of the multiple hats that philanthropists may choose to don as they work on social problems that have both charitable and public-policy components, here is a simple sketch of what tax-protected organizations are and are not allowed to take up when it comes to policy advocacy.

**Nonprofit organizations
that funders can use or create
to promote policy change:**

501(c)(3) Private Foundation
(example: Bill & Melinda Gates Foundation)
The Crux: Organization is tax exempt. Donations are tax deductible. Contributions and grants are publicly disclosed. Generally cannot lobby (that is, advocate for specific rules or legislation with elected officials or their staff) except in "self-defense." Can provide funds to charities that lobby with funds from other sources. Can directly inform public opinion and public policies

through research and communications. Prohibited from engaging in political campaigns. Main advocacy role is to conduct policy research and run public-awareness campaigns.

501(c)(3) Public Charity
(example: American Red Cross)
The Crux: Organization is tax exempt. Donations are tax deductible. Contributors can be anonymous. Can advocate for public policies. Can engage in a limited amount of lobbying. May engage in nonpartisan election activities like debates, candidate forums, and voter assistance. Prohibited from engaging in political campaigns. Main advocacy role is to push for public policies it believes in.

501(c)(4) Social Welfare Organization
(example: League of Conservation Voters)
The Crux: Organization is tax exempt. Donations are not tax deductible. Contributors can be anonymous. Can advocate for public policies without limitation. Can lobby without limitation on topics related to its mission. Can participate in political activity, including urging particular votes and depicting candidates in positive or negative ways. Also allowed to engage in active electioneering so long as that is not the "primary purpose of the group" and the electioneering is relevant to the organization's primary purpose. (These same basic rules apply to 501(c)(5) labor organizations, and 501(c)(6) business leagues—which often do similar work in the policy arena.)

527 Political Action Committee
(example: Planned Parenthood Action Fund)
The Crux: Organization is tax exempt. Donations are not tax deductible and they are capped at $5,000 per year. Donors are publicly disclosed. Lobbying can only be a secondary activity of the group. Can make unlimited contributions to political campaigns, including directly to candidates, subject only to federal and state rules and reporting. Main purpose is to directly supply campaign expenses in support of specific candidates, initiatives, or legislation.

527 Independent-expenditure PAC also known as a Super PAC
(example: American Crossroads)
The Crux: Organization is tax exempt. Donations are not tax deductible and they are unlimited. Donors are publicly disclosed. Lobbying can only be a secondary activity of the group. Can make unlimited contributions to political causes, subject only to federal and state rules and reporting, but these cannot go directly to candidates or be coordinated with candidates. Main purpose is to inform voters of the positions of candidates on public issues, or the merits of initiatives or legislation.

special protected status on the basis of sexual orientation. By the late 1990s, Gill and his allies were determined to elect Democrats to office at all levels of government.

In 1999, Bridges founded the Bighorn Center for Public Policy with $1 million of his own money. The short-lived think tank pushed successfully for new rules on campaign finance, setting the stage for the Gang of Four and its new model of policy philanthropy. Before long, they were funding an infrastructure of nonprofit organizations that issued reports, investigated conservative politicians, and generated controversy. They gave Colorado Media Matters, a left-wing media-pressure group, enough money to keep a dozen people on staff. Citizens for Responsibility and Ethics in Washington, a liberal group that publicizes politicians' questionable behavior, opened a Colorado field office. A website called ColoradoPols.com set out to influence statewide reporting. "I can't tell you how often reporters would call 36 hours after something appeared there," said Bill Owens, who was Colorado's Republican governor from 1999 to 2007.

It was an impressive effort, made even more impressive by the result—a wholesale transfer of Colorado's political allegiance from one party to the other.

Through their combination of public-policy philanthropy and traditional campaign contributions, the Gang of Four built a well-oiled machine whose central purpose was to persuade voters not to vote for conservative candidates. In an investigative story for the *Denver Post*, reporter Karen Crummy explained how the various pieces fit together: "A liberal group with a nonpartisan name like Colorado First puts out a list of polluters and demands official action. A Republican running for Colorado office is on the list. Paid liberal bloggers chatter. An online liberal publication with a newspaper-like name writes an article about the candidate and his company polluting Colorado's streams. A liberal advocacy group puts out a news release, citing the group and the pollution, which sound reputable to an ordinary voter. They mass e-mail the release and attach a catchy phrase to it like 'Dirty Doug.' At some point, the mainstream media checks out the allegations."

The overall spending by the Gang of Four and their liberal allies dwarfed that of their conservative rivals. In 2012 the *Denver Post* estimated that in PAC spending alone, liberals spent 150 *times* what conservatives did on Super PAC contributions. It was an impressive effort, made even more impressive by the result—a wholesale transfer of Colorado's political allegiance from one party to the other. Nothing is permanent in politics, and in the deep-red 2014 election Republicans finally reclaimed one of the two U.S. Senate seats in Colorado. But the other Senate seat and three of the seven House seats remained with Democrats, and the incumbent Democrat governor won re-election. Colorado is now a purple state. And the Gill/ Bridges/Polis/Stryker donor structure remains in place.

Behind the successes of the Project for the Republican Future, the New Democrats, and the Colorado liberals lay philanthropists who sensed an opportunity to change the terms of a political debate. Through wise investments in skillful policy entrepreneurs, they took ideas that seemed out of favor and filled them with life and promise. In relatively short periods of time, they achieved remarkable swings in governance.

JOHN KIRTLEY

"I wasn't involved in philanthropy at all. And I didn't do anything in politics except vote in presidential elections," says John Kirtley. For a decade, he had focused on running a venture-capital firm in Tampa Bay. But by the mid-1990s, when he was in his middle 30s, Kirtley was ready to do more. "I woke up to the need to give back."

After working at a large bank in New York City, Kirtley returned to Florida (where he had attended high school) and founded, at age 25, a venture-capital firm focused on small companies in the Southeast. He made more than enough money to live on, and began to think about giving some of it away. A friend in New York City told him about a program that paired patrons with needy Catholic schools. Even though Kirtley isn't Catholic, he signed up, because the schools were such lifesavers for children living in neighborhoods with terrible public options.

Before long Kirtley was giving both money and advice to Christ the King Elementary School, near Yankee Stadium in the South Bronx. "It was a rough area at the time," says Kirtley. "It was like a scene from Tom Wolfe's *Bonfire of the Vanities*. At night, you went there in groups because it was dangerous to go alone."

About 300 students attended the school. "The tuition was maybe $3,300, and the cost to educate was maybe $5,500," says Kirtley. "Parents took two or three jobs to pay for it." Donors made up the difference.

The sacrifices of the poor parents forced Kirtley to ask a question: "Why are they doing this, when there's a free public school just down the street?" He knew the answer: "They understood that it was the right school for their kids."

While he was involved with this one school, Kirtley read about the efforts of philanthropists Patrick Rooney and Virginia James to launch scholarship funds across the country that would help poor students attend private schools. "It made sense," he says, "so I decided to start a scholarship program in Tampa Bay."

Today, Florida is arguably America's leader in school choice. Its laws already help nearly 100,000 children attend private schools, with the number rising with each passing year. A means-tested tax-credit scholarship program assists 69,000 poor students in the 2014-15 school year. Separately, more than 27,000 special-needs students receive scholarships. This would not have happened without Kirtley's ingenious blend of philanthropy, which combines old-fashioned charity for low-income students with public-policy activism.

"Florida has come further than any other state in developing a new definition of public education," says Kirtley. "Under the old definition, we raised tax dollars, gave it all to the school districts, and assigned kids to schools by zip code. Under the new definition, we raise tax dollars but let parents direct them toward providers and delivery methods that best fit their needs."

At first, Kirtley envisioned a scholarship program for low-income students in Tampa Bay that would offer about 350 scholarships worth $1,500 apiece. "Then I got lucky," he says. He read a newspaper article about the Children's Scholarship Fund, a new initiative launched by Ted Forstmann and John Walton to help low-income students attend private schools. "They wanted to find partners for matching grants."

"I got on a plane the next day, flew to New York City, and went to their offices without an appointment." When he arrived, the staff was still unpacking boxes. "I'm your guy in Tampa," he told them. They struck a deal, allowing Kirtley to double the number of scholarships he planned to give away.

Back in Tampa, Kirtley handled the publicity for his scholarships himself—walking around neighborhoods, visiting churches, and talking on radio stations. "I knew the need was out there, but I didn't know what kind of response we'd get." When the application deadline arrived, his new fund received about 12,000 applications for 700 scholarships of $1,500 each. "It just blew me away."

Kirtley felt good about meeting a need, but the experience also troubled him. "We had to turn away a lot of good people," he says. "Parents kept calling—my phone number was listed—and asking, 'Don't you have just one more scholarship?' Not even Bill Gates could write a check big enough to respond to the need. That's when I realized that philanthropists must become involved in public policy."

This was the fall of 1998, when Florida voters elected Jeb Bush as their new governor. Bush had run on education reform, proposing a school-choice law to allow students to escape failing public schools. "I was so out of touch with politics that I didn't even know he had talked about it," says Kirtley. The following spring when the legislature considered some of Bush's ideas, Kirtley bused parents to Tallahassee. "A lot of politicians say that parents want more public-school funding. Our parents got up and said they want choice."

As they pushed for new alternatives for parents, Kirtley and his allies faced tremendous political resistance. Much of it was motivated by fear and self-defense. "One day, a black legislator who publicly opposed school choice took me into his office." He handed Kirtley a list of ten things he wanted to accomplish as a legislator. "You're right about school choice," he told Kirtley. "But if I put school choice on my list, the teacher's union will take me out, and I won't get to the nine other things."

For Kirtley, the comment was a revelation. "He was making a perfectly logical decision," he says. "I realized we had to broaden the political support for school choice. We needed more than a traditional nonprofit group that funded scholarships."

So Kirtley became a political actor. In addition to his 501(c)(3) scholarship fund, he started a pair of campaigning organizations: a 501(c)(4) to focus on communications and lobbying and a 527 group to fund elections. He picked hardball activists to run operations. One was a former public-school teacher, union leader, and lifelong Democrat. Another was a former newspaper editorialist, tasked with the job of winning hearts and minds in the media. A third was a veteran organizer in African-American communities.

Kirtley devoted millions of dollars to these efforts, both his own money and funds he raised energetically from others. In each election cycle his groups spread the word about school choice and ran advertisements educating voters about candidates who favored choice and those who opposed it. "We had a lot of tough days," says Kirtley. Yet for every step backward, the movement seemed to take two forward.

By 2010, school-choice bills had wide support, including co-sponsors among Democrats. Majorities of both the black and Hispanic caucuses had become supporters of a large expansion of Florida's school-choice programs. In an historic vote taken on the same day that Kirtley brought thousands of parents and community leaders to march in Tallahassee, the Florida Senate voted to strengthen school choice across the state.

The success helped even students who stayed put. The new schooling alternatives forced public schools to improve. "Our results indicate that private-school competition, brought about by the creation of scholarships for students from low-income families, is likely to have positive effects on the performance of traditional public schools," concluded researchers David Figlio and Cassandra Hart.

John Kirtley's philanthropic organizing now serves as a case study in how to bring school choice to the masses. "If others want to do this in their states, the first thing they should do is contact the American Federation for Children, which advises school-choice supporters around the country," he says. "Then they should be ready to do more than just fund scholarships. You also have to get involved in politics and public policy. If your goal is to change K-12 policy, you're going to have to change laws. And if legislators refuse to change those laws, then you're going to have to change those legislators."

In a bit of personal advice, Kirtley offers that "you need to steel yourself. You will be a target. It's amazing what the press will print about you. If you're in it for the accolades or to win political office, get out. This isn't for you. But if you want to improve the schooling of our children, and if you can handle the pressure, the rewards are so worth it."

Since founding the Washington-politics journal the *Weekly Standard* in 1995, Bill Kristol has seen increased philanthropic interest influencing policy, including via media outlets. "It's very hard to predict what's going to work, but the Internet gives you a much lower startup cost than in the old days. And more ability to quickly modify what you're doing."

"The *Times of Israel* is an excellent example. It's an online newspaper supported by philanthropists. The idea was to create an English-language website that would be moderate and not biased, with reporting and some opinion on developments in Israel and throughout the Jewish world. It's very high quality, not that expensive to operate, and gets good readership in America. It's affecting the coverage of the Middle East."

"Influencing foreign policy is complicated, but there have been moments when donors have made a huge difference. The Iraq troop surge in 2006 was basically invented at the donor-funded American Enterprise Institute by Fred Kagan and Jack Keane, and sold to the Bush administration as a way to turn the war around. It worked, and it's an example of a think tank making a huge difference."

"The lesson I draw from that is you need to have infrastructure in place. Foreign policy investing is investing for the long haul. It's finding good people and funding them so they'll be relevant when a rare moment arrives. Most of the time, you're not going to see a dramatic result. But when there is a crisis, the right person or organization can make a huge difference."

"It takes patience, but you can make a difference. It's harder in domestic policy, where there are huge interest groups. Winning arguments against hospitals, energy companies, whatever, it's pretty hard as a donor to make a difference. Education is probably where the highest percentage of public-policy donors are investing today, and they're up against teacher unions, bureaucracy, state legislatures and administrators. It's not easy."

"In foreign policy, there aren't as many interest groups. If you can influence a few policymakers and the Defense Department, the State Department, if you can influence a few key senators, you can actually affect foreign policy. A few employees doing two good studies, and a couple people publicizing the work on the Hill and in blog posts and articles can make a wave. You don't need to be a massive institution putting on conferences and trips with big overhead."

"I'm someone who thinks we need to spend more on defense. Are we going to affect President Obama's last budget or two? I don't think so. But there will be a huge moment when there'll be a new President and he or she will have to set the defense budget for 2017. So the Foreign Policy Initiative, a small donor-backed group I'm on the board of, is doing a big project which lays out what defense budget we need. It doesn't have a big staff of its own, but contracts with good people elsewhere to write papers, brief candidates, and so forth. I think it could have influence over the long haul."

"Donors I respect tend to be somewhat experimental in their efforts. And people shouldn't kid themselves—we can't always predict ahead of time that Fred, Jack, and Joe are going to be terrific, while John, Tom, and Mary are not going to work out. You have to be willing to invest in all six of them and then, after a year or two, say, "I'm going to double down on Fred and tell Joe it's time to move on."

"Foreign policy isn't the only place where small investments can make a big difference. Reform of higher education is another area with potential. A donor's ability to change colleges and universities is very limited—there are a lot of tenured faculty and ensconced administrators and they're not going to listen to any one donor. But if you go around the professors directly to students, you can educate a new group of leaders. It's not as good as having a great professor directly teach students, but if you can't control professors you can at least make material easily available to students. You can put things online. You can set up supplemental seminars. You can get a few professors to recommend these to students."

"So Roger Hertog has given the money to establish a political studies program in Washington. Forty-five excellent kids, six weeks, very good faculty, very good extracurricular speakers. These kids are brought to Washington and given an intensive course where they read great books, and listen to serious people, and discuss politics and philosophy and literature."

"There are other groups reaching out directly to students. They post reading lists, curated biographies, video conversations with people like Charles Murray, Harvey Mansfield, Peter Thiel, and others whose thinking extends beyond the liberal conventional wisdom. They create internships and online workshops and summer programs. They fund independent lecture series on campus."

"It's a way of going around the established institutions. It's easier to start the *Weekly Standard* than to change the *New York Times*. Does it solve the problem of the *New York Times* being biased? No. But at least people aren't stuck with them as their only source of high-quality information."

"Donors who don't want to have to deal with the Harvard administration are doing a lot to shape alternatives for students. In addition to Roger Hertog there's Jack Miller, Thomas Smith, Peter Thiel, and Jim Piereson through the Veritas Fund. In foreign policy, Paul Singer, Roger Hertog, the Smith Richardson and Bradley Foundations, and Marilyn Ware are good role models. They are people who have adopted the long view and invested in content and people."

Conflict, Consensus, and Competence

Within weeks of the 2011 swearing-in of Scott Walker as governor of Wisconsin, his state fell into political pandemonium. Noisy protesters descended on the state capital, banging drums and roaring through bull-horns all day long, waving signs that compared Walker to Darth Vader and even Adolf Hitler. Both the rotunda and the grounds outside were occupied for weeks by camped-out activists. The effort was organized by public-employee unions.

The opponents gathered to denounce Walker's budget bill, which tried to close a $3.6-billion budget gap by trimming the pension benefits and collective-bargaining powers of government workers. The political battle turned so spiteful that Democratic lawmakers went on the lam, fleeing to Illinois so that their own legislature would fail to achieve quorum. When it was all over, Walker and his budget bill had survived, but the costs of the battle were high.

Legislators of both parties faced recall attempts. There were lawsuits and counterlawsuits. Walker was forced to run again in a recall election, having to re-defeat the candidate he had beaten only 19 months earlier. By one estimate, the two sides spent more than $60 million on this battle of wills.

Wisconsin was one of the first states to grapple with a serious problem that gravely threatens scores of states and municipalities: the inability of government to keep the budget-crushing promises it has made to public-sector workers and retirees. When Walker took on that dilemma

> Intensely personal attacks on my philanthropy, wrote John Arnold, will not deter me.

frontally, public life in Wisconsin turned into a series of mad dashes from costly crisis to costly crisis. Would states like Illinois, Michigan, and California have to endure the same travails as Wisconsin in order to slay their gigantic pension dragons? Or could there be a smarter solution?

Laura and John Arnold, philanthropists based in Houston, have made it one of the highest priorities of their giving to help solve the pension crisis with as little collateral damage as possible. They agree with Governor Walker's premise that unsustainable public-pension growth is one of the gravest threats to governance today. "The economic and social costs of this looming crisis are potentially crippling to our nation," warns the Arnold Foundation website.

Despite the high stakes, though, the Arnolds believe states and municipalities can solve this problem without all the anguish Wisconsin recently went through. They have launched a major effort that provides research, technical advice, and political and communications support to government leaders who want to tame their pension and benefit budgets.

If the Arnolds succeed in this effort, they will demonstrate the tremendous potential of philanthropy to fix some of America's most vexing public-policy problems.

Their initial results are encouraging. On the same day that Scott Walker won his recall, two local elections in California quietly illustrated a less contentious way of achieving much the same result. With help from Laura and John Arnold and the Arnold Foundation, large majorities of voters in San Diego and San Jose, California, approved ballot measures to trim their pension commitments to municipal employees.

In San Diego, a city of 1.3 million residents, voters reacted against a system that had allowed librarians, for instance, to go into their golden years with annual pensions of $227,000. To pay for these eye-popping expenses the city had been hoarding money by shutting down fire stations on a rotating basis. As an alternative, two thirds of voters opted to freeze pay and create a new retirement plan for city workers.

In San Jose, fully 69 percent of voters backed a plan to make municipal employees pay for more of their benefits. Studies had shown that every household in San Jose owed $11,000 merely to cover the unfunded cost of public pensions. To allow taxpayers a bit of fiscal room so they could begin to grapple with unfunded obligations that had swelled to $245 million (more than triple what they were just a decade earlier), current city workers were asked to cover a larger share of their own retirement costs.

Both of these referendums in California had hot detractors, but neither generated quite the meltdown that had resulted in Wisconsin. The major difference was that in the two California cities reformers managed to get Democrats involved in solving the problem, including San Jose Mayor Chuck Reed. "Insolvent retirement plans threaten to fiscally implode hundreds of municipal and state governments into irrelevance," wrote Sam Liccardo, then a member of San Jose's city council, now the mayor. "Although conservatives have long called for pension and arbitration reform, I supported these measures not in spite of my progressive views, but because of them. Progressive advocacy for affordable housing, environmental stewardship, marriage equality, and immigrant rights doesn't preclude the pragmatic pursuit of fiscal reform."

Helping politicians and voters understand the pension predicaments in San Diego and San Jose, and showing that the problem could be solved with firm action now, before deficits accumulated into a Detroit-style bankruptcy, was the work of an assortment of nonprofits, including the California Foundation for Fiscal Responsibility, and California Pension Reform. And powering these groups were public-policy philanthropists. Though operating out of the limelight, on a mostly educational basis, these grantmakers gave crucial boosts to reform and innovation.

Laura and John Arnold, the husband-and-wife team from Texas, were two of the most important donors behind the successful pension reforms in San Diego and San Jose. "The Arnold Foundation really got us going," says Marcia Fritz of the California Foundation for Fiscal Responsibility, which produced studies and hosted workshops for elected officials around the state. "It's such a wonderful foundation. The grant gave us validity, let us perform the public education that needed to happen, and helped us fundraise with other potential supporters."

Many philanthropists begin their major giving toward the end of their life. Not the Arnolds. In 2012, when he was just 38, John Arnold announced he was closing the hedge fund he created. Only people who wear numbers on their backs are supposed to retire so young, joked the *Houston Chronicle*. John said he was not actually retiring, just changing careers. With Laura, a former energy lawyer, he promised to work hard giving away a fortune estimated at more than $3 billion.

"I was more excited by working at the foundation, coming up with effective ways of creating change and solving problems," he explained. Many of the problems this young couple wants to solve are problems of public policy, in areas such as pensions, education, and criminal justice. "The mission is to change the country," says Laura.

Change for the better will require improvements in public accountability, according to the Arnolds. Confronting today's unsustainable commitments on public-employee benefits and pensions is their top current priority. This effort may not be glamorous, but governments won't be stable in the future if it is left unsolved. Research done jointly by the Arnold Foundation and the Pew Center on the States finds that the total shortfall in unfunded benefits promised to government workers by states and cities is now approaching $2 trillion.

The Arnolds hired economics Ph.D. Josh McGee to conduct background research on the pension mess. The foundation began to propose solutions, and educate the public. Separately, the Arnolds started the Action Now Initiative, a 501(c)(4) organization that funds local groups willing to advocate for measures like the San Diego and San Jose ballot initiatives.

The Arnolds have already tasted success not just in those two California cities, but also in Rhode Island, where Democratic state Treasurer (now Governor) Gina Raimondo pushed pension reform through the state legislature with a range of support from the Arnolds. They also aided the successful 2010 pension reform in Utah, and have joined forces with the field-general of that battle, former state senator Dan Liljenquist, sending him around the country under the aegis of the Action Now Initiative to share the lessons learned. The couple hope to repeat these successes in other jurisdictions, defusing public-pension bombs across the country well before they lead to political explosions like in Wisconsin or economic meltdowns as in Detroit.

Their campaign is difficult to pigeonhole politically. The Arnolds themselves have donated generously to Barack Obama. Yet the president of their foundation, Denis Calabrese, was chief-of-staff to former Congressman Dick Armey, a conservative and Tea Party favorite. With pension reform, they have adopted a cause that is frequently identified with Republicans. Yet they have demonstrated clear success in working with Democrats in a variety of cities and states.

However they are labeled, Laura and John Arnold have chosen to take on some of the most intractable problems facing America. Only time will tell if their accomplishments match their ambitions; many donors have failed at public-policy philanthropy. To date, though, the couple are showing a willingness to persevere even in the face of blowback.

In a 2014 *Chronicle of Philanthropy* article entitled "Attacks and Vitriol Will Not Deter Me From Supporting Fixes to Public Policy," John Arnold reported that "In recent months, I have endured a number of intensely personal public attacks on my philanthropy—including lies... selective reporting...and juvenile insults." These criticisms, he noted, "have the clear objective of intimidating me into standing down." Saying "we will not be deterred," however, he insisted that his foundation will continue to weigh in on public issues, as a balance to selfish special interests. Reforming or removing "policies that do not work for anyone other than the few who continue to gain from them at the expense of the rest of society" would be his public contribution as a philanthropist.

TOM CARROLL

Thomas Carroll is a public-policy marathoner. At New York's Foundation for Opportunity in Education he helps connect donors with alternative schools, nonprofit reformers, and needy students. When New York passed a groundbreaking law in 1998 allowing a limited number of charter schools across the state, he knew the fight for education reform was just beginning.

He was right. As charter schools began to take root in central Brooklyn, Harlem, Albany, and Buffalo, policy battles increased. "There was political pushback from the teacher unions and local school boards that were affected."

The introduction of legislation to cap the growth of charter schools caused reformists to rally their troops. "It was the beginning of a more aggressive advocacy phase. Charter-school advocates had to create a permanent policy and political presence within New York. The value of relationships in politics is paramount. Someone who shows up on an issue for the first time and expects to compete against teacher unions or any organized lobby is at an extreme disadvantage."

"So once the charter-school law was adopted, we didn't pop champagne corks and think it was over, but rather set up a series of ongoing nonprofit organizations funded by donors to handle the intellectual, policy, advocacy, and political side of advancing charter schools. Some of the charter networks looked at politics with great disdain. But as they started to suffer some of the indignities of the political process, they became more active."

"Over the last 15 years, it has become much more of a fair policy fight. There is now a pretty substantial set of education-policy donors in the state that, depending on the year, can match or exceed what the teacher unions spend. Because of that, there are mature advocacy organizations, getting more sophisticated every year, working to make our state's education policy more innovative. Donors no longer view it as, 'Oh, we just have to do this for a couple of years and then we can move on.' They see that there has to be a permanent ongoing effort funded at a fairly substantial level."

"There needs to be a broad constituency behind education reform. In New York, charter schools came in under a Republican governor, and there have been three Democratic governors since. We still had growth in charter schools, because great care was taken to make sure that the movement was perceived as a bipartisan effort benefitting children statewide."

"For my current work on behalf of a tax credit for donations that allow children to attend a school of their choice, I'm pulling together a coalition that's very broad. We have more than 80 community groups including the Brooklyn NAACP, the Urban League in Buffalo, the New York City Hispanic Chamber of Commerce, and more than 20 labor unions. The religious coalition includes the Catholic Church, Orthodox Jews, evangelical Christians, and Muslims. We joke when we have meetings that nobody is allowed to talk about any other issue, or the room could descend into a bar brawl. But this is one issue that everybody comes together on." (In his 2015 State of the State Address, New York's Democratic Governor Andrew Cuomo expressed support for Carroll's education tax credit.)

It takes patient donors to build these kinds of coalitions. "Michael Bloomberg, as the largest philanthropist in New York City, used to annually convene New York's top politics and policy donors, of both parties, and give them a little printed card of what he viewed as the top five priorities. Charter schools were always on the list. He would educate the donors that whenever you're raising money for any politician in New York, you need to ask them about these five issues."

"The biggest mistake donors make in this area is an assumption that politics is linear and predictable. Politics works in a zig-zaggy way. Donors, like all people, want instant gratification. We need patience. The charter-school law had three defeats before final approval. We're now in a phase, with a New York City mayor who's hostile to education reform, where a lot of political slugging is going to go on for a long time."

"That means people have to make donations with more risk. Giving on the other side of the mayor is an uncomfortable place for a lot of business people in New York. In New York, 501(c)(4) donors can be publicly disclosed, unlike the rest of the country, so there are no quiet checks. It's out in the open, so people have to get over being timid about controversy. They have to realize that's the price of moving forward on reform."

"On any public-policy issue where you have a well-financed, determined opponent with political capacity, 501(c)(3) charitable activities alone are simply not going to be enough. Donors who want to be successful policy advocates have to be willing to get engaged in politics, and be comfortable with a high level of uncertainty and risk. Some people just don't have the stomach for it."

"A tremendously high percentage of charitable giving on education reform currently goes to things like setting up charter schools or paying private-school tuitions for poor kids. A relatively small percentage goes to advocacy. I think the ratio needs to be rebalanced a bit. I think givers of charity should focus somewhat more on changing the policy environment in which district schools, charter schools, and private schools operate."

FRED KLIPSCH

"You know what's unacceptable?" says Fred Klipsch. "It's unacceptable that kids from poor families or living in the wrong zip codes don't get educated. We've known about this problem for decades but we've decided not to talk much about it."

Klipsch is an ideal figure to raise the volume on such conversations: His name is linked to the speaker company whose products are found in everything from miniature earbuds to massive home-theater systems. And his home state of Indiana has become a national leader in educational innovation partly because of the loud-and-clear messages that Klipsch has helped introduce into public discussions there.

Klipsch is quick to credit others for the Hoosier State's successes—former governor Mitch Daniels and former superintendent of public instruction Tony Bennett in particular. But his steady encouragement and support of their work made a crucial difference. And he has devoted the final phase of his career to going beyond talking about the problem of education and actually doing something about it directly, as a public-policy philanthropist.

"I'm a product of public schools," says Klipsch. "My dad worked in a factory. I went to grade school in the inner city of Indianapolis. I got a good education—this was back in the days when we made sure everybody got a good education." He graduated from high school in 1959 and went on to Purdue University. "Sometime after that, we let the teacher unions hijack the schools and then take over the state legislature."

For years, Klipsch paid far more attention to his businesses than to public policy. "I've been my own private equity firm for 50 years," he says with a smile. He bought a handful of nursing homes in the 1970s, and later moved into health-care real estate. In 1989, he purchased a small speaker company owned by a second cousin in Arkansas. It already had the name Klipsch, but Fred moved the firm to Indianapolis and transformed it in just about every other way, pushing it to become the top-selling maker of high-performance speakers in the United States.

In the 1990s, a fellow Indiana businessman approached Klipsch about improving education. The late Pat Rooney ran the Golden Rule Insurance Company. As a philanthropist, he was tireless in creating scholarships to help low-income students escape failing public schools and attend effective private ones. Klipsch agreed to get involved.

"We raised money and helped kids," says Klipsch. "That felt good." The Educational CHOICE Charitable Trust generated millions of dollars in donations and gave away thousands of annual tuition stipends. Over time, Klipsch succeeded Rooney as chairman of the group, which deliberately stayed out of politics. Over time, however, Klipsch began to sense that scholarships treated a symptom rather than offering a cure.

"I knew we weren't doing enough," he says. "Public education is a state-funded political monopoly. It costs the most and delivers the least. Our best students don't match up with the best students in other countries. Our average students are even worse off, on a relative basis. We've abandoned the concept that teachers are accountable and school boards are responsible. There's no competition."

In 2006, Klipsch became determined to introduce a bit of competition—through the arenas of politics and public policy. He started a pair of nonprofit groups, now called the Institute for Quality Education (concentrating on policy development) and Hoosiers for Quality Education (focused on politics and elections). Philanthropists who want to shake up dysfunctional public institutions and policies cannot ignore the rough and tumble of politics, Klipsch insists. "A policy arm without a political arm will fail," he says.

When Klipsch leapt into the politics of education in 2006, Democrats controlled Indiana's general assembly. Within four years, the GOP captured a majority—and later it went on to win a supermajority. Collaborating with Governor Daniels and Superintendent Bennett, Republicans then pushed through a series of major reforms, including merit pay for teachers, charter-school expansion, and tax credits for donors of scholarships. By 2014, Indiana was sponsoring the country's second-largest school voucher program, allowing nearly 20,000 students to attend private schools rather than failed public alternatives.

"You need to focus on politics, but you can't overlook policy," says Klipsch. Coming up with good ideas is essential. So is excellent communication. "We don't talk about 'reform,'" says Klipsch. "In the science of messaging, that's a negative word. Teachers hear it and think we want to put them out of their jobs. That's not the case. We try to promote what works, and we talk about providing a quality education.

That's what most teachers want as well, even if their union leaders make it appear otherwise."

After developing, marketing, and enacting new policy ideas, there comes the essential implementation. "Once policies are in place, you have to help with their execution," Klipsch notes. Just because a state sponsors vouchers doesn't mean that families will realize they're available—especially if officials aren't committed to a program's success. "So you may have to make sure families know that they're eligible to take advantage. You can't leave this up to the politicians. Once they enact a policy, they move on. The successful execution will come back to you."

It may seem like the struggle never ends—and that's correct, Klipsch warns. There's always a new challenge: "This effort will take a couple of decades, not a couple of years. It's a hard journey. You can't just wave a magic wand and solve all problems."

Klipsch continues to donate generously to the groups he oversees. He also seeks allies, fundraising among successful men and women who share the vision of Indiana as a blazer of new paths to educational excellence. "I go after major givers," he says. "Most of my donors are successful businessmen. About 60 percent of our budget comes from 20 to 25 individuals."

Motivating fellow donors, he says, involves repeating a version of the argument that inspired him to become a public-policy philanthropist. "Our society allows a lot of students not to get educated and says it's okay. But if you see a bus hit a lady in the street, and then walk around without helping her—maybe you bear some responsibility for her death," he says. "That's how we should think about public education. And those in a position to become philanthropists in this area need to become leaders. People say they can't do anything to fix public education, but that's just wrong."

The Power of Invention

At a 2002 dinner hosted by the Heritage Foundation in honor of former British Prime Minister Margaret Thatcher, Heritage president Edwin Feulner noticed a tear welling in the eye of beer mogul Joseph Coors. The old man leaned over, gestured to the assembly of 900 national leaders, and said, "Heritage is my legacy." This was a powerful statement. Coors, after all, had led an extraordinarily successful life in business, turning his grandfather's regional beer company into America's third-largest brewer. Yet he held this product of his public-policy philanthropy in even higher regard.

Sometimes, investing in good work done by the top existing organizations is the best way for philanthropy to take on problems in public policy. Other times, though, a public-policy challenge may require a fresh approach that only a new organization can provide. This entails a high level of risk for donors. Just as most small businesses shutter within five years of their start, most nonprofits fail to thrive. Yet the flip side of risk is reward, and a smart investment in an unproven idea can lead to dramatic results. Without risk-taking philanthropists willing to back new creations, vital organizations like the Heritage Foundation and the Brookings Institution would not exist, leaving serious holes in national policy debates.

The story of the Heritage Foundation begins in the late 1960s and early 1970s, when conservatives in Congress complained that they could not keep up with liberals. Their rivals enjoyed the services of the Brookings Institution and other well-established organizations that reinforced the seemingly inexorable growth of the federal government. Conservatives lacked competing idea-generating groups. When several Congressional staffers learned that Joseph Coors was interested in helping conservative political causes, they invited him to Washington, D.C., and arranged a meeting with a handful of senators and congressmen. The lawmakers explained how much they needed a new action-oriented, fast-moving think tank, and urged Coors to fund one.

The brewer was intrigued, but torn by the alternative of making a safer investment in the American Enterprise Institute, a free-market think tank that had already enjoyed solid success for several decades. Coors was ultimately persuaded that a new think tank was needed. The capability conservatives were then missing was offering timely and conveniently bite-sized information to Members of Congress—before they had to make legislative votes.

In 1971 and 1972, Coors contributed $250,000 to a new venture, first called the Analysis and Research Association but soon retitled the Heritage Foundation. The support from Coors not only paid the initial bills but also gave other public-policy philanthropists confidence to make their own donations. If the Heritage Foundation was good enough for Coors, they reasoned, it was good enough for them as well. William Brady, the Samuel Roberts Noble Foundation, and Richard Mellon Scaife became significant backers. Many more followed, underwriting the Heritage Foundation's steady growth as it provided conservatives with the quick and reliable issue-research that was so badly needed.

Coors was known as the first American beverage company to package its product in aluminum cans. Now the Heritage Foundation became the first think tank to pour its research aimed at members of Congress into quick and convenient eight-page "backgrounders" on the topic of the moment. "A congressman or other public official had to be able to fit a Heritage paper in his briefcase and read it on the go," said William Simon, the Olin Foundation president and former Treasury Secretary. "By so doing, and I know this from personal experience, Heritage reshaped the world of think tanks and Washington policymaking."

Joseph Coors continued to make large donations to the Heritage Foundation his whole life long, believing that good organizations deserve ongoing support from philanthropists rather than abandonment. He also served on its board, where he persuaded the think tank to act more like a

> Coors identified a need, realized that existing institutions could not meet it, and discovered a capable group of policy entrepreneurs worthy of a major investment as they built something entirely new.

business than a charity. He demanded that it create an operating reserve, and hammered away at the supreme importance of marketing, even for merchandise as ephemeral as ideas. By the time Coors died in 2003, just a few months after the tribute dinner for Margaret Thatcher, the Heritage Foundation had become one of the most influential public-policy organizations in the country. In 2013, it had an annual budget of $77 million.

Coors identified a need, realized that existing institutions could not meet it, and discovered a capable group of policy entrepreneurs worthy of a major investment as they built something entirely new. His venture was especially successful, but the effort was hardly unique. The creation of new groups to satisfy unmet needs is one of the major paths to success in public-policy philanthropy.

Indeed Heritage, as mentioned, was a response to the earlier creation of the Brookings Institution, whose success inspired admiration and envy. Heritage never tried to mimic Brookings, but it sought to provide its conservative allies with data and research needed to win battles on Capitol Hill as effectively as the Brookings Institution did in its own way for liberals. In serving as Heritage's founding angel, Joe Coors was actually following in the footsteps of Robert Brookings.

An amazingly successful salesman who took advantage of the business boom in St. Louis following the Civil War, Brookings retired in 1895 at the age of 47, then devoted much of the rest of his life to improving society. An early foray into traditional charity did not go well: He asked police officers to point him toward needy families at Christmastime, only to discover that the officers received kickbacks from the families Brookings tried to help. He went on, however, to become one of his generation's great philanthropists in public policy.

While serving on a public commission during the First World War, Brookings observed the desperate need in government for reliable economic data. When the fighting was over, Brookings acted. Instead of starting a brand-new organization, he took control of a moribund group, the Institute for Government Research, and injected new life into it. He gave it not just money but also leadership, raising funds from friends in order to build an organization capable of supplying the federal government with the basic information Brookings felt it needed.

He was dogged in enlisting other donors. "Do you want things to go on in the haphazard fashion of the past? Do you want a log-rolling or a scientific tariff? Do you want pork-barrel bills or a budget?" he would ask his friends.

Brookings did not intend to push a personal program or ideology. His passion really was the gathering and distribution of facts. His biographer, Hermann Hagedorn, called Brookings the "Maecenas of research," referring to a Roman patron of arts and culture.

"Nearly every interest in the country is now organized and has permanent representation in Washington, all striving to further their own interests," Brookings wrote to John Rockefeller Jr., one of his supporters. "We are the only research activity in Washington which is just simply collecting evidence in the interest of the truth, and making our findings known." One of his organization's early accomplishments was the creation of a more orderly federal budget process, something government seemed unable to accomplish itself before philanthropists came to the rescue.

In addition to funding and promoting the Institute for Government Research, Brookings started a new organization in 1922: the Institute of Economics. It would advocate for specific policies. In 1927, the two institutes merged, becoming the Brookings Institution. For all practical purposes, it was the first modern think tank, mixing basic research with policy advice aimed at improving government.

Robert Brookings died in 1932, so although he glimpsed his group's potential, he did not see it become hugely influential. Eventually, though, its scholars and researchers helped create the Marshall Plan, the United Nations, and the Congressional Budget Office. It defended, refined, and reinforced many of the institutions of the New Deal and Great Society. And it remained relevant over many decades—in 2012, a University of Pennsylvania survey named it the world's leading think tank.

Other prominent think tanks have creation stories that remind us how often powerful forces in public policy begin with acts of philanthropy. In 1977, oilman Charles Koch provided the seed money for Ed Crane to start the Cato Institute, which would become the dominant research organization for libertarians. They wanted their own version of Heritage or Brookings: "not an above-the-fray educational institute, but an in-the-debate public-policy house," as Brian Doherty put it in *Radicals for Capitalism*. Cato opened in San Francisco, moved to Washington in 1981, and established a reputation for sound work on Social Security privatization, school choice, and free trade.

The Manhattan Institute was willed into existence by philanthropist Antony Fisher (see 1978 entry in this book's Annex). It has been generously supported by many of the country's most prominent public-policy donors throughout the decades since its founding. The Manhattan Institute played an important role in thinking through welfare reform, crime control, entitlement and budget issues, and many other topics of public governance. It was a strong influence on Rudy Giuliani's great successes as mayor.

A generation later, liberals who had become disenchanted with the perceived moderation and passivity of Brookings, which had always been reluctant to embark on starkly partisan projects, founded the Center for American Progress, a group with no such shyness. The former chief of staff in the Clinton administration, John Podesta, relied on funding from banking entrepreneurs Herb and Marion Sandler to start a nonprofit organization with two distinct wings—a 501(c)(3) that conducts traditional policy research, linked with a 501(c)(4) that engages in partisan advocacy.

In the *New York Times*, Podesta described CAP as "a think tank on steroids." Others were more specific: "With the Center for American Progress, Podesta was trying to create something new: a think tank that doubled as a campaign war room," wrote Byron York in *The Vast Left Wing Conspiracy*. The center's initial donors had hoped it would help Democrats capture the Presidency in 2004. That didn't happen, but the group helped to pave the way for Democratic success in the congressional elections of 2006, as well as the race for the White House in 2008.

CAP's aggressive partisan style was so influential that its *bête noire* offered the ultimate compliment: In 2010, the Heritage Foundation imitated the center's main innovation. Heritage launched a parallel 501(c)(4) action group of its own.

DICK WEEKLEY

"Making money is fun, but nothing compares to this," says Dick Weekley, the homebuilder who brought legal reform to Texas as a public-policy philanthropist. "Other than family, trying to make society better is the most rewarding thing you can do in life."

In the early 1990s, Weekley didn't know any of this. He just knew that his home state of Texas faced a litigation crisis and somebody had to fix it. "I wanted to help, but had no time to lead the effort," he says. "But since nobody else agreed to take the time to lead, I finally drew the black bean."

That's a Texan's way of saying he drew the short straw—the reference comes from the 1840s, when a group of Texas Republic soldiers tried to escape from their Mexican guards. The Mexicans recaptured 176 of them and, as punishment, condemned roughly one out of every ten to death. They filled an earthen jar with 159 white beans and 17 black beans. The men who drew black beans were shot.

It's a grim metaphor, and Weekley didn't consider himself fortunate when he agreed to take on the most powerful special-interest group in his state— the Texas Trial Lawyers Association, known as "the Trials." For a generation, the Trials had preyed on hospitals and businesses, driving up the cost of everything. "There was no effective opposition," says Weekley. "It seemed like this problem was in the process of destroying the state, as well as the country, if it didn't get solved."

The organization he helped found, Texans for Lawsuit Reform, enjoyed early success though. And it then continued to be politically relevant. Today, TLR remains one of the most powerful reform forces in the state, and a model for other philanthropists.

Weekley was born and raised in Houston and attended Southern Methodist University, graduating in 1967. After serving in the Navy for three and a half years, including a tour of duty in Vietnam, he returned to Houston to work at a real-estate company. It wasn't exactly his dream. "I just needed a job and was offered one in real estate." Yet it turned into a calling: Two years later, Weekley started his own firm, and later expanded into homebuilding and commercial development. By the late-1980s, he was a wealthy man.

In 1993, though, Weekley attended a presentation detailing how litigation was driving businesses out of Texas, how doctors were leaving their medical practices or retiring early, and how businesses were reluctant to expand in the state because of out-of-control and abusive lawsuits.

At first, Weekley and several of his friends, also successful businessmen, tried to address the problem by supporting existing organizations. Nothing seemed to work, though. "Before long, we recognized that we needed to try something different—we needed a new organization that would think out of the box and go about things in a new way," he says.

That's when he drew the black bean. Weekley became the full-time volunteer leader of Texans for Lawsuit Reform, founded in 1994. "I thought it would take a couple of years," he says. "Then two years turned into 22."

He recalls a conversation with his brother, David, who is his business partner. "David asked me if I wanted to spend my time building more shopping centers, or if it was more important to change Texas. It dawned on me that there were things more important than simply making money."

Although Weekley and his allies had a vision, they were not sure how to achieve it. "I felt like I had been dropped into the middle of the Atlantic Ocean and didn't know whether to swim north, south, east, or west. I didn't know anything about public policy or politics. I was in the real-estate and development business!"

"We started by assembling a bunch of capable people in a room and deciding, initially, what the biggest problems were. Then we worked on which of the various solutions were the most efficacious. Finally we figured out how to piece things together to accomplish our goals."

One of the group's first insights was to reject the established methods of changing public policy. "The conventional business lobby wasn't enough," says Weekley. "The weakness of that model starts with their aversion to risk. Nobody wants to make an enemy or become a target."

"Moreover, mainline business lobbies spread their resources across a wide spectrum of issues and concerns. In the case of lawsuit reform, they are going up against an extremely wealthy group of personal injury lawyers with a narrow self-interest. The lawyers had been working the legislature for decades and had massive influence. There was a total mismatch of capabilities. That's why there was a need for a new organization with a new approach that provided a laser-like focus on lawsuit reform."

A year after the launch of Texans for Lawsuit Reform, a breakthrough was achieved. "That's the year we broke the lock," says Weekley. "It wasn't just one piece of legislation. It was the cumulative effect of putting eight bills together." The eight separate pieces of legislation that got passed reined in the unbridled power of the Trials in a variety of ways—from capping punitive damages, to prohibiting venue shopping.

There remained plenty to do. "We still had huge holes to plug," says Weekley. Over the next several years, Texans for Lawsuit Reform pushed their legislative allies for more reforms. (See 1994 entry on Annex list of Major Projects in U.S. Public-Policy Philanthropy.)

Arguing for bills on their merits went only so far, though. "We also needed to engage in politics, and help to elect legislators who had the courage to vote with their conscience and their constituents for lawsuit reform. A lot of state reform groups focus on research and advocacy. And that's important. But it's not enough," says Weekley. "You need to help elect legislators who have similar beliefs, and back them politically."

So in addition to performing the traditional work of a think tank, Texans for Lawsuit Reform created TLR PAC, which funded candidates willing to solve the state's litigation problems. In 2002, it played a key role in the Republican takeover of the Texas House of Representatives, which Democrats had controlled since Reconstruction. A flood of reforms followed, making Texas courts more balanced, and fairer to retailers, manufacturers, and doctors. By 2006, the Pacific Research Institute's "U.S. Tort Liability Index"—which evaluated every state on its legal climate—ranked Texas as best in the nation.

That same year, Texans for Lawsuit Reform published *Template for Reform*, describing how Weekley and his allies met their objectives. The document, which Weekley uses like a playbook, is available on the group's website (tortreform. com). He summarizes some of its lessons for other philanthropists who might be contemplating taking on an entrenched public problem.

First, he encourages thinking big: "We're totally against gradualism and halfway measures. We kept hearing that this was how things were done in Austin—one bill at a time, always watered down, legislative session after legislative session. We didn't accept that. We weren't willing to wait for decades."

It's important to brace for a fight that can turn dirty. "There are vested interests on the other side, and often tens of billions of dollars at stake when you change public policies. It's going to get rough." He tells stories of journalistic hit jobs, office break-ins, phone lines being tapped, and even death threats.

Volunteer leadership is essential. "Unless there are committed volunteers at the top, people won't get out of their chairs to help," says Weekley. Much of his work involves raising money to meet multimillion-dollar budgets. "A lot of days, I feel like a university president, laying out a vision and asking for donations," he says. "But this isn't a one-time task, like chairing a campaign for a campus building or a church. The effort is constant."

In addition to promoting legal reform, Weekley has been a leader in local efforts to improve the quality of life in Houston. He has, for instance, helped create more parks and green space in his growing city. In 2014, the Texas Business Leadership Council named its annual policy-reform prize the Richard Weekley Public Policy Leadership Award.

Drawing the black bean, apparently, was Dick Weekley's lucky day. Does he ever think he might have made more money if he hadn't become a public-policy philanthropist? "Maybe I would have," he says. "Or maybe I would have gone bankrupt. I have no regrets about any of this. I'm really happy to have made this choice of how to spend my time."

Policy Player Profile
PAUL BREST

Paul Brest, former dean of the Stanford law school and retired president of the William and Flora Hewlett Foundation—one of America's largest givers—is painting a mental picture. "Suppose you're supporting a social program to reduce teen pregnancy, or to improve outcomes for disadvantaged kids in a charter school. After the program is established you can not only measure the outcomes (pregnancies, test scores), but also expect to see similar results year after year. Once you've built a good program, success is a pretty linear process."

"With policy advocacy, progress is totally nonlinear. You're trying to persuade policymakers to do something. It may or may not happen, depending on the political environment as much as on anything you do. And even after a policy is adopted, there remains the question of whether it's going to be implemented. So it's much harder to proclaim success via public-policy philanthropy than it is with a typical social intervention."

When the Hewlett Foundation decided to act on global warming during Brest's tenure, they encountered this abstract problem as a practical reality. "Our efforts started with a decision that global warming was a problem. We decided, first, through grantees, to encourage policymakers to adopt policies that would mitigate climate change. And, second, we provided technical assistance to help different sectors reduce carbon dioxide emissions (supporting, for instance, organizations encouraging transportation efficiency, appliance efficiency, and more efficient cities)."

"At the magnitude that we felt it needed to be done, we decided the campaign to mitigate climate change called for a separate organization. That was the genesis of ClimateWorks." The official ClimateWorks goal was a giant one: To slash emissions of carbon dioxide and other greenhouse gases by 50 percent by the year 2030.

"We thought it would be helpful to combine forces with other funders who were trying to achieve the same ends, so there were two other major co-funders at the beginning. One was the Packard Foundation, and the other was the McKnight Foundation. Over time, other foundations and wealthy individuals either funded ClimateWorks or funded organizations in parallel."

"ClimateWorks is a re-granter. Hewlett and the other funders put hundreds of millions of dollars into the organization, and it then made grants, in effect substituting for our own staff in doing the grantmaking." (For some additional details, see 2007 entry on Annex list of Major Projects in U.S. Public-Policy Philanthropy.)

"ClimateWorks was heavily involved in encouraging countries to reach an international agreement in Copenhagen in 2009. It didn't succeed." Rather than setting up an international regime of carbon-dioxide controls, the U.N. conference collapsed in disarray.

"It's not a surprise that it failed. Given how complicated and costly carbon limits would be, the likelihood of success was very small. But we thought that the magnitude of the success if it happened justified the cost. It's not very different from an early-stage venture capitalist who thinks the likelihood of success is not very great but hopes that every once in a while, there'll be a home run."

"Imagine you're a philanthropist responding to malaria. An intervention that has a high probability of success is providing people with malaria bed nets for use at night. You have data and can be pretty sure how much that's going to reduce malaria. But your could also try to end malaria by investing in developing a malaria vaccine. That has a low probability of success, but if you get it, the effects would be large. That's the way philanthropists should think about risky investments."

"Philanthropists, like other people, tend to be somewhat risk-averse. And they love to see obvious successes. So many would rather buy the bed nets that they know are going to make a difference, and it's only foundations like Gates who take a risk on a vaccine. An alternative option would be a mix of grants—fund some things where the outcome is certain, so you feel psychologically good about that, plus some risky things."

"The worst possibility is when the board says, 'Yes, we're willing to take a high risk,' and then the initiative fails and they feel really bad about it and blame the foundation president and staff. At Hewlett, when Copenhagen crashed, the board never blamed the staff. The board said, 'We knew this was risky. It didn't work.' And they moved on."

"Philanthropists should take risks when the risk has the possibility of making a real difference. Government policymakers avoid risky decisions because they're worried about getting re-elected and reappointed. Foundations have the wonderful advantage of not being accountable."

"We often think of the lack of accountability as a source of criticism, but actually the independence of donors is a great source of power. The power ought to be used wisely. But I think taking risks that politicians won't is a very good use of philanthropic resources."

Working through
the Courts

The Heritage Foundation and the Brookings
Institution may differ in ideological orientation,
but they share one important feature in common:
They are both general-service think tanks that work
on a broad range of topics, pumping out research
and analysis on everything from military security to
health care to bank regulation. Visiting their websites
is like shopping at Walmart or Target: They stock a
little bit of everything. This offers advantages—

convenience, economies of scale, powerful branding. Yet customers sometimes prefer specialty stores.

Moreover, think tanks are mostly oriented toward influencing Congress, the President, and the legislative process. But of course there is another branch making public policy in America, and that is the courts. Starting in the 1960s and '70s, liberal philanthropists pioneered the concept of single-issue public-interest law firms. Suing at every opportunity, often on novel grounds, these litigators exerted enormous influence on public policy, especially in the area of civil rights.

Philanthropists funding lawsuits as a way to improve public policies was not a brand-new concept. Booker T. Washington secretly financed the *Giles v. Harris* case way back in 1903, and throughout the rest of his life paid for other litigation aimed at undoing racial disenfranchisement. (See more detail in the 1903 entry of the Annex to this book.) But paying for lawsuits openly and on a vast scale was something new in the

> For more than a century, philanthropists have been funding lawsuits as a way to improve public policies.

1960s. In our current era of freewheeling litigation, legal activism continues to be a powerful strategy, offering large openings for philanthropists who want to take a more narrowly focused approach to changing public policies.

In the early '60s, the Ford Foundation was America's biggest philanthropy, and the foundation's grants pushed a fairly mainstream liberalism. As the civil-rights revolution unfolded, though, the foundation began to promote rapid social change. The foundation made a particular leap into activism when it hired McGeorge Bundy as its new president in 1966.

A national security adviser in the Kennedy and Johnson administrations, Bundy was an enthusiast for the re-engineering of society by government. At the Ford Foundation, "Mac," as he was known to friends, was literally a limousine liberal: "Every morning at 8:15 a limousine ferried Mac downtown to his spacious office in the Ford Foundation headquarters," writes Kai Bird in *The Color of Truth*. From there, Bundy steered Ford into a dramatic new phase, spending about $200 million each year—vastly more than any other player, and more than most other players combined—with large sums going to some quite radical efforts. Achieving quick alterations of public policy was goal No. 1.

McGeorge Bundy had become convinced that racism was the biggest problem in America. Leading a moral and political crusade with race issues at its center became his obsession. Racial grievance groups became the favorite recipients of Ford's enormous cash flow, rising from 2.5 percent of the foundation's grants in 1960 to fully 40 percent by 1970.

Bundy thought the Ford Foundation was much too conventional and timid. "What really large and constructive forces has it let loose in our society?" he asked. The aggressive agenda that Bundy wanted to promote actually outstripped the ability of the traditional institutions of liberal public policy to carry out the spending. So Ford created many new groups. Each had a special emphasis, and there was a powerful overall interest among them in using litigation battles as a tool for uprooting and re-seeding various fields of public policy. Many of these new activist legal groups owed their existence entirely to the foundation's giving.

"The civil rights movement has long received support from varied private sources, including foundations, corporations, and individuals," wrote Robert McKay of New York University Law School. "But litigation work has received a relatively small share of that total, with the bulk of support going to the more traditional areas of research, scholarship grants, and the strengthening of institutions weakened by discrimination." Ford's innovation, McKay noted, was in actively triggering litigation.

The foundation and its surrogates would seek out parties with standing to sue, initiate challenges, pay powerful legal teams to build cases, and try to leave behind large and lasting precedents. "Many people, including elements of the organized bar, have long felt that to provide financial assistance for the conduct of litigation, regardless of the metis of the case, might be an inappropriate intrusion in the judicial process," wrote McKay. The Ford Foundation's went much further than just paying for litigation. It fomented public-interest litigation, and created groups whose entire mission was to reshape public policy through lawsuits.

The effort kicked off in 1967 with big grants to groups like the Lawyers' Committee for Civil Rights Under Law, and the NAACP Legal Defense Fund. One of the first products of this campaign was to establish the principle of "disparate impact"—which maintained that policies of colorblind neutrality could be considered discriminatory if they coincided with unbalanced racial outcomes. Soon, Ford-powered litigation created policies of direct racial preference in public contracting, education, and employment.

The real groundbreaking philanthropy was what came next. The Ford Foundation created several ethnic action groups from scratch. An important one was the Mexican American Legal Defense and Educational Fund, which received more than $2 million in startup cash in 1969, and heavy ongoing support in succeeding years. Its major achievement was to argue that African Americans were only one of many groups discriminated against in American life.

Before long, voting-rights law evolved to guarantee the creation of majority-Hispanic jurisdictions, even at the price of gerrymandered district lines. Ethnic fillips were added to racial preferences and quotas. MALDEF prevailed in *Plyer v. Doe*, in which the Supreme Court decided that public schools must open their doors to illegal aliens. The group filed lawsuits to require that English learners receive public-school instruction in Spanish. Support from the Ford Foundation was crucial in making all of this possible.

And MALDEF was just one extension of Ford's civil-rights crusade. The foundation also founded several other litigation engines in the early 1970s. The Puerto Rican Legal Defense and Education Fund worked to establish native-language instruction as a legal right for language-minority children. The Native American Rights Fund frequently clashed with the federal government over tribal lands.

Soon, women were also defined as an aggrieved group (though not a minority, since they make up more than half of the population). Ford launched the Women's Law Fund. It gave birth to the Women's Rights Project at the American Civil Liberties Union. The Minority Women's Employment Program was set up at the NAACP-LDF, and the Chicana Rights Project got funding at MALDEF. The most influential of these was the ACLU's endeavor, co-founded by Ruth Bader Ginsburg. Her strategy was to file lawsuits based on clever readings of the 14th Amendment's equal protection clause, leading judges to wipe out gender distinctions in everything from employment to family law.

By creating numerous heavily funded public-interest law firms that would litigate on civil rights, the Ford Foundation met Bundy's objective of achieving dramatic results within a relatively short period of time. These groups left a permanent large mark on public policy.

This tidal shift inspired a response from thinkers with different approaches to race and ethnic issues. Thomas Sowell, Abigail Thernstrom, Linda Chavez, and others commenced research or started organizations, often with their own (much more modest) philanthropic funding. They argued that racial preferences and quotas violate the principle of equal opportunity that is the best base for civil-rights protection. Right-of-center donors tried to offer help that could balance some of the Ford Foundation's legal activism.

While conservatives did not embrace public-interest law as quickly or as fully as liberals, they did make some early efforts in the field. In 1968, the National Right to Work Legal Defense Foundation began to help workers fend off compulsory unionization via court cases. In the 1970s, several broad-spectrum conservative public-interest law firms were founded on a regional basis. The most successful was the Pacific Legal Foundation, started in 1973. Its initial backers were allies of California Governor Ronald Reagan (who became frustrated by legal efforts to block welfare reform), and business leaders responding to environmental litigation. Before long, a number of similar organizations sprang up.

These initial efforts from the right were weak, however. A memo prepared in the early 1980s by the staff of the Olin Foundation stated the problem bluntly: "The bright hopes of ten years ago that conservatives could create effective counterparts to the liberals groups that have taken their policy agendas to the courtroom, such as the American Civil Liberties Union and the Sierra Club, have produced more disappointments than success. The loose network of law firms has not been conspicuously effective, well-organized, or stable."

Conservative philanthropists concerned with the imbalance in the courts found few existing nonprofits they could turn to. So in the 1980s they created new forms. Attorneys Michael Greve and Michael McDonald circulated a proposal to open the Center for Individual Rights, a different kind of public-interest firm. Having witnessed how weak staffing, a limited regional emphasis, and overreliance on corporate patronage had caused previous forays by conservatives into public-interest law to fail, they proposed to build a firm that defined itself not by particular issue but as a defender of liberty, with enough horsepower to establish important legal precedents.

Greve and McDonald rounded up initial support from the Bradley, Olin, and Smith Richardson foundations, then went to work. The main legacy of the Center for Individual Rights today is the lawsuits they filed in opposition to use of racial preferences to manipulate the student bodies of public universities. In 1996, the center prevailed in *Hopwood v. Texas*, a federal case that notched a clear victory against color-coded admissions. Seven years later, the center took a pair of cases involving race and admissions to the Supreme Court, but suffered a setback when the justices accepted race-based admissions at the University of Michigan for certain purposes.

By this time, however, conservative foundations had built an infrastructure of civil-rights organizations and arguments that challenged race-conscious public policies in both courts of law and the court of public opinion. One of the new organizations they financed, the Center for Equal Opportunity led by Linda Chavez, issued a series of reports that published data on the admissions scores of students at public universities broken down by race and ethnicity—showing, despite fervent denials from officials, that skin color and ancestry were huge factors in determining which students got accepted and which got excluded.

Evidence of this sort changed the public mood. In 1996, California voters approved Proposition 209, also known as the California Civil Rights Initiative, which banned the use of race in public contracting, employment, and university admissions. Relying on donated support, Ward Connerly of the American Civil Rights Institute led the campaign. He later became involved in similarly successful measures in Arizona, Michigan, Washington, and elsewhere. Efforts to push federal legislation, however, went nowhere. Increasingly, the left and right approaches to civil rights were locked in uneasy stalemate.

There continued to be opportunities for savvy donors to refine the law, however. The Project for Fair Representation matched plaintiffs and attorneys over a period of years to test the legitimacy and boundaries of racial affirmative action in college admissions, the drawing of voting districts, and other areas. Thanks to philanthropic support, the group was able to take cases all the way to the U.S. Supreme Court, winning rulings that placed new limits on the use of racial preferences.

In 1991, a new right-of-center public-interest law firm called the Institute for Justice began to define civil rights in fresh ways. The group suggested, for instance, that parents have a civil right to educational choice for their children. Philanthropist Charles Koch had pledged up to $1.5 million for the creation of a "national law firm on liberty." The Institute for Justice never needed the full Koch pledge, because it quickly raised additional funds from other sources, especially as it began accepting and winning cases.

IJ rapidly became one of the leading firms pursuing "public interest" cases in the courts, usually for no fee. It aggressively litigated in four areas: economic rights, free speech, private property protection, and school choice. It has taken numerous cases all the way to the U.S. Supreme

Court. In *Zelman v. Simmons-Harris* the high court endorsed public funding of private-school vouchers. In *Kelo v. City of New London* the justices rejected IJ's call to forbid use of eminent domain for economic development, but a public backlash stirred up by the case compelled state legislatures around the country to restrict the use of eminent domain via new laws—highlighting the success of IJ's model combining good lawyering with strategic research, media savvy, and political activism.

The organization's second donor, retired investor Robert Wilson, helped fuel it to new heights when, after years of making annual gifts of $35,000 and promising more only "when the time is right," he issued a challenge grant in 2008. He would donate $15 million if IJ would raise a matching $30 million. This double infusion allowed the organization to expand significantly and become one of the nation's leading litigants for liberty.

> With reform via legislation having proved inadequate, a donor hacked out a new path around the entrenched interest groups—and toward a policy solution executed by the courts.

Philanthropists have also been active in supporting litigation that tests the legality of various provisions of President Obama's Affordable Care Act. Donor have supported petitioners and groups filing supporting briefs in challenges to Obamacare's funding mechanisms, the operation of state exchanges, the allowability of its Independent Payment Advisory Board, the extent of employer mandates, the law's infringements on religious freedoms, and other issues. These questions strike at the very heart of the Affordable Care Act, and its Constitutionality and durability will not be settled until these donor-supported suits have been adjudicated.

The latest signal moment in donor-funded public-policy litigation came in 2014. Silicon Valley entrepreneur David Welch and his wife had spent years trying to improve public schools in their home state of California. They tried traditional education grants, funding new teaching methods, bringing technology into schools. They soon realized that in many public schools, incompetent teachers made necessary educational improvements impossible.

So in 2011 Welch founded a group called Students Matter, and gathered facts about the forces blocking school reform. He found nine students who reported that their education suffered after they were stuck in classrooms with poor teachers. Between 2011 and 2014, Welch spent several million dollars hiring a top-flight legal team and building a court case that California's teacher-tenure laws—which grant permanent employment after just 18 months on the job, make it nearly impossible to fire even the most terrible teachers, and require school districts to lay teachers off based on seniority rather than competence—deprive students of the right to be educated as guaranteed by the state constitution. Welch was also canny enough to put up the funds for an accompanying public-relations campaign to fend off a massive counterattack by teacher unions, which, predictably, was quick in coming.

In 2014, a judge of the Los Angeles Superior Court ruled that "there are a significant number of grossly ineffective teachers currently active in California classrooms" and that this causes thousands of students to fall years behind in math and reading. "The evidence is compelling. Indeed, it shocks the conscience," wrote Judge Rolf Treu in his *Vergara v. State of California* decision striking down seniority-based job protections for unionized teachers.

The state appealed, a process that could take three years. Almost immediately, though, other philanthropists and education reformers began to consider similar donor-funded lawsuits to take on rigid teacher tenure in states like New York, Connecticut, New Jersey, New Mexico, and Oregon. With traditional reform via legislation having proved inadequate to solve a damaging public problem, a donor hacked out a new path around the entrenched interest groups—and toward a policy solution executed by the courts.

CLINT BOLICK

For lawyer Clint Bolick, understanding the power of philanthropically funded "public interest" litigation begins with a history lesson. "For decades, starting with the creation of the NAACP Legal Defense Fund and the founding of the ACLU early in the twentieth century, followed by the rise of groups in the 1960s and '70s that deployed lawsuits against ethnic and environmental grievances, the Left had free rein in the courts. There really were no conservative organizations that were active at all."

"Starting in the late 1970s, the U.S. Chamber of Commerce added a little bit of balance with some conservative public-interest litigation. Initially, theirs was very much a defensive strategy, designed to blunt the highly effective liberal, environmental, and civil rights organizations that were basically setting all the new standards in our courts. Out of that came the first generation of conservative public-interest law firms, organized on a regional basis with the idea that each group would focus on issues important in their area."

"These entities had very mixed success. They tended to receive a large percentage of their giving from corporations, and I would characterize them as pro-business rather than pro-free enterprise. They didn't attract great talent, did not win many cases, and had a limited impact. Several fell by the wayside. The two that remain today are Pacific Legal Foundation and Mountain States Legal Foundation, which have evolved into effective organizations. Chip Mellor and I, before we co-founded the Institute for Justice, both worked at Mountain States Legal Foundation, and we were frustrated by its defensive agenda and narrow pro-business approach at that time. So we started thinking about what a more effective conservative public-interest law firm could look like."

After a season in the Reagan administration, Bolick and Mellor had their chance. "We put together a game plan for what would become the Institute for Justice. It was the birth of a second generation of conservative public-interest law firms. Our model differed from the original versions in several important respects. It was national rather than regional. It set goals rather than responding to the Left's agenda. It developed constitutional precedents that we wanted to achieve."

"We believed our mission would attract support from foundations and individual contributors—donors with less of a mercenary self-interest, and more desire to establish legal principles. We received our seed funding from Charles and David Koch. They gave us a five-year commitment, and we moved very quickly to diversify the funding base to include other foundations and individuals."

The surge of donor interest exceeded Bolick's expectations. "No one had really tried to get individual donors invested in litigation. And it turned out that donors were very moved by the stories of the people we represented. It was more action-oriented than research-oriented work, and people felt invested in the cases that we filed."

"We wanted to avoid dependence on a small number of large contributors. It was very important for us to have autonomy, and I think our donors appreciated that we weren't dominated by contributors who might be able to influence the work we were doing. We started with the Kochs by going to them with a detailed game plan. They invested in it instead of coming up with their own plan or imposing or suggesting one. They were not deeply involved in strategy. They didn't have previous experience in public-interest litigation. I think we were their first model."

"The Kochs have evolved in their philanthropic pursuits. Today they are bringing together individual donors and bundling supporters in effective ways. An individual contributor who has $100,000 to invest in the freedom movement oftentimes will not go very far, but the Kochs have learned how to connect that donor with like-minded fellows. They have also encouraged investment in judicial races across the country, which is very, very important."

"The donor base is broader today. I received my very first seed funding, long before the Institute for Justice, from the Bradley Foundation. I opened the Washington, D.C. office of Landmark Legal Foundation—one lawyer with an idea—and they took a risk on me. Bradley has continued to be visionary in strengthening state-based policy organizations and making them more sophisticated and comprehensive in their approach, adding the litigation side, the lobbying side, the investigative journalism side, whatever they don't have. The Randolph Foundation, Searle Freedom Trust, Dan Peters, and the Challenge Foundation are among those who have been especially open to taking risks. So pioneer donors don't have to go it alone quite so much anymore."

After years building court cases at IJ and the Alliance for School Choice, Bolick joined a new wave of public-interest litigators a few years ago. "The third generation is the Goldwater Institute model, started in 2007. It was the first time a litigation organization was attached to a state-based policy organization. Our focus is on state constitutional litigation, which is a very useful supplement to federal litigation. We use litigation to extend and complement policy work, and we share infrastructure, fundraising, communications, and research with the wider policy organization. This Goldwater model has now been replicated in ten states."

Given the increasingly liberal politics of the federal court system, Bolick sees state courts as today's primary opportunity. "The state courts and state constitutions are really the virgin territory for conservative public-interest law groups. I see vast expansion opportunities there. State constitutional litigation is still very much in its infancy, and there is much untapped potential."

"Free-market reform is now likelier to come from the states than the federal government. The freedom movement should be litigating in all 50 states."

"States are incubating ideas that have potential to spread rapidly to other places. For example, I'm very, very excited about the *Vergara v. California* case that knocked down teacher tenure since it has created so many dysfunctional schools. I've been working with activists in California to develop a follow-up to *Vergara* that would challenge public-school attendance zones and push for open school enrollment in California."

"You look at what's possible in a given state context, pull together a first-rate legal team, and use the courts to accomplish something that you could never accomplish in the political arena. One thing a number of litigation organizations are focusing on is reining in the power of public-employee unions. In different states that means different things. So here in Arizona we've challenged the widespread practice where employees who were hired to be cops or firefighters are instead paid to work for their unions. They are still on the public payroll but report every day to union headquarters. We were the first to challenge so-called 'union release,' and so far, knock on wood, we've been successful."

In all future cases, litigation should be coupled with media campaigns. "Every good lawsuit filed by a public-interest law firm should be accompanied by an equally aggressive and sophisticated media agenda. Sometimes you lose a case in the courtroom and win in the court of public opinion, as we did in the *Kelo* case, where eminent domain powers were abused. Quite apart from what transpires in the courtroom, a lawsuit can be a catalyst for policy change in the legislature that would not have happened without the lawsuit."

Combining litigation and policy in one organization can also yield outsized results. "I think that both sides make the other more successful. When we go to court challenging a corporate subsidy, we have a team of economists who help us identify the most vulnerable corporate subsidies. On the other hand, any time we walk into a legislator's office, they know that we're not just bringing them a good idea. We may sue if we're not successful in the legislative arena. We have big litigation guns if necessary."

Compared to other branches of public-policy philanthropy, funding litigation is fairly easy to assess for failure or success. "Litigation organizations have somewhat of an advantage over policy organizations here, because it's much easier to measure victory in tangible terms." Bolick says this suits his personal temperament and interests. "I love issues that are resolved, and the benefit of litigation is that you can win a complete victory without sacrificing your principles in the way that passing legislation often requires. A lot of donors would rather go for broke and risk loss when the alternative is partial victory. For people who see things in black-and-white rather than shades of gray, litigation is where they can make an investment with potential for a serious payoff."

SEAMUS HASSON & BILL MUMMA

At the Becket Fund, founder Seamus Hasson and president Bill Mumma have relied on donors who understand the long-term importance of their strategy. Providing free, first-rate legal representation to practitioners of all religious faiths when they come under social pressure has been Becket's mission from the beginning. In the process, the nonprofit law firm not only aids individuals under duress, but sets precedents in our top courts that protect the religious freedoms of all Americans.

Religious liberty became a passion of Seamus Hasson very early. "I actually went to law school with the idea of creating a public-interest firm that would defend religious liberties. It dawned on me how important that was in our country. At the time, religious freedom was a divisive issue. One side was saying religion is bad for you, almost like smoking. It's something you can do in private if you really want to, but whatever you do don't do it in public. On the other side, the common argument was simply, "This is a Christian country," which was legally and historically incorrect."

"So we had a growing problem. Courts were stripping people of their right to follow their conscience and express themselves religiously. But the public counterarguments were weak. What was needed was a defense of religious pluralism."

"The answer is that religion is a natural keystone in human culture. And a good thing. I founded the Becket Fund to supply that answer, and to represent all religions, not just Christians, not just Protestants, not just Catholics, but all the religions. Anglicans to Zoroastrians, I like to say. We don't endorse the faiths, just the individual's right to practice sincere religion. We even stand up for a person's right to be wrong," states Hasson.

"Many potential donors said we'd get more supporters if we focused on just Christians. But there were already people doing that. And they weren't winning the culture war. Fortunately we found donors willing to try a new tack: the Randolph, Bradley, and Olin foundations, and one little old lady."

"Our first notable case involved the *Beginners Bible*. Zack was a first grader in a New Jersey public school. The teacher had an activity where students brought their favorite books to read in front of the class. His favorite book was a cartoon version of the Bible, and he wanted to read the story of Jacob and Esau. It didn't even mention the word God. But his teacher told him he had to sit down and be quiet, that he couldn't read that publicly in school."

"Zack's mom felt this was a violation of freedom of expression. So we went to war. About the same time, and also in New Jersey, we fought for a Muslim police officer who wanted to grow his beard. Our donor roster grew after these cases. We started with a $300,000 annual budget and quickly rose to $5 million," Hasson concludes.

Several other top-flight public-interest law firms focused on protecting religious freedom have grown up in parallel with the Becket Fund over the past two decades. For instance, the very same year Hasson founded Becket, the Alliance Defense Fund was created to offer a counterbalance to the ACLU on issues of church and state. Now known as the Alliance Defending Freedom, the group has been influential in Supreme Court decisions, legal training, public education, and other areas.

Becket Fund president Bill Mumma notes that "by definition, religious liberty is about the law, so building a religious-liberty movement requires law firms. A range of firms have grown up, employing different philosophies about how best to protect religious freedom, but they aren't antithetical to each other. They all take on different aspects of the fight. Our mission is very focused on higher-level appeals that will set a precedent."

"A donor might say, 'The local school district stomped on this poor Christian teacher. You ought to take that case. This person is suffering.' That's true, yet it may not be a case the Becket Fund can take. If it's in an area of law that has already been established in favor of the teacher our answer is 'Get yourself a good lawyer. You're going to win.' Our limited resources need to be reserved to carving out new protections and precedents in areas where the law is not yet clear in favor of religious liberty."

"We have relied on donors who are already knowledgeable about the law, and understand we don't make these choices because we are or aren't sympathetic to the person involved. They understand the importance of strategy and case selection and the long process of appeal to set a precedent."

"At the same time, our donors are not passive. Some of them have been helpful in terms of identifying cases. Some recommend clients, and have people reach out to us."

"For future litigation, one of our areas of interest is the Blaine Amendments. In the early 1900s, Senator Blaine tried to pass a Constitutional amendment that would prevent public money from going to

Catholic schools. His federal effort failed, so he went to the states and asked them to add Blaine amendments to their state constitutions, prohibiting public funding of church-connected schools."

"The Ku Klux Klan got involved. Anti-Catholic sentiment was really hot. The public feeling eventually passed away, but Blaine amendments remain on the books in states all across America. Now instead of Protestants fighting Catholics over these amendments, it's anti-religious groups who want to keep them fighting defenders of religious freedom who want them repealed. Helping the religious-freedom side win will require a long campaign."

"Another effort we're pursuing with donor support is to protect people's ability to practice their profession without committing practices that are contrary to their religious views. This is an issue in health care, where nurses and doctors are sometimes forced to agree to participate in abortion, for instance. If an employer were to say 'no Catholic doctors allowed,' that obviously would be impermissible. But conscience rights for religious professionals are not well protected."

"Another frontier is at universities that are now saying it's discriminatory for student groups to require their leaders to share the central convictions of the group. A Christian student association cannot require its president to believe in Jesus Christ. If a group of atheist students show up at the public meeting and vote an atheist as the president of the Bible study, it has to be accepted. We think that's a violation of religious liberty."

Philanthropists interested in religion will increasingly find it impossible to avoid law and public policy, says Mumma. "All the religions of the world occupy themselves with marriage, births, raising of the family, sickness, old age, death. As governments grow bigger and intrude more and more in these areas, government enters space that was formerly staked out by religious organizations. It dictates issues where people look to religion for answers. This clash is intrinsic to the expansion of the government. So legal action and political action are required to sort this out."

"If defenders of religious freedom have the resources to fight, I am optimistic about what will happen over time. But it's like tuning a piano or a guitar. Every so often you have to go back and tighten the strings."

Lead Donors

Success in public-policy philanthropy requires potent ideas and competent institutions, but most of all it requires wise people capable of leading troops through the treacherous, quicksilver process of inducing useful social change. Charles Loring Brace once said that only astute "practical philanthropists" could orchestrate this. He himself was an excellent example of the type.

Born in 1826 to a prominent Connecticut family, Brace graduated from Yale and considered a career in the ministry. For a time, he worked as a missionary in New York City, trying to assist adults who had fallen on hard times or into prison. The experience disillusioned him: He feared that many of his charges were beyond help.

Brace believed it would make more sense for volunteers and philanthropists to focus on children: "As Christian men, we cannot look upon this great multitude of unhappy, deserted, and degraded boys and girls without feeling our responsibility to God for them," he wrote. Brace found his true calling as an urban youth reformer, a vocation he pursued for the rest of his life through the Children's Aid Society, which he founded in 1853.

"Something must be done to meet the increasing crime and poverty among the destitute children of New York," wrote Brace in his first circular for the society. "These boys and girls, it should be remembered, will soon form the great lower class of our city. They will influence elections; they may shape the policy of the city; they will, assuredly, if unreclaimed, poison society all around them."

Brace's solution was to establish trade schools, lodging houses, and rural camps—anything that would take orphaned and abandoned children off the streets and give them opportunities to improve themselves, before they turned into the hopeless adults he had encountered through his initial missionary work. Self-improvement was a constant theme of his work: "The worst evil in the world is not poverty or hunger, but the want of manhood or character which almsgiving directly occasions."

Self-improvement, he believed, sometimes requires a drastic change of scenery. So his Children's Aid Society popularized the practice of resettling troubled youngsters with adoptive families in the Midwest and far West, where urban pathologies were absent, and work was available and sometimes highly rewarding. This activity was known as "placing out," and led to the advent of "orphan trains"—groups of children who left the east coast for a new life in the American interior.

It was a controversial practice. A few abolitionists condemned it as a new form of slavery. Some Southerners regarded it as an abolitionist plot to make slavery uneconomic in the territories by bringing in surplus labor. Modern-day critics are more likely to concentrate on the permanent separation of children from their parents: Not all of the passengers on the "orphan trains" were orphans, and many were in fact surrendered by mothers who could not support them.

By the time the practice ceased in 1929, the Children's Aid Society had placed out at least 150,000 children. Combined with other groups that copied this strategy, the total number of children relocated from east coast urban poverty to rural life out west may have approached 200,000. "To judge the success of placing out is not easy," writes Marilyn Irvin Holt, a historian. "The Aid Society had no rigid criteria, since its purposes were bound to ideals of self-help and self-improvement, impossible qualities to measure."

Brace knew his work depended on the generosity of others. He raised the funds for the Children's Aid Society through "incessant publicity." He once commented that he wrote so many articles for newspapers and magazines, calling attention to the problems his group tried to address, that he often felt like a "daily editor."

Brace's first major financial supporter was Margaret Astor, wife of businessman William Astor, who offered a gift of $50. By 1870, Brace was raising $200,000 per year. "A State charity has the advantage of greater solidity and more thorough and expensive machinery," wrote Brace.

> He foreshadows a type of figure who would become important in philanthropy: the charitable activist who doesn't just rustle up money, but leads, acts as an impresario, and inspires.

"But, as compared with our private charities, the public institutions of beneficence are dull and lifeless. They have not the individual enthusiasm working through them, with its ardor and power. They are more like machines."

Brace foreshadows a type of figure who would become important in philanthropy: the charitable activist who is not just someone who rustles up money, but leads, acts as an impresario, and inspires. A century after Brace took up the cause of children, another example of the type emerged in New York City. Louis Schweitzer was at a Manhattan dinner party in 1960 when a friend shared a startling statistic: Across the river in Brooklyn at that very moment, more than 1,000 boys had been sitting in jail for at least ten months, waiting for their trials to begin, simply because they were too poor to make bail. Schweitzer was astonished by this. He became determined to learn more, and possibly do something about it through his own action and philanthropy.

Born in 1899, Schweitzer had immigrated to the United States from Ukraine at the age of four. His immigrant father thrived in America and built a fortune running a company that manufactured cigarette paper. Louis trained as a chemical engineer and took over the family firm. He also put his wealth to a variety of colorful uses. He bought a theater in New York for his wife, a stage actress. When he learned about a cabbie who by sheer coincidence shared his name, he acquired a taxi medallion and gave it to the driver, asking him simply to split the proceeds and take Mrs. Schweitzer to the theater when she needed a lift. For his favorite barber, Schweitzer purchased a shop in the basement of the Chrysler Building, on the condition that he could get his hair cut for free, after hours, when he would not have to wait in line.

Schweitzer was also passionate about the Bill of Rights. He was concerned that the languishing of so many unconvicted boys in Brooklyn didn't match the Sixth Amendment's promise of a "speedy and public trial," and the Eighth Amendment's pledge that "excessive bail shall not be required." So he hired young journalist Herb Sturz to help him look into the matter. They visited detention centers around the city and encountered some wretched squalor.

Before long, Schweitzer recognized that an amateur operation would not suffice. They needed a nonprofit group, possibly to run a bail fund. So, in 1961, he and Sturz founded the Vera Institute.

Schweitzer possessed an extensive list of powerful contacts and secured an appointment with Robert Wagner, the mayor of New York City. At Gracie Mansion, Wagner saw the promise of a criminal-justice reform that would not cost his administration any money. During the meeting, the mayor called the city's chief magistrate, Abraham Bloch, and handed the phone to Sturz, who made his pitch for new bail funds. This led to another conversation with a different judge, John Murtagh, who pointed out that the core problem was a lack of good information. Judges, he said, were often forced to make bail decisions based on nothing more than the names of defendants and the charges filed against them. He suggested that Vera examine the character of defendants and make informed recommendations about which of them could be released on their own recognizance.

To outsiders it may have seemed an unlikely collaboration. Schweitzer was a liberal. Judge Murtagh had a tough-on-crime reputation. In 1970, the left-wing Weathermen terrorist group tried to kill him and his family by firebombing his house, while he was presiding over a trial of Black

Panthers. But the two men were united by an interest in true justice—dealing appropriately with the innocent as well as the guilty, and not letting them become confused.

What soon emerged was the Manhattan Bail Project, sponsored by the Vera Institute and funded initially by Schweitzer and later by the Ford Foundation. (By 1966, Schweizer had contributed $200,000 and the Ford Foundation had given $376,000.) Sturz oversaw the development of a fact-finding process that aimed to learn more about defendants. It relied on a four-page questionnaire: Were they married? Did they have jobs? Had they served in the military? What were their ties to the community? Did they have a prior arrest record?

Armed with this information, plus recommendations from the Vera Institute's investigators, judges suddenly found themselves able to make better decisions about bail. As the months passed and the results trickled in, the Vera model began to show strong results: Judges who worked with Vera's data were much more likely to release defendants, and very few of them failed to appear in court later.

"By mid-1964, Vera workers had interviewed 10,000 defendants and recommended 4,000 of them for release. Of the 2,200 or so who had been released without bail, the proportion of no-shows was 0.7 percent—less than one fourth the typical rate when money bail was imposed," wrote Sam Roberts in his book on the subject. Liberals and conservatives alike appreciated a reform that both improved justice and saved money.

Data-based bail reform quickly spread through the five boroughs of New York City, then to other locales like Chicago, Des Moines, St. Louis, San Francisco, and Washington, D.C., and next to 15 states. It even prompted copycats in Canada and Great Britain. Finally, in 1966, the success of Vera led to congressional passage of the Bail Reform Act. Schweitzer attended a ceremony in the East Room of the White House when Lyndon Johnson signed the bill, where the President noted the power of "one man's outrage against injustice."

Success requires much more than outrage, of course. Schweitzer identified a problem that few others knew about or cared to address. He sought the expert advice of knowledgeable officials. He marshaled hard evidence, not rhetoric, to make his case. He made a wise staffing decision with Sturz. He used his connections to influential political actors. And Louis Schweitzer exerted real personal leadership. In all of this he demonstrated again the power of people in public-policy philanthropy.

ART POPE

When Governor Pat McCrory of North Carolina took office in 2013, one of his top priorities was tax reform. And with fellow Republicans controlling the Tar Heel State's executive and legislative branches simultaneously for the first time since Reconstruction, he had an opportunity to succeed. Within a few months, the North Carolina government had passed what *Forbes* magazine called "one of the most impressive tax-reform packages in any state in years." State income and corporate taxes became both lower and flatter, with promises of more cuts to come. In 2014, McCrory became one of just four governors in the country to earn a grade of "A" on the Cato Institute's fiscal-policy report card.

Partial credit for this accomplishment belongs to Art Pope. As McCrory's budget director and in-house fiscal expert for two years, Pope was an essential part of the governor's team. Yet he was also more than that. Pope was the indispensable philanthropist who helped create the underlying conditions for the success of tax reform and other policy shifts in North Carolina. Beginning in the late 1980s, he methodically funded the development of an intellectual, legal, economic, and media infrastructure capable of generating conservative innovations in public policy for his state. He built what the *Washington Post* labeled "a state version of what his friends Charles and David Koch have helped create on a national level."

"My goal is to improve the lives of the people of North Carolina, and the United States," says Pope. The primary vehicle for these efforts has been the John William Pope Foundation, named for his father. Since its creation in 1986, it has donated more than $60 million to think tanks and other organizations across North Carolina. This collection of groups, says the *Washington Post*, represents "a sphere of influence that has put [Pope] at the epicenter of North Carolina government and moved his state closer to the conservative vision he has long imagined."

Pope's main job is to run Variety Wholesalers, which owns and operates a chain of nearly 400 retail-merchandise stores throughout the South. His father started the company and Pope always knew he'd play an important role with it, but early in life he also demonstrated an interest in ideas and politics. He majored in political science at the University of North Carolina at Chapel Hill, read the books of free-market economist Friedrich Hayek on his own—"because none of my teachers assigned them"—then went to law school at Duke. He worked in the administration of Governor Jim Martin, a Republican elected in 1984.

Government, however, became an exercise in frustration for Pope. "The state had been Democratic for so long that everything was oriented toward Democratic priorities," he says. "There was nowhere to look for good public-policy ideas."

Martin's administration needed something like the Heritage Foundation and other free-market think tanks that were then generating ideas for President Reagan, but with a focus on Raleigh rather than Washington. Pope wasn't immediately sure about how to build one. As he left the government to work at Variety Wholesalers, however, his father asked him to establish the Pope Foundation, with one of its goals being to defend the system of free enterprise that made the company's success possible. "We want other people to have a chance to prosper, too," says Pope. He decided that the family foundation might best serve its public mission by providing officials in North Carolina with good public-policy ideas.

The first step was to start a think tank: the John Locke Foundation (named for the English philosopher of liberty). The Pope Foundation provided seed money in 1990, and then generous long-term support. Today, the JLF is widely recognized as one of the most successful and influential state-level think tanks in the country. The foundation also created the Civitas Institute, which promotes citizen involvement in public policy, a public-interest law firm known as the North Carolina Institute for Constitutional Law, and the Pope Center for Higher Education Policy, which focuses on colleges and universities.

The Pope Foundation also gives a good deal to traditional charities. "If a person is starving and homeless, he needs food and shelter. So we support humanitarian causes," says Pope. The foundation's beneficiaries include the likes of the Salvation Army, homebuilder Habitat for Humanity, and StepUp Ministry, which offers job training and life skills. The foundation also promotes education (by supporting various schools) and character training and individual improvement (via the Boy Scouts and Girl Scouts, for instance).

"These are important projects," he says. But "if we want a long-term cure for poverty, we need to promote a just society through individual liberty, limited and constitutional government, and the voluntary exchange of goods under the rule of law. That's how we can do the most good for the most people in the long term, by promoting good public policy."

Pope suggests that the famous parable about teaching a man to fish so he can eat for a lifetime, rather than just giving him a meal, is "all true. But there's more to it." Donors should help the poor become owners and producers and participants in America's thriving world of business. "Does the fisherman have access to capital, a right to sell his catch in a marketplace, and rules that protect his efforts to better himself?" This comes back to public policy.

Pope also participates in traditional politics. He is a donor to candidates. He has been a candidate himself—serving several terms in North Carolina's legislature, and running unsuccessfully for lieutenant governor. His latest stint as budget director was an appointed post.

But all of this traditional politics has only confirmed in Pope's mind the need for philanthropists to support longer-range, detailed, unglamorous, but useful public-policy research. "The budget director," for example, "doesn't have the time or the resources to engage in broad public-policy research. That's why think tanks and similar organizations are so helpful."

When North Carolina's tax reformers took charge in 2013, they didn't have to invent an agenda from scratch. Instead, they could draw on years of investigation and advocacy, much of it supported by the Pope Foundation. "These things take time," says John Hood, who headed the John Locke Foundation for many years before becoming president of the Pope Foundation in 2015. "You can't parachute in with a new plan and expect immediate success. You need to build an infrastructure for ideas. You need to develop relationships over time. Tax reform worked in 2013 partly because we were forming relationships with legislators back when they were county commissioners in the 1990s."

Pope emphasizes that good public-policy groups don't serve partisan interests. They promote valuable ideas to lawmakers of all political persuasions. Back in 2009, amidst the Great Recession, "when Democrats needed ideas for cutting the budget, they knew they could turn to the John Locke Foundation," he notes.

Thirty years later, Art Pope has solved the problem he encountered in the 1980s—the absence of mechanisms for generating reform ideas in North Carolina from the problem-solving Right. "In a generation, we've shifted the public-policy debate in North Carolina from the center-left to the center-right," he says.

What's the most important lesson Pope can share with philanthropists who might want to achieve similar results in their own states? "Find great people—you have to invest in great people," he says. "You also have to risk failure. If you don't make a few errors along the way, you're probably not trying hard enough."

Philanthropists also need to understand that just as central planners can't actually steer an economy, ideas may take their own unexpected courses. "When we started the John Locke Foundation, we had no idea where we'd be now," says Pope. The result is better than he probably ever dared to imagine.

The rest of the country has taken note. As the *Washington Post* observed in 2014, "There is no one in North Carolina, or likely in all of American politics, quite like Art Pope."

Give Locally,
Achieve Nationally

New York City's influential data-based bail reform,
described in the last chapter, is an excellent illustra-
tion of how philanthropists who solve local problems
in creative ways can then find their contributions
echoing on the national stage. Another crystalline
example of this is the Bradley Foundation's sponsorship of school-choice successes in Milwaukee.
Bradley pried open the door for much more school
choice across the nation.

In a 1990s presentation to the Council on Foundations, Bradley president Michael Joyce and his staff encapsulated the ideal that underlay all of the foundation's philanthropy: "Individuals coming together in communities as proud, self-governing, personally responsible citizens, capable once again of running their own lives and affairs, freed from the paternalistic oversight and interference of bureaucratic elites." School choice fit this vision perfectly. Its goal was to liberate parents from unresponsive bureaucracies and give them the tools to make educational choices themselves on behalf of their children.

The battle still rages. Defenders of the status quo continue to resist the decentralization and de-monopolization of public schooling. Some jurisdictions now offer parents wide and wondrous choices, while others allow nothing but the conventional assigned public school. Growing numbers of places, though, fall somewhere between those two poles. (For

Today's explosion of new school offerings would be hard to imagine absent the pioneering Milwaukee experiments of the Bradley Foundation.

much more detail on how philanthropists have advanced school choice and education reform generally, see The Philanthropy Roundtable's several guidebooks on giving to schools, and our list of Major Achievements in Education Philanthropy.)

Scores of cities and states are now tinkering with alternatives like charter schools, privately funded tuition vouchers, state education tax credits, mechanisms for including religious schools among family options, and choice (rather than assignment) of district schools. Places like Washington, D.C., and New Orleans that were one-size-fits-all, single-option educational deserts a decade ago are now bursting with variety and excellence. The U.S. will never go back to the old factory-style public-school model of the past.

Today's explosion of new school offerings would be hard to imagine absent the pioneering Milwaukee experiments funded during the 1980s and '90s by the Lynde and Harry Bradley Foundation. Since 1985, Bradley has spent more than $75 million on school choice, primarily for schools serving the lowest-income families. The foundation's efforts proved both that there is an enormous appetite among urban parents for better educational choices, and that inventive independent schools of various kinds can take children who were moldering in conventional public schools and propel them into mainstream success.

Bradley's money was invested in exceptionally canny and creative ways, so as to bring success on both local and national levels. The local grantmaking, focused on neglected students in Bradley's own backyard, was the indispensable beginning. It shifted school choice from the realm of promising theory to proven practical strategy. It produced a gratifying crop of poster children illustrating the human fruits of an approach that respects the right of a parent to seek the school match that best fits her child.

When future historians look back at the last quarter century, they will identify the school-choice experiments that began in Wisconsin as one of the great success stories of public-policy philanthropy in our era. The lessons for other public-policy philanthropists are many: Ground your investments on solid intellectual work by fresh-thinking scholars. Seize political opportunities. Build broad coalitions, including with unexpected allies. Make bold investments and sustain them. Work across a wide range of fronts—not only offering direct aid but also paying for the intellectual, communications, political, and legal work needed to build, sustain, and protect the charitable breakthrough. Donors who understand these precedents will be better equipped to instigate or accelerate policy reforms in other areas as well.

The story begins long before the Bradley Foundation became a force in philanthropy. In 1955, economists Milton and Rose Friedman proposed giving the parents of school-age children vouchers worth "a sum equal to the estimated cost of educating a child in a government school, provided that at least this sum was spent on education in an approved school.... The injection of competition would do much to promote a healthy variety of schools."

A separate movement for school choice began to emerge in black communities in the 1960s and 1970s. The activists who supported it were not reading the libertarian theories of the Friedmans. Instead, they saw vouchers as tools for empowering parents to exert more control over schools in poor neighborhoods that were doing little more than warehousing students.

Neither the libertarians nor the black activists got much traction on their own. Then in the late 1980s and early 1990s the Bradley Foundation managed to marry the two movements. By offering generous private financial support, the foundation moved the discussion beyond rhetoric into real life, and linked two strange bedfellows in a powerful alliance.

Bradley's engagement started in 1986 when it provided a grant of $75,000 to launch research by John Chubb and Terry Moe, two scholars who wanted to look deeply into the alarming failures of America's urban schools. Four years later when Chubb and Moe were completing their work, the foundation ramped up its investment with a new gift of $300,000 to make sure that their results were distributed widely and given a full public airing.

Politics, Markets, and America's Schools became one of the most important books on education in a generation when it was published in 1990. Chubb and Moe marshaled a range of evidence to show that centralized government schools, shackled by bureaucracy and teacher unions, were incapable of performing as well as decentralized schools. Using data from the Department of Education, the authors showed that public education's problems were so fundamental that solving them required a new set of schools that relied on competition. "We believe existing institutions cannot solve the problem, because they *are* the problem—and that the key to better schools is institutional reform," they wrote. They called for something along the lines of what the Friedmans and the black activists had suggested.

The book was persuasive on its own terms, but it gained special notice because it was published by the Brookings Institution, a liberal think tank known for its conventional, establishmentarian tendencies— exactly the sort of place that isn't supposed to favor a system-shocking idea like school choice. This wasn't the predictable product of a conservative think tank driven by ideology, so it attracted special attention from the media and policymakers.

The Bradley Foundation had known its grant to obscure scholars operating in a different ideological milieu was risky. "There were some questions around the board table about whether we should support Brookings," recalls Bradley vice president Dan Schmidt. "But it was definitely the right thing to do." In the end, the gamble paid off in spades.

Around the same time, the Bradley Foundation helped start the Wisconsin Policy Research Institute, a conservative think tank devoted to state issues. The new organization produced a series of reports calling attention to the need for school reform in Wisconsin. This included one report written by Chubb that previewed the arguments he would make in his book with Moe.

That set the stage for the next important development: a 1988 budget proposal from Wisconsin Governor Tommy Thompson to start a school-choice program. It went nowhere because conventional partisan politics got in the way. Thompson was a Republican, and his natural allies on school choice were black community leaders who were predominantly Democrats. There was no existing mechanism for political collaboration.

Undaunted, Thompson began a deliberate campaign to reach across the aisle. He put on a school-reform conference in Milwaukee that featured Chubb and Moe. He attracted the interest of a black Democratic state legislator named Polly Williams. She knew about school choice from her days as a community activist, when she saw choice as an attractive alternative to desegregation policies that had bused many black children from their neighborhoods to put them in predominantly white schools.

Working with Thompson, Williams proposed legislation that would create a school-choice pilot program for poor families. It was small and limited, affecting only about 1,000 students and restricted to non-religious schools. But it was a start. And it would grow.

The first phase of the Bradley Foundation's commitment to school choice involved helping create the conditions for this breakthrough legislative success. The second phase involved fending off counterattacks. The new pilot program immediately came under fierce legal challenge. Bradley provided $500,000 between 1988 and 1992 to bring in attorney Clint Bolick, then with the Landmark Legal Foundation, to defend the program in the courtroom. In 1992, the Wisconsin Supreme Court ruled that the school-choice program was valid under the state constitution. Reformers had jumped a critical hurdle.

Yet new challenges awaited. Blocked by law from attending Catholic or other religious schools, voucher recipients found that their actual options for finding seats were quite limited. In the program's first year, only 341 students were able to use their vouchers. So in 1992, the Bradley Foundation donated $1.5 million to Partners Advancing Values in Education. This group provided private scholarships to low-income students who wanted to attend private schools, including religious ones. Local business leaders in Milwaukee chipped in another $2.5 million. The short-term goal was to help students get educated. The long-term goal was to build a political constituency that would favor expansion of the state's school-choice pilot.

PAVE announced it could offer 1,900 children private scholarships. Twice that number of applications poured in. "The Bradley Foundation was important to us on an intellectual level, convincing us that we were running a demonstration project rather than a charity," said Dan McKinley of PAVE. "When all those applications came in, and we had to turn away so many people, it became clear to us that we had to fight for public policy."

The private scholarships provided by PAVE were received with hosannas. Milwaukee families were stirred to new hope for an even wider solution. Three years later, the Bradley Foundation realized its goal. The state of Wisconsin approved a much larger school choice program that would provide publicly funded vouchers to as many as 7,000 students. And it would let them attend religious schools.

Opponents convinced the Wisconsin Supreme Court to issue an injunction against the expanded program just days before the start of the school year. Families' plans were smashed. In order to allow students who had been promised state-funded vouchers to follow through on their enrollments in alternative private schools, PAVE raised $1.9 million in philanthropic money in just nine days, much of it coming from the Bradley Foundation. Children who would have been stranded in a legal limbo were saved for that school year.

It was just a one-year emergency rescue, though. The legal challenge orchestrated by the ACLU still hung over the choice families. Then Wisconsin's attorney general, tasked with defending the public program passed by state legislators, announced that he was politically opposed to school choice.

The Bradley Foundation responded rapidly to this legal crisis. It donated $350,000 to allow Governor Thompson to hire Kenneth Starr, a former U.S. solicitor general regarded as one of the best lawyers in the country, to defend the state statute. The judicial war rumbled on for two years. Meantime, private philanthropy kept the existing choice students from being bounced out of their schools.

Finally, in 1998, the Wisconsin Supreme Court came down in favor of the expanded school-choice program. The Bradley Foundation hailed the result in a statement: "Low-income parents in Milwaukee today have been given a freedom previously reserved for the affluent. They will use it to add immeasurably to their children's lives through education, and, in doing so, they will fully satisfy the aspirations that have caused the Bradley Foundation to place parental choice in education first and highest among its policy objectives."

The Milwaukee school-choice program continued to weather attacks. As of 2015 this included ongoing litigation by the ACLU, echoed by threats from the Obama administration's Justice Department, this time using disability law as a wedge to try to shut down the tuition payments. But the program has become a familiar part of education in the city, relied on by thousands of families.

To make sure that the offer of school choice is not a hollow one due to lack of capacity at alternative schools, the Bradley Foundation has spent generously to help Milwaukee' private and religious schools expand so they could enroll more low-income students. This included a 2001 gift of what was up until then Bradley largest grant ever: $20 million to PAVE to help expand school capacity. Since then, Bradley has made an even larger commitment to choice: $27 million to the Charter School Growth Fund,

> School choice in Milwaukee expanded from a small pilot project into a thriving mainstream reality, and the city became a beacon for the whole country.

which provides financing, business advice, and other assistance to charter schools that serve minority and low-income populations.

By the 2014-15 academic year, more than 26,000 students (a quarter of all the school-age children in the city) were attending 113 schools under the Milwaukee Parental Choice Program. They received vouchers worth up to nearly $7,000, allowing them to choose from a panoply of participating schools. A comprehensive analysis of the program revealed not only that participating parents were happy, but that even families who weren't involved benefited, because the increased competition the program produced forced modest achievement gains in Milwaukee's public schools. Vouchers allowing students to attend private schools, in other words, also improved the public schools those students left.

Academic achievement rates among participating students were modest. Voucher students showed a small edge in reading, but not in math. Results in areas like student safety, family satisfaction, and education perseverance, however, were rosier. School-choice students graduate from high school and enroll in college at significantly higher rates than equivalent public-school peers. Moreover, school choice saves money: Because the vouchers the state provides are not nearly as generous as what it gives to public schools on a per-student basis, the program saves taxpayers more than $50 million every year.

As school choice in Milwaukee expanded from a small pilot project into a thriving mainstream reality for an entire large city, Milwaukee became a beacon for the whole country. School choice there was studied intensively by both the advocates and enemies of reform. The U.S. Supreme Court's ruling in 2002 that school choice is constitutional removed one more major barrier to its spread to other places. While choice is still not as common as supporters would like, programs based on Milwaukee's model of low-income assistance now exist in Florida, Indiana, Pennsylvania, Louisiana, Ohio, D.C., Georgia, Mississippi, Oklahoma, Utah, and other places. The explosion of charter schooling across the U.S. was also heavily inspired by the Milwaukee success.

Bradley's example in the arena of school choice demonstrates the value, in public-policy philanthropy, of boldness, patience, and unswerving devotion to a cause. The foundation was indispensable in transforming school choice from mere concept to active movement. The size and power of the vested interests in America's educational bureaucracies will prevent school decentralization and choice from ever coming easily. But if the reform effort continues to expand, it will be due almost entirely to philanthropists who have been willing to invest for the long haul.

BETSY DEVOS

"I was optimistic educational choice would happen much more quickly than it has," says Betsy DeVos, reflecting on her work of more than a quarter century. "I've learned that this is a generational battle and change takes a long time."

She should know. Her activism began in the 1980s, when her family began to support low-income families at a private school in Grand Rapids, Michigan. Since then, she has continued to push for school choice as both a philanthropist and a political leader. "Education is the biggest issue we face as a nation," she says. "Too many children don't graduate from high school. When children don't develop to their full potential, it's such a waste."

For philanthropists drawn to efforts to improve public policy, the first step can be the hardest. "Getting involved in reform can be intimidating," DeVos admits, because politics is controversial. Her solution is to focus on personal lives rather than political schemes. "I'm always encouraging people to come with me and visit schools that work," she says. "Look into the eyes of the children who are benefitting from a good education—and then think about how we're denying the same opportunity to the ones who aren't here. I just have to see the faces of these kids. It makes all the criticism worth it."

DeVos didn't plan to become a champion of school choice. "Our interest evolved," she says, referring to herself and her husband, Dick DeVos, the son of a co-founder of Amway and himself a successful businessman.

"When we had young children, we knew that we could provide them with a good education," she says. "We knew we had a choice." She also recognized that many other parents lacked the financial means to make their own choices about where to send their children to school. "We became aware of the Potter's House, an urban Christian school in Grand Rapids," she says. "We were struck by how hard many of the parents worked to pay the tuition."

The DeVoses started to sponsor needy students on an individual basis, and their philanthropic commitment to the school grew. "We kept returning to the fact that we could choose the right school for our kids—and our belief that other parents should have the same options for their own children, no matter what their zip codes."

In 1990, Dick DeVos won election to Michigan's State Board of Education, and the DeVoses began a decade of intense political activity.

"Every night at the dinner table, we talked about improving opportunities for education." Betsy joined the boards of two nonprofit groups that promoted school choice: the American Education Reform Council, and Children First America. "Our initial goal was to persuade people about the wisdom and logic of choice," she says.

In 1993, the couple helped Michigan pass its first charter-school bill. Three years later, Betsy became chairwoman of Michigan's Republican Party—and used her position to call for additional reforms. Michigan's constitution expressly forbade tax dollars from supporting private schools, so in 2000 she and Dick led an effort to amend it through a ballot initiative. Proposal 1, as it was called, would have lifted the ban, and promised vouchers to students in the worst-performing schools across the state. On Election Day, however, voters rejected it by a margin of two to one. "We were a little premature," she says. "People weren't ready for it."

After suffering such a stinging defeat, many philanthropists might have given up. DeVos, by contrast, gained new appreciation for the fact that transformational change requires patience. She resolved to keep going. "It took a long time for our education system to get where it is today," she says. "It's going to take a long time for us to change it."

The DeVoses made one more major foray into electoral politics: Dick ran for governor as a Republican in 2006. He lost to the Democratic incumbent, Jennifer Granholm. (The loss was partly due to counter-efforts by another policy-oriented philanthropist and politics funder, Jon Stryker—see the 2006 entry on our Annex list of Major Projects in U.S. Public-Policy Philanthropy.)

Through it all, Betsy remained committed to education reform. She helped to fund and lead several organizations working to expand school choice across the country. At present she is on the board of the Great Lakes Education Project and is chairwoman at the American Federation for Children. The AFC seeks to empower children by breaking down barriers to educational choice so families can find and pay for the school that is best for their student. The federation works with state allies to eliminate caps on charter schools and school choice programs, push tax credits and school vouchers through legislatures, and otherwise create new options for low-income children trapped in poor public schools.

"I'm much more optimistic today about the prospects for educational choice," she says. "Hundreds of thousands of students benefit from it right now, and we're continuing to see positive steps in more and more states.

We won't be turned back now. The opposition will continue to fight, but the momentum has shifted." She points to Florida, Indiana, and Louisiana as three states that have enjoyed special success.

After decades of involvement as a policy-reform donor, what lessons has DeVos learned? First, that charitable efforts must be backed by practical political activism—or even the best ideas are likely to be ignored. Changing policy always makes enemies, so reformist donors must cover the backs of legislators willing to stand up to the status quo.

"This is really important: You need to devote dollars to politics, advocacy, education, and implementation. That means three different kinds of groups all working under the same umbrella and toward the same strategic vision. You can have the same board and staff, though you have to be meticulous with how you allocate time. You need to be careful about documentation."

The approach of many donors, DeVos argues, is too narrow: They support 501(c)(3) groups that fund scholarships for children, and that inform legislators about the benefits of school choice. "That matters, but it's not enough. You can't neglect the political side. We need to elect allies and defeat the politicians who stand in the way of reform. We also have to put money behind legislation."

Personnel matters, too. "Lots of people give to organizations that are staffed with highly paid consultants whose primary interest is in keeping their retainers—and from these groups, we don't see a lot of production. They don't put a lot of lead on their targets," she suggests. "We need people with passion, who are dedicated to the issue because they care about it deeply and stretch every dollar as far as they can."

In recent years, DeVos has dropped the familiar term "school choice" in favor of another: "I refer to it as 'educational choice,' because 'school' suggests a building and you don't need a building to learn," she says. "A lot of educators and entrepreneurs are getting away from the batch-processing method of education. We're not just talking about helping low-income kids have access to better schools anymore, but also about using new technologies and methods."

Digital learning excites her in particular. "It's really just getting started," she says. "Children pick up technology so quickly. I was bored in high school, and I bet a lot of students are bored today. Sitting in a classroom and listening to a lecture isn't the only way for students to be taught. We can find ways to use technology to make learning fun."

"In the future, education will look a lot different," DeVos argues. "We're going to see options that we can't even imagine right now because nobody has thought of them yet." Nothing is inevitable, though, and philanthropists can be important influences. New representatives bearing new ideas may be the most pressing need. "We have to get involved in politics and public policy to make sure these options can flourish—so that children can flourish."

Prepare to Be Surprised

Serendipity is not a strategy. Yet some of the greatest achievements in public-policy philanthropy were unexpected. One of the secrets to successful policy-oriented philanthropy is to position yourself so you're ready if the stars suddenly align and an opportunity for action opens up.

As the Second World War came to an end in 1945, the United Nations was born—but it was born homeless, or nearly so. Its initial conferences took place in San Francisco, where a group of governments signed its charter. The next year, the General Assembly and Security Council met for the first time, in London. Other gatherings occurred at Hunter College in New York City and at Lake Success on Long Island.

As the new body searched for a permanent home, preferably in the United States, nothing seemed quite right. A committee proposed a tract in New York's Westchester County, but the idea found little favor. The U.N., many felt, needed to be in a major urban location. Manhattan would be ideal, but large blocks of unbuilt real estate were almost impossible to assemble. Philadelphia and San Francisco stepped forward as candidates. The idea of a European location, perhaps Geneva, also presented itself.

John Rockefeller Jr. had taken an interest in the U.N. from its earliest beginnings in 1944, when Allied diplomats met at Dumbarton Oaks in Washington, D.C., proposing a successor organization to the ineffectual

> One of the secrets to successful policy-oriented philanthropy is to position yourself so you're ready if the stars suddenly align and an opportunity for action opens up.

League of Nations. Rockefeller's son Nelson was involved in an effort by New York City's government to find a headquarters for the new assembly. A suggestion of the 1939 World's Fair grounds in Flushing Meadows went nowhere, simply because it was not Manhattan. Nelson proposed Rockefeller Center, but his father overruled him, not wanting to break leases with existing tenants.

The U.N. finally set a deadline for a decision: December 11, 1946. On the day before the vote, Nelson and his brothers were holed up trying to find a solution. They considered surrendering their own portions of a family estate in Tarrytown, just north of the city. With 15 hours to go, Nelson phoned his father and began to explain the Tarrytown concept. "Is this what the United Nations prefers? Is this the ideal location?" asked the elder Rockefeller. "No," said Nelson. "What is?" asked the father. "New York City, of course," said Nelson.

Within minutes, John Rockefeller Jr. made a different proposal: He would buy the "Zeckendorf property"—17 acres along the East River in Manhattan, already planned for development—and give it to the U.N. His sons tracked down the owner at a nightclub and worked out a deal on the spot worth $8.5 million. The next morning, with time running out, the elder Rockefeller signed the papers at his breakfast table. The U.N. immediately accepted. At last it had found a home, thanks to the generosity of one of America's leading philanthropic families.

The elderly Rockefeller was of course a shrewd businessman. Perhaps he felt that taking the Zeckendorf property out of commercial circulation would increase the value of Rockefeller Center, which was still relatively new and had space for tenants. Yet the donation was clearly offered with an idealistic spirit: Rockefeller hoped that aiding the creation of the U.N. could help prevent the eruption of a third world war.

The subsequent performance and value of the U.N. as an international institution is of course highly debatable. Yet the fact remains that although the U.N. was mostly passive throughout the Cold War and any number of other conflicts, there was at least no global cataclysm after it started meeting regularly. And the organization's location in New York as made possible by public-policy philanthropy has provided the United States with many benefits, like easy access to foreign diplomats, and American acculturation of global elites. The Rockefeller gift made a difference. And it reveals that some of philanthropy's best achievements are unplanned, ad hoc, and last-minute.

Another ad hoc grant that produced a big effect, despite being much tinier, was made by the John M. Olin Foundation in the early 1980s. A group of conservative law students at Chicago, Harvard, and Yale wanted some balance to the overwhelming liberalism of most law schools, and an alternative to the left-wing National Lawyers Guild that coordinated activism among attorneys across the country. The dissenters decided to call themselves the Federalist Society. The founders proposed an inaugural academic conference at Yale in the spring of 1982. The Institute for Educational Affairs, an organization that often served as a vehicle for the disbursement of Olin funds, awarded $15,000 to the project.

The event featured speakers like future Supreme Court justice Antonin Scalia, D.C. Court of Appeals judge Robert Bork, Ted Olson of the Department of Justice, and Richard Posner, the influential scholar of law and economics. The audience numbered about 200 law students, including some from as far away as California, Colorado, and Louisiana.

"When we started the Federalist Society, we didn't know we were starting the Federalist Society," said Lee Liberman Otis. The gathering turned out to be more than just a conference. The successful launch event encouraged the organizers to set up campus chapters that could organize more dissident gatherings. Before long, the leaders were raising funds, hiring staff, and growing rapidly in size and influence. Within a year and a half of the conference at Yale, private donors had seeded the Federalist Society with $103,000, with almost two thirds of it coming from the Olin Foundation. The organization quickly created a new balance of intellectual and ideological power within many of the nation's best law schools, and as alumni graduated it eventually brought the same realignment to the legal profession itself.

At a 1988 event, President Reagan argued that the Federalist Society was changing the country, by reviving "the value and concepts of law as our founders understood them." Within another decade, worried liberals were quizzing nominees at Senate confirmation hearings about whether they had ever participated in Federalist Society events. In 2013 the group had nearly 60,000 members, raised $12 million, held 1,500 events with speakers at law schools, and sponsored discussions at more than 75 lawyers' chapters around the country. The Olin Foundation's initial contribution of $15,000 (and lifetime investment of more than $5.5 million) paid off handsomely.

Many philanthropists regard the Federalist Society as so successful at shifting the tides within a major profession that they have tried to replicate its accomplishments in other fields. In 2007, the Ewing Marion Kauffman Foundation supported creation of the Benjamin Rush Society, which seeks to organize medical students and doctors. Soon that group was also receiving support from donors like the Achelis and Bodman Foundations, the Searle Freedom Trust, and the Paul Singer Family Foundation. Not long after, investor-turned-philanthropist Marilyn Fedak launched the Adam Smith Society, which works with students and professors at business schools. And in 2009, Roy Katzovicz, Roger Hertog, and other philanthropists joined with the Bradley Foundation to build the Alexander Hamilton Society, which focuses on informing professionals in the fields of foreign policy and national security.

It remains to be seen if these most recent groups will thrive as the Federalists have. If even one of them becomes a permanent presence in its profession, though, that could have deep and lasting effects on our society. Public-policy philanthropy often cannot be predicted. But sage giving can sometimes have wonderfully serendipitous effects. And often for a comparatively modest investment.

"It doesn't take that much capital," said Hertog. "We're not building with bricks and mortar. We're building intellectual capital—and that provides the highest return on investment that you can have."

ANNEX

Major Projects in U.S. Public-Policy Philanthropy

(1833-2014)

1833

American Anti-Slavery Society

The powerful religious and moral revival in America during the early 1800s, known as the Second Great Awakening, spawned an outpouring of voluntary giving and the creation of many new charitable societies aimed at spreading Christianity and reducing social ills like drunkenness, violence, and slavery.

One of the most consequential of these new charities was the American Anti-Slavery Society. It was established in 1833 with financing from major philanthropists Arthur and Lewis Tappan and Gerrit Smith, along with many small donors mobilized by an army of religious female fundraisers. Within two years the society had 200 local chapters, and there were 1,350 by 1838, mobilizing an estimated 250,000 members. Given the controversial cause, historian Kathleen McCarthy calls this "a stunning level of recruitment, accounting for almost 2 percent of the national population within the scant space of five years in an era of primitive communications." As a fraction of the national population, the society was larger than today's Boy Scouts, National Rifle Association, National Wildlife Federation, or Chamber of Commerce.

In the process, abolitionism became a national crusade. Advocates presented the following arguments for reform: No one has the right to buy and sell other human beings. Husbands and wives should be legally married and protected from involuntary separation. Parents should maintain control of their children. It is wrong for slaveowners to be able to severely punish a slave without trial. Laws prohibiting the education of slaves must be repealed. Planters should pay wages to field hands instead of buying slaves.

In the summer of 1834, slavery apologists reacted violently to this new opposition. During a riot in New York City, leading AAS donor Arthur Tappan escaped with his life only by barricading himself and his friends in one of the family stores well supplied with guns. The home of his brother Lewis Tappan was sacked that same evening, with all of his family possessions pulled into the street and burned while some leading citizens looked on passively.

Despite their narrow escapes, the Tappan brothers were undeterred. Lewis left his house unrepaired, to serve, he said, as a "silent anti-slavery preacher to the crowds who will flock to see it." More substantively, the Tappan brothers decided to flood the U.S. with anti-slavery mailings over the next year. They had founded and subsidized several important magazines to popularize anti-slavery arguments, including the high-circulation *Emancipator*, the children's magazine the *Slave's Friend*, the *Record* illustrated with woodcuts, William Lloyd Garrison's the *Liberator*, and the journal *Human Rights*.

These publications and other abolitionist tracts and papers were now flurried across the country by the American Anti-Slavery Society. The campaign was powered by $30,000 of donations. It targeted ministers, local legislators, businessmen, and judges, using moral suasion to make the case against enslavement. The society's publications committee, headed by Lewis Tappan, mailed over a million pieces in the course of ten months, harnessing new technologies like steam-powered presses plus the religious enthusiasms of thousands of volunteers to mobilize public opinion.

As McCarthy notes, defenders of slavery had "kept the leavening potential of civil society in check...watchfully curbing any trend which might contribute to the development of alternative, independent power bases." So the enemies of abolition struck back against this civil information campaign. In his 1835 message to Congress, President Andrew Jackson called for a national censorship law to shut down mailing of these politically "incendiary" writings. He encouraged his postmaster general to suppress the deliveries or at least look the other way while local postmasters did, and in many places abolitionist tracts were pulled out of the mail and subscribers were exposed and threatened.

Arthur and Lewis Tappan and other philanthropists subsidizing the effort were subject to additional violence. Lewis was mailed a slave's ear, a hangman's rope, and many written threats. An offer of $50,000 was made for delivery of his head to New Orleans. A Virginia grand jury indicted him and other members of the American Anti-Slavery Society. As his only weapon, Lewis carried a copy of the New Testament in his breast pocket.

These thuggish reactions helped turn public opinion against slavery, especially among Northern churchgoers, and fueled the rapid spread of AAS chapters described above. The Tappans, meanwhile, continued their dogged efforts to change national policy on this issue. See their contributions, for instance, in the nearby 1841 entry on the *Amistad* decision, and the 1846 entry on the American Missionary Association. Combining abundant generosity with personal passion and a genius for organizing and public relations, the Tappan brothers made giant contributions to the most consequential public-policy reform in the history of the United States.

Further reading

• Kathleen McCarthy, *American Creed: Philanthropy and the Rise of Civil Society* (University of Chicago Press, 2003), pp. 134-145.

• University of Missouri-KC monograph on Lewis Tappan, law2.umkc.edu/faculty/projects/ftrials/trialheroes/Tappanessay.html

• Lewis Tappan, *The Life of Arthur Tappan* (Hurd and Houghton, 1871)

—————————— **1841** ——————————

Amistad Decision

In 1839, a group of Africans captured by Spanish slavers and then sold into bondage in Cuba rose against the crew of the ship transporting them, the *Amistad*. They eventually came to shore on Long Island, where they were put on trial for murdering a crewmember. Abolitionist financier Lewis Tappan immediately recognized this as a potential teaching moment for public understanding of slavery.

Tappan collected donations from some fellow abolitionists and set off for Connecticut, where the 36 Africans were locked up. The defendants were clothed and fed by Tappan and questioned with the aid of interpreters he brought in. Tappan subsequently retained respected lawyers to represent their interests, and hired Yale students to tutor them in English, American manners, and Christianity.

After criminal charges were dismissed, the case was referred to civil trial. Lewis Tappan initiated a suit charging the Spanish ship owners with assault and false imprisonment of the Africans, which got the Spaniards arrested. The case became a national and international cause célèbre, drawing large crowds and banner headlines.

The courtroom struggle eventually reached its final appeal before the U.S. Supreme Court, and Tappan convinced former President John Quincy Adams to join the all-star legal team. Ultimately, though five of its nine justices were Southerners who either owned or had owned slaves, the court ruled that the Africans were kidnap victims, not property, with a right to defend themselves. They were declared wholly free.

Lewis Tappan had almost single-handedly financed and organized the defense. He had attended every day in court. He had engineered much of the publicity and reporting that had transfixed many Americans in sympathy with the Africans. Some months later he helped finance the excursion which returned the Africans to their native lands. Hundreds of donors moved by the *Amistad* trial also donated funds, which were used to supply the returnees and help them resettle. Abolitionism had turned a corner toward a wide popular following.

Further reading
- Trial archive at the University of Missouri-Kansas City, law2.umkc.edu/faculty/projects/ftrials/amistad/amistd.htm

— 1846 —

American Missionary Association

Led by a mix of evangelical pastors and funded by Lewis Tappan and other public-minded philanthropists, the American Missionary Association was created in upstate New York in 1846. It promulgated Christian principles, opposed slavery, educated blacks, and promoted racial equality. By linking eastern abolitionists with those in Ohio, Illinois, and other parts of the "West," the group exerted an important influence on American politics and culture.

The association supported missions for runaway slaves in Canada and for liberated slaves in Jamaica. It paid teacher salaries for schools serving African Americans in border states. It helped American Indians, Chinese immigrants in California, and the poor in Hawaii, Sierra Leone, Thailand, Egypt, and other overseas locations. The AMA helped anti-slavery ministers plant hundreds of new churches across the Midwest.

In the lead-up to the Civil War, Lewis Tappan and other AMA leaders denounced the Democratic Party as pro-slavery, and nurtured anti-slavery political parties that eventually coalesced in the birth of the Republicans. After the war the AMA aided freedmen, and founded schools. The association also chartered eight colleges that became the core of what are now referred to as America's historically black colleges and universities. By 1888, 7,000 teachers trained by the American Missionary Association were instructing hundreds of thousands of pupils in Southern states.

Further reading
- Bertram Wyatt-Brown, *Lewis Tappan and the Evangelical War Against Slavery* (Louisiana State University, 1997)
- Historical notes, amistadresearchcenter.org/archon/?p=creators/creator&id=27

— 1848 —

Adding Active Resistance to Abolitionism

The long, hard campaign to ban slavery was the first, and still largest, triumph of public-policy philanthropy in the U.S. When it began in earnest in the 1830s, private donations from hundreds of thousands of

Americans were used for everything from dogged journalism, literature creation, and tract distribution, to the creation of schools for slaves and former slaves, to special events like the *Amistad* trial (see 1841 entry). From the beginning there were also acts of civil disobedience, as by the volunteers and financial donors who aided furtive transport of escaped slaves to northern states or Canada via the Underground Railway.

As decades passed, some abolitionists edged closer to active, physical resistance. Gerrit Smith's family had partnered with John Jacob Astor in the fur trade and became the largest landowners in New York state. But Gerrit lived simply so that he could give most of his money to favorite causes, primarily his passion for eliminating slavery. Smith donated to every kind of anti-slavery effort. He was the main funder of Frederick Douglass's newspapering. He paid large sums to buy the freedom of slaves and whole slave families. He supported the building of schools. He gave money and land to create a village of new freedmen surrounding his own home in central New York state.

Smith was not a vindictive man, as shown by the fact that he also bailed Jefferson Davis out of jail after the Civil War, and argued against criminal prosecutions of Southerners, in order to hasten national healing. In the decades of stalemate before the war, however, Smith became frustrated with mainstream efforts to change public law on slavery. In 1848 he met for the first time with John Brown, who was countenancing lawbreaking.

In 1850, Smith organized and underwrote the Cazenovia Convention that urged Americans to disobey and nullify the Fugitive Slave Law. Its resolution calling on slaves to use all means necessary to escape, including stealing and force, was written by Smith. Over the next decade, Smith brought John Brown to his home for meetings several additional times, and he secretly began to finance Brown's running of guns into Kansas, and then his attack on the federal arsenal at Harper's Ferry. "I can see no other way," he said.

These violent acts of resistance were an exception to Smith's mostly pacific philanthropy, and they led him to a nervous breakdown. But they were part of his indefatigable use of his personal fortune to end legal slavery, and of course the Harper's Ferry attack ultimately sparked the Civil War. Gerrit Smith's abolitionist philanthropy totaled about a billion dollars of donations, in current value. There is no question that this giving accelerated the most important national policy change that our nation is ever likely to undergo.

Further reading
• Gerrit Smith entry in National Abolition Hall of Fame, nationalabolitionhalloffameand-museum.org/gsmith.html

— 1889 —

Jane Addams Pushes Social Reform

After visiting the Toynbee Hall settlement house in London, where she saw university men living among the poor, Jane Addams returned to the United States determined to build something like it. In 1889, she opened Hull House in an immigrant neighborhood on the South Side of Chicago. Its mission was to defeat poverty and encourage assimilation through education, services, and counsel supplied by successful members of the community.

At first Addams operated Hull House from her inheritance. Later, she received contributions from individuals such as Anita Blaine, Louise Bowen, and Mary Smith. In 1895, with the help of private philanthropy, she published *Hull House Maps and Papers*, a collection of articles calling public attention to the Chicago housing and working conditions that Hull House aimed to alleviate.

Over the years, Addams shifted from her initial focus on direct, personalized, positive intervention in the lives of the poor, and toward more collective and impersonal action. She pushed for legislation on housing regulations, law-enforcement issues, factory inspections, child labor, women's suffrage, worker's compensation, prostitution, international pacifism, and other topics. She took high-profile roles in the Progressive Party, the Women's International League for Peace and Freedom, and the founding of the American Civil Liberties Union.

Further reading
• Jean Bethke Elshtain, *Jane Addams and the Dream of American Democracy* (Perseus Books, 2002)

— 1892 —

John Muir Guides the Sierra Club to Activism

A difficult upbringing under a fanatical father turned John Muir into a loner and wanderer who spent long stretches isolated from other people in remote places. Once he had formulated his own quasi-religious gospel of nature, however, he recognized that he needed to enlist other people, and ideally government, in his crusades against exploitation of natural areas. So in 1892 he and some like-minded activists founded the Sierra Club. He was president for 24 years, until his death.

One of the Sierra Club's founding goals—"to explore, enjoy, and render accessible the mountain regions of the Pacific Coast"—echoed the purpose of the Appalachian Mountain Club started on America's opposite coast 16 years earlier. (See 1876 entry on the Roundtable's list of philanthropic Achievements in Nature.) But the Sierra Club's third goal became its distinguishing characteristic: "To enlist the support and cooperation of the people and government in preserving the forests and other natural features of the Sierra Nevada." Rather than becoming an operating entity aimed at the enjoyment of land, the Sierra Club turned into a protectionist group focused on lobbying.

Sustained in its early years by small donations, the group eventually reached a dominant financial and political position amidst the growth of the environmental movement. Muir's popular writings on nature continued to attract followers long after his death in 1914. And in recent decades new generations of activists have been inspired by the radicalism of his previously unpublished work, which includes rejections of people-centric policy, capitalism, nationalism, and Christianity. The Sierra Club is now a large national organization at the center of environmental politics, with a budget exceeding $100 million.

Further reading

• Donald Worster, *A Passion for Nature: The Life of John Muir* (Oxford University Press, 2008

• Franklin Rosemont, "Radical Environmentalism," in *Encyclopedia of the American Left*

--- **1902** ---

Rockefeller Sends the South to High School

When John Rockefeller put up a million dollars to create the General Education Board in 1902, his mission was to improve public education in the Southern states—particularly high schools. In many places (rural towns, black districts) public high schools didn't even exist, and where they did they were usually inadequate. State law actually prevented Georgia from using public dollars for secondary education.

In addition to devoting millions of its own dollars to building up decent high schools, the GEB created a strategy aimed at getting governments to meet their educational responsibilities. In particular, the GEB asked state universities to appoint professors of secondary education onto their faculties, paying for their salaries and expenses with Rockefeller money. Once in place, these specialized educators lobbied legislators and the public on the importance of improving high schools.

With remarkable speed, these state-college professors were able to build convincing cases, overcome local resistance, and convince lawmakers to pass enabling statutes. In the case of Georgia it required an amendment to the state constitution. After securing successes at the state level, the GEB-backed education professors began encouraging local communities to improve their schools. They promoted bond proposals to finance local construction of schools. They pushed for a longer academic year. They suggested improved curricula.

Across the South, the GEB transformed attitudes toward secondary education. The charity played an essential role in the creation of 800 public high schools, and improved many others. For the first time, high schools became widely available to ordinary Southerners. The GEB subsequently focused on improving colleges, universities, and professional schools, spending almost $325 million before closing its doors in the 1960s.

Further reading

• Duke University case study, cspcs.sanford.duke.edu/sites/default/files/descriptive/general_education_board_support.pdf

1903

Booker T. Washington's Secret Litigation Donations

Born into slavery, Booker T. Washington went on to become the best-known African American of his generation, primarily as the leader of the Tuskegee Institute, which prepared thousands of black students for skilled occupations. Washington was a prolific fundraiser and received support from Northern industrialists who admired his self-help philosophy and his practical organizing skills. Among his "sainted philanthropists" were Andrew Carnegie, Collis Huntington, John Rockefeller, Julius Rosenwald, and Jacob Schiff.

Some critics, however, particularly modern ones, have complained that Washington's reluctance to stir up social conflict was too accommodating. Long after he died in 1915, though, historians discovered that Washington had another non-public face. He was also a philanthropist himself, secretly making personal donations to fund legal challenges to Jim Crow laws.

Washington quietly supported the *Giles* cases of 1903 and 1904 that took on black disenfranchisement. They went all the way to the Supreme

Court before ultimately failing in their claims for black voting rights. In the *Rogers* case of 1904, Washington supported a winning argument. The Supreme Court ordered the retrial of a convicted black man because qualified blacks had been deliberately kept off the jury.

Major legal and political advances for black Americans would not arrive until decades later, but the modest gains of Booker T. Washington's hidden philanthropy gave him and others solace. He credited the *Rogers* decision, for example, with giving "the colored people a hopefulness that means a great deal."

Further reading

• Louis Harlan, "The Secret Life of Booker T. Washington," *Journal of Southern History*, Vol. 37, No. 3 (August 1971)

1910

Carnegie Endowment for International Peace

"To hasten the abolition of war, the foulest blot upon our civilization." That was the utopian aim when Andrew Carnegie handed over a $10 million startup grant in 1910 to create the Carnegie Endowment for International Peace. The charter written by the optimistic Carnegie actually made plans for what the organization should do next after it ended armed conflict: "When the establishment of universal peace is attained, the donor provides that the revenue shall be devoted to the banishment of the next most degrading evil or evils, the suppression of which would most advance the progress, elevation, and happiness of man."

Pacifists dominated Carnegie's initial board, and rosy hopes abounded. In the 1920s, the endowment pushed for the adoption of the Kellogg-Briand Pact, whose signatories foreswore the use of war to resolve conflicts. Nicholas Butler, president of the Carnegie Endowment for International Peace actually won the Nobel Peace Prize in 1931 for his promotion of Kellogg-Briand. The pact's real-world effect, however, was nil: Its signatories included Nazi Germany, imperial Japan, and the Soviet Union.

Disappointed in its efforts to ban war, the endowment turned its attention in the 1950s and '60s to promoting the United Nations and training young foreign-service officers from newly independent countries. In the 1970s, in what the organization called a "second founding," the endowment moved from New York to Washington, D.C., and began to focus on influencing U.S. foreign policy. It launched the Arms

Control Association to advocate for disarmament, and took control of *Foreign Policy* magazine, a voice for liberalism in international affairs.

Additional think tanks have been spun off of the endowment, including the Henry Stimson Center (a similar group promoting liberal security policies), the Institute for International Economics (now the Peterson Institute), and the Migration Policy Institute. In 2007, the endowment announced plans to become "the world's first global think tank," opening offices in Moscow, Beijing, Beirut, and Brussels. All of this has been possible because the group maintains an endowment of more than $300 million, thanks to Andrew Carnegie's original investments.

Further reading

- Joseph Wall, *Andrew Carnegie* (Oxford University Press, 1970)
- Centennial history, issuu.com/carnegie_endowment/docs/centennial_essaybook?e=0

1911

Mothers' Pensions

Early in the twentieth century, concerns about poor children led a ragtag alliance of progressive politicians, early feminists, and dissident philanthropists to promote what they called mothers' pensions—direct government aid to impoverished mothers of minor-age children. Mainstream organizations such as the Russell Sage Foundation and the National Conference of Charities and Corrections opposed the initiative, fearing that public relief would encourage dependency, invite political corruption, and deflate private anti-poverty efforts that involved extensive personal contact and behavioral counseling.

A group of Jewish philanthropists, led by Hannah Einstein of the United Hebrew Charities, dissented from these concerns within the charitable establishment, however. They pushed for direct government payments, and some activists like Jane Addams joined them. In 1911, Illinois passed the first statewide program of mothers' pensions. Thanks to continuing pressure on legislatures, 40 states had approved their own versions by 1920.

Funding proved more difficult. Most of the programs focused on widows with children, as opposed to unmarried women, because they were regarded with the most sympathy. Critics also complained that the pensions were too stingy. The mothers' pension movement cast a long shadow, though—providing the model for the Aid to Families with Dependent Children welfare payments created in 1935 as part of the Social Security Act, and establishing the precedent for the subsequent rise of a dense system of federal payments to individuals lacking income.

Further reading
- Theda Skocpol, *Protecting Soldiers and Mothers: The Political Origins of Social Policy in the United States* (Harvard University Press, 1992)
- *Social Service Review* history of mothers' pension movement, jstor.org/stable/30021515

1916

Brookings Institution

Robert Brookings made a lot of money in St. Louis manufacturing and selling housewares, then devoted much of his fortune and energy to building up Washington University and other institutions in his home city. At the start of World War I he agreed to serve as co-chairman of the War Industries Board, where he became the link between hundreds of private companies and a federal government trying to organize emergency war production. The experience convinced him that federal policymakers needed better economic data and better informed civil servants.

So in 1916 Brookings organized the Institute for Government Research, the first private organization aimed at bringing a factual and scientific approach to policymaking and governance. Other donors to the effort included J. P. Morgan and John Rockefeller, and companies like Fulton Cutting and Cleveland Dodge. Brookings also established the Institute of Economics in 1922 and a graduate school in 1924.

In 1927 the three organizations merged, becoming the Brookings Institution, which is generally regarded as the first think tank. Brookings researchers later contributed to the Marshall Plan, establishment of the United Nations, creation of the Congressional Budget Office, and many other national efforts. Employees of the Brookings Institution often moved back and forth between government posts and their perches at the think tank.

Although normally associated with mainstream liberalism, the Brookings Institution has also contributed to causes associated with conservatism. These include welfare reform, school choice, tax reform, and regulatory rationalization. A University of Pennsylvania survey has named the Brookings Institution the world's leading think tank.

Further reading
- Hermann Hagedorn, *Brookings: A Biography* (Macmillan, 1936)

1919

Private Scholarly Institutes to Guide Government

In its early years, Andrew Carnegie's main foundation, the Carnegie

Corporation, had a Republican board that was anxious to improve the quality of American governance without increasing the size of government. Toward this end, the corporation began to make grants creating independent advisory groups that aimed to elevate the quality of information available to government officials. Beginning in 1919, Carnegie and allied funders set up a whole series of private research institutes and scientific councils that, as historian Ellen Lagemann puts it, "would be accessible to the federal government but not controlled by it." The aim was to encourage an "associative state," where experts supported by private philanthropy could improve the policymaking process and help solve national problems while preserving America's traditionally limited sphere of government action.

Carnegie and Rockefeller funds led this effort by establishing the National Research Council during World War I. It was tasked with helping solve important military problems by serving as a "department of invention and development." Drawing on numerous scientists, the council brought the government many military advances, including nascent sonar systems for detecting submarines, intelligence tests used to classify army recruits, and range finders for airplanes. In 1919 the Carnegie Corporation donated $5 million to make the National Research Council a permanent adviser to government, under the wing of a revived National Academy of Sciences. A headquarters building and a permanent endowment were created with the Carnegie money, and today the NRC conducts hundreds of studies every year to guide and improve federal operations.

Other donors followed this with similar efforts to capitalize private think tanks and advisory organizations with the aim of refining government policies and enhancing the performance of public agencies. Thanks to philanthropic money from Ford, Russell Sage, Rockefeller, Eastman, Rosenwald, and many others, independent organizations like the RAND Corporation, the Social Science Research Council, and the American Council of Learned Societies began to appear, elevating governance via better information.

Further reading

• Ellen Lagemann, *The Politics of Knowledge: The Carnegie Corporation, Philanthropy*, and *Public Policy* (University of Chicago Press, 1992)

1919

Hoover Institution

Fresh from leading humanitarian relief efforts during World War I, future President Herbert Hoover founded the Hoover Institution on

War, Revolution, and Peace at Stanford University in 1919. His goal was to create an archive on the Great War so that future generations would learn its lessons. With an initial gift of $50,000, Hoover funded scholars to travel to Europe so they could hunt down relevant historical documents and bring them back to Stanford. The Hoover Institution soon focused on other aspects of twentieth-century history—most notably the Russian Revolution and the development of the Soviet Union. Hoover encouraged ambitious scholarship and publication, with an eye toward warning Americans about the dangers of communism.

Following his one term as President (1929-1933), Hoover returned to his namesake organization. He eventually came into conflict with the increasingly liberal faculty at Stanford, and in 1959 wrested control of the Hoover Institution from the professors, ensuring its independence while maintaining a link to the university. His statement to the Stanford trustees that year outlines the mission of his organization:

> "This Institution supports the Constitution of the United States...and its method of representative government. Both our social and economic systems are based on private enterprise from which springs initiative and ingenuity.... Ours is a system where the Federal Government should undertake no governmental, social or economic action, except where local government, or the people, cannot undertake it for themselves.... This Institution is...to recall man's endeavors to make and preserve peace, and to sustain for America the safeguards of the American way of life."

Major donors to the Hoover Institution in its early decades included Alfred Sloan Jr., Jeremiah Milbank, and the Lilly family. Over time, the organization grew into an important think tank. Its experts provided public-policy advice to Ronald Reagan when he was governor of California. Top-flight scholars took up residence—like Robert Conquest, Milton Friedman, and Thomas Sowell.

Even as it became an important policy generator, the institution remained true to its historical mission, providing a home for the papers of Friedrich Hayek, for Hoover himself outside of his years in national government (those records are at his Presidential library in Iowa), and for rich archives in areas like communism, war and peace, intelligence, business and commerce, and more.

The Hoover Institution's current budget is about $40 million, with half of that covered by earnings on its endowment of several hundred million dollars, and most of the rest coming from philanthropic gifts.

Further reading

• George Nash, *Herbert Hoover and Stanford University* (Hoover Institution Press, 1988)

— 1921 —

Building the ACLU

Charles Garland, age 21, told the executor of his father's estate that he would not accept the inheritance left to him because it came from "a system which starves thousands." When they saw press reports describing this decision, radical activists Upton Sinclair and Roger Baldwin urged Charles to accept the money and devote it to left-wing political causes. Baldwin, who had just founded the American Civil Liberties Union, managed to persuade the young man. Garland used his father's money to establish the American Fund for Public Service, commonly known as the Garland Fund, in 1921.

A board was appointed whose members included the prominent socialist Norman Thomas and Benjamin Gitlow, a founding member of the Communist Party USA. Garland attached few requirements, letting the trustees decide how to disburse the money. The fund resolved not to support political parties or religious organizations, preferring radical journalism, labor unions, and Marxist causes.

The ACLU turned out to be the fund's most consequential grantee. Garland money was crucial in helping the ACLU grow into an influential policy organization promoting free speech, secularism, gay rights, and other liberal causes. By 2014, annual spending by the ACLU topped $133 million.

The Garland Fund dissolved in 1941 after spending all of its assets.

Further reading

• Gloria Garrett Samson, *The American Fund for Public Service: Charles Garland and Radical Philanthropy*, 1922-1941 (Greenwood Press, 1996)

• Merle Curti, "Subsidizing Radicalism: The American Fund for Public Service, 1921-41," *Social Service Review* (September 1959)

— 1936 —

Laying the Intellectual Foundation for Racial Equality

In 1935, the board of the Carnegie Corporation expressed interest in "Negro problems" in the United States, and the extent to which they could be reduced through education. This led to a decision to commission a study of the issue. For reasons of objectivity, the foundation sought a European scholar to conduct the work, settling in 1936 on Swedish economist Gunnar Myrdal, who had spent 1929 and 1930 in the U.S. as a Rockefeller Foundation Fellow, and who later went on to win the Nobel Prize in economics. The Carnegie Corporation arranged a two-month tour of the South for Myrdal, guided by a knowledgeable official of Rockefeller's General Education Board. They gave Myrdal $300,000 of funding, with which he commissioned 40 research memoranda from experts in different aspects of race issues. Beyond this, the foundation gave Myrdal wide latitude for his investigation.

Drawing from the 40 research papers and his own observations during his Southern tour, Myrdal wrote a 1,500-page book called *An American Dilemma*, which the Carnegie Corporation published in 1944. The book took a basically positive view of the potential of black Americans and the ability of U.S. society to transform itself to accommodate them as productive and equal citizens, and strongly influenced the public view of race relations. It sold over 100,000 copies, and its second edition published in 1965 influenced the civil-rights activism of that time. The study was cited in five different Supreme Court opinions, including the *Brown v. Board of Education* case that ushered in full racial integration.

Further reading

• Gunnar Myrdal, *An America Dilemma: The Negro Problem and American Democracy* (Harper & Row, 1944)

1946

RAND Corporation

There was recognition after World War II that one of the important factors allowing the U.S. to win the war was an unprecedented mobilization of scientific and industrial resources by a combination of private companies, philanthropists, and government. (See, for instance, 1940 item on the creation of radar on the Roundtable's list of Prosperity Achievements.) In 1946 the U.S. Army launched an effort to institutionalize such cooperative research, calling it Project RAND (for research and development, or R&D) In 1948, the Ford Foundation provided a $1 million interest-free loan, plus a guarantee of a private bank loan, to allow the organization to become an independent nonprofit called the RAND Corporation. This was the first of many grants from Ford to RAND.

National-security issues dominated RAND's initial research agenda. Its first report, involving satellites, was issued a decade before *Sputnik*. The group's experts subsequently formulated nuclear strategies, proposed new weapons, and started fresh fields like terrorism studies and systems analysis (which aims to improve organizational decision-making). RAND's early research on computers helped develop the Internet.

The nonprofit gradually evolved into a broad "think tank" (one of the first progenitors of such organizations). Today, RAND remains active on military topics but also studies everything from obesity to educational accountability. In 2013, it had revenues of $263 million, with about half coming from the Pentagon and most of the rest from non-military government agencies. Roughly 10 percent came from private and philanthropic sources.

Further reading

• RAND history from *Invention & Technology,* rand.org/pubs/reprints/RP1396.html

• Alex Abella, *Soldiers of Reason: The RAND Corporation and the Rise of the American Empire* (Harcourt, 2008)

1946

Rockefeller Keeps the U.N. in U.S.

When the United Nations was created in 1945, after the trauma of World War II, it lacked a home. The organization initially met in cramped quarters at Manhattan's Hunter College and on Long Island. The inadequate arrangements forced the new body to look for permanent accommodations in other cities or overseas. Switzerland was a possibility. Hours before a final decision was due, John Rockefeller Jr. swooped in with an irresistible offer: He would buy 17 acres along the East River in Manhattan and donate it to the international organization. The U.N. quickly accepted the multimillion-dollar gift.

Rockefeller was motivated by a hope that the U.N. could help avert future catastrophes like the previous world wars, and that having the organization in the United States made it less likely that the organization would stray into mistaken or irrelevant policies. He also saw practical benefits: New York City would enjoy economic benefits, American diplomats would have easy access to counterparts in a convenient location, and U.S. intelligence could keep an eye on foreign officials.

Further reading

• Raymond Fosdick, *John D. Rockefeller Jr.: A Portrait* (Harper & Brothers, 1956)

• Peter Collier and David Horowitz, *The Rockefellers: An American Dynasty* (Holt, Rinehart, and Winston, 1976)

1947

Volker Bolsters Economic Liberty

William Volker was a millionaire by age 47, and could have been so earlier had he not begun each workday by meeting with anyone who asked and writing checks to help many of them, giving away perhaps one third of his income. He had been powerfully impressed as a young boy when his German-immigrant family arrived in Chicago shortly after the Great Fire and saw "a vast spontaneous system of relief supported by charitable persons." When he grew up he did his part to keep such neighborly assistance alive. "Mr. Anonymous" was a devout Christian and very active in the civic life of his adopted Kansas City, Missouri.

In 1910, Volker helped the Kansas City government create the nation's first municipal welfare department. He was soon disillusioned, however, by political manipulation of the funds. "Political charity isn't charity," Volker concluded. Later in his life Volker discovered the free-market thinker Friedrich Hayek, whose analysis of the ways government is often kidnapped by special interests helped Volker make sense of his experience.

When Hayek, amidst Western Europe's flirtation with Marxism, was trying to organize a meeting of free-market economists in Mont Pelerin, Switzerland, he worried that no Americans would attend due to the high cost of travel. Volker's foundation came to the rescue with a check that allowed 17 Americans to fly across the ocean for the 1947 gathering. The American attendees included Milton Friedman, Henry Hazlitt, Leonard Reed, George Stigler, and Ludwig von Mises (who was not an American but was teaching in New York). The Mont Pelerin Society, as the resulting group came to be called, went on to become a leading hub of free-market thinking. Eight of its members have won the Nobel Prize in economics. Many others have held important government posts in the U.S. and elsewhere.

Under the influence of Volker's nephew and business partner, Harold Luhnow, the Volker Fund continued to play a role in the re-emergence of free-market thinking during the twentieth century. At a time when few other philanthropists showed any interest, it supported organizations that made the case for liberty in the Western cultural tradition, like the Foundation for Economic Education, the Institute for Humane Studies, and the Intercollegiate Studies Institute.

In 1956, the Volker Fund sponsored a series of lectures by Milton Friedman that evolved into his seminal book *Capitalism and Freedom*.

"This series of conferences stands out as among the most stimulating intellectual experiences of my life," wrote Friedman in the preface. The Volker Fund also underwrote the fellowship that allowed Friedrich Hayek to teach at the University of Chicago for many years (which helped cement that campus as a center of classical liberalism and home for subsequent scholars like Milton Friedman, George Stigler, Ronald Coase, Gary Becker, Eugene Fama, Robert Fogel, Lars Hansen, and Robert Lucas—all winners of Nobel Prizes in economics), as well as grants that supported Ludwig von Mises at New York University.

Further reading

• Herbert Cornuelle, *"Mr. Anonymous": The Story of William Volker* (Caxton Printers, 1951)
• R. M. Hartwell, *A History of the Mont Pelerin Society* (Liberty Fund, 1995)

1950

Philanthropists vs. Communism

During America's Cold War with the Soviet Union, many philanthropists hoped that our confrontation with the Soviet Union could be settled peacefully through a competition of ideas rather than with weapons. In the end, it was. Early on, the big foundations—Carnegie, Ford, and Rockefeller—spent tens of millions of dollars creating new "area studies" programs at universities to churn out experts with the language, cultural, and historical skills needed for diplomacy, analysis, popular communications, and intelligence-gathering in communist countries. (See 1952 item on the Roundtable's companion list of philanthropic Achievements in Education.)

Many foundations battled Marxist ideas in partnership with the Central Intelligence Agency. The initial meeting of the Congress for Cultural Freedom, a group of anti-communist liberals, was held in Berlin in 1950, sponsored by a mix of philanthropic money and secret CIA grants. "Friends, freedom has seized the offensive!" declared Arthur Koestler, author of the influential book *Darkness at Noon* and a CCF organizer.

The CCF would thrive over two decades, growing to employ 280 staffers and operating in 35 countries, making the positive case for cultural and economic liberalism. The goal was not only to confront the Soviet Union, but also to fend off communism in countries like Greece and Turkey, and to balance the communist parties that actively vied for influence in elections in France, Italy, and other western European nations. The CCF published a number of anti-communist magazines, including *Encounter*, a well-read London-based literary journal founded by poet Stephen Spender and intellectual Irving Kristol, whose contributors included individuals like Albert Camus, George Kennan, Isaiah Berlin, Vladimir Nabokov, Arthur Koestler, Jorge Luis Borges, and V. S. Naipaul.

More than a hundred U.S. foundations worked with the CIA in funding such causes early in the Cold War, out of patriotic duty and alarm over the spread of totalitarianism. When parts of the American press began to criticize these efforts in the later 1960s, CIA funds dried up and foundations began to refuse to cooperate, especially as liberals abandoned anti-communism during the Vietnam War. Much of the intellectual capital that allowed the West to successfully resist the spread of communist governance, however, was built up during the opening stages of the Cold War by this quiet partnership between philanthropists and intelligence analysts.

Further reading

- Peter Coleman, *The Liberal Conspiracy: The Congress for Cultural Freedom and the Struggle for the Mind of Postwar Europe* (Free Press, 1989)

- Frances Stonor Saunders, *The Cultural Cold War: The CIA and the World of Arts and Letters* (New Press, 1999)

- *Philanthropy* magazine article, philanthropyroundtable.org/topic/excellence_in_ philanthropy/victory

---

1952

Rockefeller III Births the Population Council

When global population passed 2½ billion in the early 1950s (it is now more than 7 billion), John Rockefeller III was among those who feared that catastrophe might follow. He believed his family foundation bore some of the responsibility for rising numbers—because its health programs had reduced death rates in poor countries. So he convened a panel of experts for advice on blunting population growth. They called attention to the cultural, religious, and political sensitivities that would complicate any intervention into matters of sex and fertility, and the Rockefeller Foundation refused to adopt "overpopulation" as an area of interest.

John III, however, was adamant. With a personal grant of $100,000 he founded a new group called the Population Council, and followed that soon after with a $1.25 million donation. Soon, the Rockefeller Brothers Fund joined the cause. Before long, the Ford Foundation pitched in $600,000, followed by a $1.4 million Ford grant later in the 1950s. (Ford continues to be a significant donor to the council today.) Eventually the Rockefeller Foundation itself became a major donor. Foundations like Mellon, Hewlett, Packard, and Gates became involved later, and the Population Council now operates in scores of countries, spending $87 million in 2013.

At its beginning, the Population Council was associated with eugenics. Its first president, Frederick Osborn, was a founding member of the American Eugenics Society. Eugenics and alarm about population growth were entwined for decades, and there has been no shortage of wealthy philanthropists willing to spend money to reduce births among poor families in other countries.

This topic has always generated controversy. In 1959, reacting to a proposal for U.S. government funding for fertility control in other countries, President Dwight Eisenhower declared that he "could not imagine anything more emphatically a subject that is not a proper political or governmental activity." But by 1965 President Lyndon Johnson was asserting that "five dollars invested in population control is worth a hundred dollars invested in economic growth."

Coercive measures controlling family size in China, India, and other countries led to protests and suspensions of international funding on several occasions. Even amidst backlashes against eugenics, coercive fertility control, and population alarmism, donors ranging from the MacArthur and Scaife foundations to Ted Turner and Warren Buffett have made large donations to a cause they viewed as a crisis. And government agencies like the World Bank, United Nations, and the U.S. Agency for International Development have also been heavily committed to reducing births in foreign countries. Fully 58 percent of the Population Council's $75 million of grant revenue in 2013 came from governments. Most of the remainder came from donors.

Further reading

- Peter Collier and David Horowitz, *The Rockefellers: An American Dynasty* (Holt, Rinehart, and Winston) 1976
- Matthew Connelly, *Fatal Misconception: The Struggle to Control World Population* (Harvard University Press, 2008)

--- **1954** ---

AEI Guards Free Enterprise

Founded in 1938 by a group of businessmen aiming to strengthen "free, competitive enterprise," the American Enterprise Association had been only mildly effective when William Baroody arrived in 1954, quitting a comfortable job at the U.S. Chamber of Commerce to do so. Within a generation, he transformed the think tank—renamed the American Enterprise Institute—into one of the great conservative forces in Washington, rallying corporate and philanthropic dollars to make it happen.

Libertarian economist Milton Friedman became an AEI academic adviser, and conservative intellectuals like Irving Kristol, Arthur Burns, Antonin Scalia, Herb Stein, and Michael Novak began long associations with the think tank. At a dinner honoring Baroody's twentieth anniversary at AEI, President Richard Nixon sent a message that praised Baroody for breaking liberalism's "virtual monopoly in the field of ideas." By the time of Ronald Reagan's election, AEI had a budget of $8 million and a stable of innovative thinkers. It helped fill the new administration with personnel like Jeane Kirkpatrick, an AEI foreign-policy expert who became Reagan's ambassador to the United Nations.

AEI's finances sagged in the 1980s, but new president Christopher DeMuth revived donations and lifted the organization to a further peak during his 22 years at the helm. He built around scholars and fellows like James Q. Wilson, Charles Murray, Lynne Cheney, Glenn Hubbard, Leon Kass, Robert Bork, Michael Barone, John Bolton, Newt Gingrich, Christina Sommers, and Arthur Brooks. He built a large paid circulation for the institute's monthly current affairs magazine the *American Enterprise*. AEI researchers led policy in many areas: a group convened by Michael Novak set groundwork for the 1994 welfare reform; Frederick Kagan helped the Bush Administration develop the successful troop surge in Iraq; Peter Wallison gave advance warnings of the looming crisis in housing finance, and the government role in causing it.

Economist Arthur Brooks became AEI's president in 2009. He greatly expanded the institute's communications capacities, continued to add scholars, became a nationally popular speaker, book writer, and commentator himself at newspapers like the *New York Times* and *Wall Street Journal*, and demonstrated a flair for fundraising. A total of $100 million in gifts will allow the group to renovate an historic building on Washington's "Think Tank Row" into its new headquarters. In 2014, AEI raised $41 million, 41 percent of that donated by individuals, 34 percent coming from foundations, and 19 percent contributed by corporations.

Further reading

• AEI 2014 Annual Report, aei.org/wp-content/uploads/2014/12/2014-Annual-Report-.pdf

1957

Spawning Birth Control

Katharine McCormick had grown up in a prominent Chicago family, struggled through eight difficult years to become the second woman to graduate from MIT, then married the emotionally disturbed youngest son of Cyrus McCormick (reaper of the International Harvester fortune). Their marriage was probably never consummated and her husband soon spiraled into horrifying mental illness and decades of institutionalization. Katharine poured her energies into the nascent women's movement. She became an officer of the National American Woman Suffrage Association, was heavily involved in organizing and funding the campaign to ratify the Nineteenth Amendment to the Constitution, and became vice president of the League of Women Voters after ratification.

When her mother died in 1937, Katharine inherited $10 million, and the death of her husband in 1947 left her additional tens of millions. It took five years to conclude family battles and pay inheritance taxes, but once the estate was settled Katharine was rich. She asked Margaret Sanger (the founder of what would become Planned Parenthood and a friend made through suffrage politics) for advice on where she might make a difference with her money.

Sanger had long dreamed of a means of preventing pregnancy that would be as easy as taking an aspirin, so in 1953 she introduced McCormick to a scientist she thought might be able to pull off such a creation. Gregory Pincus was a brilliant biologist but so unobservant of conventional ethical scruples that he had been fired by Harvard and was scraping by in a small lab of his own in Worcester, Massachusetts. At their first meeting, McCormick wrote a check to Pincus for $40,000. She funded him steadily thereafter at $150,000-$180,000 per year—eventually investing more than $2 million in his quest to develop a daily birth-control pill.

McCormick was the sole and entire funder of this work. In today's dollars her contributions come to approximately $20 million. And she was involved in more than just funding. She brushed off suggestions from Sanger and others that she support broad basic research, and spread her contributions across many labs. McCormick wasn't seeking scientific advance; she wanted a consumer product available as soon as possible. She eventually moved from California to Massachusetts to monitor development of the pill and pushed constantly for the researchers to speed the drug trials.

At a time when 30 states still had laws on the books that nominally forbade the sale of contraceptives, the philanthropist and her scientists were intentionally obscure about much of their work. Live trials were conducted on women without their consent or even knowledge. And the drugs had been tested on only about 60 women, for a year or less, when Pincus announced publicly that they had a working birth-control pill. He did this to generate public pressure for FDA approval, which followed quickly in 1957.

The pill was subsequently credited with kicking off the Sexual Revolution and sparking dramatic changes in family life, economic behavior, and social order. Katharine McCormick's indispensable impetus in bankrolling creation of the pill has often been overlooked, but she herself reveled in her accomplishment—even getting a prescription, as a matron in her 80s, so she could buy some of the first birth control in her local pharmacy. Not because she needed it, but because she wanted it.

Further reading

• PBS film, pbs.org/wgbh/amex/pill/peopleevents/p_mccormick.html
• Jonathan Eig, *The Birth of the Pill* (Norton, 2014)

1958

Pastor Robinson Blazes a Path for the Peace Corps

Drawing on the long American tradition of religious missionary work abroad, Harlem minister James Robinson founded Operation Crossroads Africa with donated money in 1958. Several trips to Africa had convinced him of the need for an interracial service program that would assist poor Africans on a people-to-people basis outside of political considerations. During the summer of 1958, about 60 American students traveled to Cameroon, Ghana, Liberia, Nigeria, and Sierra Leone, where they built schools, assisted with manual labor, and formed friendships with the locals. They each collected donations, and put in money out of their own pockets.

The Crossroads service model and its philanthropic projects were an inspiration for the Peace Corps. "This group and this effort really were the progenitors of the Peace Corps," said President Kennedy in 1962. Weak management has slowed the program in recent decades, but more than 11,000 volunteers have served in Operation Crossroads Africa since the nonprofit's creation and about 50 students still go abroad to work on village projects each summer.

Further reading
- Damon Freeman, "James Robinson," in *Notable American Philanthropists* (Greenwood Press, 2002)
- Gerard Rice, *The Bold Experiment: JFK's Peace Corps* (University of Notre Dame Press, 1985)

1959

Law School Clinics Institutionalize Political Activism

Beginning in 1959, the Ford Foundation gradually established a network of law-school-based legal clinics that became a powerful tool of liberalism. Many professors resisted the effort at first, because the clinics are expensive to operate and can distract students from their academic training. As the Ford Foundation poured millions of dollars into establishing legal clinics during the 1960s, however, faculty opposition collapsed. The number of law schools allowing students course credit for clinical work leapt from just 12 in 1968 to 125 in 1972 (out of a total of 147 law schools in the country).

From the start, the agenda was much more than offering useful vocational training to students. The goal favorably cited in a contemporary Ford Foundation report was to "reinforce the social consciousness of certain law students and professors through confrontation with injustice and misery." The clinics, which were openly built on political activism, would also be a tool for changing the cities where they operated. The one at Columbia University Law School pledged to use the law to fight "poverty, racism, inequality, and political tyranny."

Over time, many Ford-funded, student-fueled clinics opened across the country, and they were remarkably successful at pushing liberal policies. Among many other achievements, Ford-funded clinics forced New Jersey to fund abortions, compelled Princeton University's eating clubs to admit women, and put the public schools of Berkeley, California, under judicial control in order to take over the disciplining of black and Hispanic students.

Further reading
- *City Journal* reporting in 2006, city-journal.org/html/16_1_law_schools.html
- Steven Teles, *The Rise of the Conservative Legal Movement: The Battle for Control of the Law* (Princeton University Press, 2008)

1960

Pierre Goodrich and the Liberty Fund

Pierre Goodrich was a successful Indianapolis businessman; as son of a former governor he had a deep interest in public affairs; and he loved to read the great classic books. Convinced that a commitment to human liberty and moral goodness needed to be nurtured anew in each generation, he established the Liberty Fund in 1960. Its mission, he wrote, was to contribute "to the preservation, restoration, and development of individual liberty through investigation, research, and educational activity." When Goodrich died in 1973 he left most of his estate to the fund; further bequests from his widow gave it assets of about $300 million.

Through most of the 1970s the Liberty Fund was a grantmaking foundation. In 1979, it transformed itself into an operating foundation that sponsors its own programs. By 2014, it had hosted about 3,500 small, invitation-only conferences for scholars and students on topics such as "Liberty and Markets in the Writings of Adam Smith" and "Shakespeare's Conception of Political Liberty." It had also published more than 300 new editions of classic books, such as *Democracy in America* by Alexis de Tocqueville and *Human Action: A Treatise on Economics* by Ludwig von Mises. In addition to the conferences and books, the Liberty Fund maintains a free online library of important writing on freedom, dating back hundreds of years, and including 459 authors writing in a wide range of fields.

Further reading

• Dane Starbuck, *The Goodriches: An American Family* (Liberty Fund, 2001)

• David Lasater and Leslie Lenkowsky, "Pierre Goodrich," in *Notable American Philanthropists* (Greenwood Press, 2002)

1960

Putting Bail on a Scientific Footing

When Louis Schweitzer heard that a thousand boys had languished in a Brooklyn prison for at least ten months without trial, he was astonished and disappointed. Schweitzer, an immigrant from Ukraine who had thrived in the United States, thought of the Eighth Amendment in the U.S. Constitution's Bill of Rights with its prohibition on "excessive bail." The boys were not necessarily guilty, but they were too poor to pay bail.

Schweitzer engaged the services of Herb Sturz, a young journalist who had written on the Bill of Rights, to examine the problem. This was the birth of the Vera Foundation. Its first effort was called the Manhattan Bail Project.

With a seed grant of $95,000 from Schweitzer, then $25,000 in each of the next two years, Sturz examined the backgrounds of thousands of defendants, trying to determine which ones posed flight risks (and therefore required incarceration) and which ones could be released with reasonable confidence that they would show up for trial. Factors like work history, family structure, previous criminal history, military service, and so forth were tested in various weightings. With the cooperation of New York City Mayor Robert Wagner, which Schweitzer procured, a three-year experiment was run where more than 3,500 accused people were released without bail, based on the recommendations of Vera. Only about 60 of them failed to appear at trial for reasons within their control.

Based on these results, New York courts overhauled their bail procedures, informed by the Bail Project algorithms. In 1966, crediting the influence of the Vera Foundation's work, President Lyndon Johnson signed the Bail Reform Act. Vera eventually turned its attention to other areas, spinning off a series of nonprofit groups involved with employment, drug addiction, immigration, and victim services. Now known as the Vera Institute for Justice, the group is a $31 million-per-year organization that studies criminal-justice policy and supports demonstration projects. At this point only one third of the Institute's funding comes from private donations, the rest is now provided by federal or state governments.

Further reading

• Sam Roberts, *A Kind of Genius: Herb Sturz and Society's Toughest Problems* (Public Affairs, 2009)

1962

Disarmament Lobbies

The arms control and disarmament movement is a product of philanthropy. The earliest influential donor was Andrew Carnegie, an internationalist and pacifist who felt sure that war could be banished through stronger international laws and group efforts for peace. (See 1910 entry on the Carnegie Endowment for International Peace.)

Another longstanding donor-supported organization with a focus on disarmament is the Council for a Livable World. Founded in 1962 as a 501(c)(4) advocacy organization, the nonprofit is active in lobbying against military spending and in favor of dovish defense policies. It was a major backer of the nuclear-freeze movement (see 1981 entry), and has throughout its history been heavily involved in steering giving to candidates for political office who are devoted to disarmament. The organization has a special fund that earmarks campaign donations, and a separate Peace PAC.

In 1980 the council spun off a sister organization, the Center for Arms Control and Non-Proliferation. It promotes pacific positions on homeland security, defense budgets, and weapons development, and urges accommodation to the nuclear-weapons programs of Iran and North Korea. The center is largely supported by individual donors.

Another prominent voice for disarmament is the Arms Control Association. It was established in 1971 by the Carnegie Endowment for International Peace as part of its effort to modernize the pacifist message. The association continues to receive Carnegie funding, as well as grants from funders like the Ford, MacArthur, Mott, and Hewlett foundations, and the Ploughshares Fund.

Further reading

• Council for a Livable World history, livableworld.org/who/legacy

---

1964

A Report Card for Schools

As policymakers began to focus on improving the performance of public schools, they felt the need for accurate ways to track student achievement. In 1963, U.S. Commissioner of Education Francis Keppel turned to the Carnegie Corporation for help. The foundation immediately sponsored a pair of conferences, and in 1964 created the Exploratory Committee on Assessing the Progress of Education.

Over a short period of time, Carnegie spent more than $2.4 million to develop a set of standard tests that would allow U.S. educational performance to be reliably measured and assessed over time. Carnegie's grants led to the National Assessment of Educational Progress, now known as "the nation's report card." The NAEP tests are taken by American students every two years, and have become "the largest nationally representative and continuing assessment of what America's students know and can do in various subject areas." If educators, policymakers, media, and the public are to gauge the improvement or decline of American schools—accurately, over time, without ax-grinding or wishful thinking—there has to be a consistent, widely accepted yardstick. NAEP is that accountability device, and it has been essential to the rise of the educational excellence movement over the last 30 years.

Further reading

• History of NAEP's creation, nagb.org/content/nagb/assets/documents/publications/95222.pdf

• Ellen Condliffe Langemann, *The Politics of Knowledge: The Carnegie Corporation, Philanthropy, and Public Policy* (Wesleyan University Press, 1989)

— 1964 —

Buffett Billions for Abortion

The biographer of billionaire investor and donor Warren Buffett describes him as having "a Malthusian dread" of population growth among the poor. In 1964 he set up an Omaha foundation centered on stopping that growth, both domestically and abroad, and to this day, the *New York Times* summarizes, "most of the foundation's spending goes to abortion and contraception." Buffett has put more than $3 billion into the foundation, which he heads along with his children, and whose domestic and international programs are both directed by veteran abortion activists. (For other causes, Buffett channels his money through the Bill & Melinda Gates Foundation.)

Buffett has put time and energy as well as money into this issue. He and his investment partner and fellow donor Charlie Munger were quite involved in *People v. Belous*, a 1969 case paving the way for abortion in California on privacy grounds, which was cited during the *Roe v. Wade* debate. After abortion was allowed in California but still illegal in most states, Buffet and Munger set up a "church" which they dubbed the "Ecumenical Fellowship," and used it as a kind of underground railroad to transport women to Los Angeles and other cities for quick abortions. The Buffett Foundation has even promoted the partial-birth method of abortion (in which a later-term child is partially delivered but dismembered before emerging from the birth canal). The foundation financed early lawsuits and legal work to overturn bans on partial-birth abortion. These went all the way to the U.S. Supreme Court before a federal ban ultimately was upheld.

After examining his foundation's IRS filings, the Media Research Center reported that Buffett's grants to abortion groups just from 1989 to 2012 (with the tax returns from 1997 to 2000 missing) totaled at least $1.3 billion. And the Buffett Foundation's spending in this area was accelerating rapidly as the 2000s unfolded. Beneficiaries of Buffett's giving include Planned Parenthood ($300 million), NARAL, National Abortion Federation, Catholics for a Free Choice, Abortion Access Project, Population Council, Marie Stopes International, Center for Reproductive Rights, and dozens of other such advocates.

Buffett Foundation donations were instrumental in creating the abortion drug RU-486 and pushing it through clinical trials. The family foundation has funded many programs that teach clinicians how to perform abortions. And it has given hundreds of millions of dollars to groups that provide contraception, sterilization, and abortion to poor women overseas.

Further reading

- *Inside Philanthropy* on Buffett Foundation, insidephilanthropy.com/home/2014/2/4/whos-who-at-the-secretive-susan-thompson-buffett-foundation.html
- *New York Times* magazine touches on Buffett funding for abortion, nytimes.com/2010/07/18/magazine/18abortion-t.html?pagewanted=all
- 2014 Media Research Center calculation of total giving, mrc.org/articles/warren-buffett-billion-dollar-king-abortion

---

1965

Making a Case for Government Arts Spending

Founded by businessman Edward Filene in 1919, the Twentieth Century Fund (rechristened the Century Fund in 1999) shaped the course of arts philanthropy by sponsoring the work of Princeton University economists William Baumol and William Bowen. In a 1965 academic paper, they described a phenomenon that has earned the nickname "Baumol's cost disease." A society's rising wealth threatens its artistry, they argued, because the wages of artists increase but not their productivity. "The output per man-hour of the violist playing a Schubert quartet in a standard concert hall is relatively fixed." To continue flourishing, the professors contended, the art world would require subsidies from the government.

Baumol and Bowen turned their Twentieth Century Fund work into a 1966 book, *The Performing Arts: The Economic Dilemma*, that became a kind of bible for advocates of public spending on the arts. A few other philanthropists were promoting a similar line: The Rockefeller Brothers Fund underwrote a study led by Nancy Hanks (who subsequently became the second chairman of the National Endowment for the Arts) that also pressed for federal funding of the arts.

The NEA had just been set up by the federal government in 1965. Its initial appropriation of a mere $3 million immediately spiked upward. The endowment's budget reached $175 million in 1992. Its involvement in political controversies later reduced its annual funding, but in 2014, the NEA received more than $146 million in federal support.

Further reading

- Baumol and Bowen 1965 paper, pages.stern.nyu.edu/~wbaumol/OnThePerforming-ArtsTheAnatomyOfTheirEcoProbs.pdf

• Abridged version of Rockefeller/Hanks Report, images.library.wisc.edu/Arts/EFacs/ ArtsSoc/ArtsSocv03i3/reference/arts.artssocv03i3.rockefeller.pdf

1966

Ford Invents Advocacy Philanthropy

From the time of the Gilded Age—when many political and journalistic careers were built by taking shots at robber barons—wealthy donors and large foundations tended to be skittish about taking up controversial political causes. It wasn't until the 1960s that public-policy philanthropy became popular, and the individual who did most to light that fire was Ford Foundation president McGeorge Bundy. Having moved into his post directly from the Johnson White House, it was a short step for Bundy to plunge his new employer into racial issues, ethnic politics, environmental lawsuits, welfare policy, and feminist litigation. The foundation didn't lobby directly, but formulated ideas and promoted strategies that would lead to legislation, regulations, and court cases advancing liberal policies like affirmative litigation, disarmament, and welfare transfers. (For some details, see the five Ford-related entries on this list between 1967 and 1972.)

Bundy viewed this effort as an extension of earlier policy-related maneuvering by Ford. In the 1950s and '60s, Ford funding powered much of the urban renewal movement—which demolished slums, built new government-run subsidized housing, and launched an array of social programs for residents. Ford programs were picked up directly by Lyndon Johnson as germs of his "Great Society" expansion of welfare spending and social activism.

But the aggressiveness with which Bundy moved into advocacy philanthropy (including paying for enormous amounts of litigation) produced lots of friction and political backlash. Ford's 1968 funding for radical community school boards in New York City, for instance, was a spectacular failure that inflamed race relations in that metro area for an entire generation. Resentment over what was viewed as the Ford Foundation's overaggressive involvement in political questions spurred heavier regulation of foundations in the Tax Reform Act of 1969, and new controversy about whether charitable donations should even be tax deductible.

Further reading

• *Philanthropy* magazine article, philanthropyroundtable.org/topic/excellence_in_ philanthropy/foundations_and_public_policy

1967

Race-rights Lawsuits

In 1967, the Ford Foundation decided to become a major funder of the civil-rights movement. By 1970 it was spending 40 percent of its grantmaking on minorities. Much of the money went to advocating for new government policies or spending aimed at economic enrichment of minorities. Another important slice went to litigation for civil-rights causes.

The foundation started with a 1967 grant of $1 million to the NAACP Legal Defense and Educational Fund. This organization had been involved in the 1954 desegregation suit *Brown v. Board of Education* and many other cases since its establishment in 1940. With Ford as a backer, the NAACP-LDF ratcheted up the lawsuits, and migrated from a commitment to equal opportunity and toward an embrace of equal results.

In 1971, the LDF's *Griggs v. Duke Power* case established the principle of disparate impact—which held that even policies of color-blind neutrality would be considered discriminatory if they produced uneven racial outcomes. The NAACP-LDF went on to become a major promoter of racial preferences in public employment, contracting, and education.

The organization also functioned as an incubator of politicians and advocates. Obama Attorney General Eric Holder, Massachusetts Governor Deval Patrick, Harvard Law School professor Lani Guinier and others worked for the NAACP-LDF. In 2013 it had a budget of about $16 million.

Further reading

• Richard Magat, *The Ford Foundation at Work* (Plenum Press, 1979)

1968

Carnegie Pushes a "G.I. Bill" for the Poor

In 1967, the Carnegie Corporation announced formation of the Carnegie Commission on Higher Education, headed by Clark Kerr, who had just been fired as president of the University of California for failing to overcome campus unrest. The commission was promised at least five years of funding and the effort ended up running for a full dozen years, with the foundation devoting about $12 million to its work.

Between 1967 and 1979 this initiative churned out 37 policy reports and 137 research and technical reports. The most consequential result was a push for greater federal responsibility for higher education. "One of the most urgent national priorities for higher education," insisted a

1968 clarion call, "is the removal of financial barriers for all youth." The recommendations were characterized as a "G.I. bill" for the poor.

Members of Congress duly proposed legislation based on the Carnegie suggestions. Within a few years, the federal government had established an elaborate apparatus of grants and loans for college students. Today, Pell Grants are probably the best-known element of the system. In 2014, nearly 9 million students received about $30 billion in federal Pell Grants.

Further reading

- Retrospective on the Carnegie Commission and Council on Higher Education, cshe. berkeley.edu/sites/default/files/shared/publications/docs/ROP.Douglass.Carnegie.14.05.pdf
- Ellen Condliffe Langemann, *The Politics of Knowledge: The Carnegie Corporation, Philanthropy, and Public Policy* (Wesleyan University Press, 1989)

1969

Ethnic-rights Lawsuits

Upon deciding to make a major push for black rights during the 1960s, the Ford Foundation started funding the NAACP Legal Defense and Educational Fund (see 1967 entry). It quickly expanded that effort by setting up similar organizations to launch lawsuits on behalf of other minority groups. (This went beyond lawsuits alone. Ford also funded groups like the Mexican American Youth Organization, a militant arm of the Chicano movement that preached separatism, disseminated revolutionary literature, sponsored visits to Cuba, and registered voters.)

One ethnic litigator receiving Ford Foundation money was the Mexican American Legal Defense and Educational Fund. MALDEF received its first Ford grant in 1969: $2.2 million of startup sponsorship. By 1973, MALDEF had attracted additional donors, but the Ford Foundation still supplied about half of its budget. The group plunged into voting-rights battles, guaranteeing the creation of Hispanic-majority jurisdictions around the country. In 1982, it won a Supreme Court ruling that public schools must open their doors to illegal aliens. The organization filed lawsuits on affirmative action, immigrant rights, and election redistricting. It had a budget of more than $6 million in 2013.

The Native American Rights Fund was also bankrolled by Ford, starting with a pilot grant of $155,000 in 1970, another $95,000 the next year, and a three-year grant of $1.2 million in 1972. NARF had grown into a $9.4 million-per-year organization by 2013.

The Ford Foundation also supported the creation of the Puerto Rican Legal Defense and Education Fund in 1972. Many of its lawsuits focused on language rights. Today the group is known as LatinoJustice, with a budget just under $3 million. It frequently works in conjunction with NAACP-LDF and MALDEF.

Between 1967 and 1975, the Ford Foundation spent $18 million specifically to create and build up civil-rights litigation groups; their lawsuits redirected many aspects of American public policy and social practice in ensuing years.

Further reading

• Robert McKay, *Nine for Equality Under Law: Civil Rights Litigation* (Ford Foundation, 1977)

• Duke University case study, cspcs.sanford.duke.edu/sites/default/files/descriptive/civil_rights_litigation.pdf

1970

Environmental Lawsuits

Environmental conservation was a part of the Ford Foundation's program as early as 1952, when it provided seed money to Resources for the Future to conduct economic research on nature issues. Over the years, Ford dedicated tens of millions of dollars to RFF. In the 1960s, however, the foundation's focus shifted.

Ford had been experimenting with shaping public policy by sponsoring litigation from public-interest law firms like the NAACP Legal Defense and Educational Fund (see 1967 and 1969 entries). Now it sought to apply this lawsuit model to the new environmental movement. One of its initial grants supplied $100,000 to the Rachel Carson Fund of the Audubon Society to sue for restrictions on the use of DDT for mosquito control.

In 1970, the question of whether groups dedicated to filing environmental lawsuits should quality as tax-exempt was resolved in favor of the activists, and the Ford Foundation began a period of vigorous financial support. A grant of $410,000 launched the Natural Resources Defense Council, and by 1977 that group had received $2.6 million of Ford money—which it used to sue the Army Corps of Engineers over dams, push for the expansion of the Clean Air Act, and block oil drilling in the Arctic National Wildlife Refuge. By 2013, NRDC was raising $113 million per year.

The Ford Foundation also helped launch the Environmental Defense Fund ($994,000 in grants between 1971 and 1977), the Sierra Club

Legal Defense Fund ($603,000 over the same period), and the Southern California Center for Law in the Public Interest ($1.6 million). These donations built a network of legal institutions that allowed environmental activists to become involved in countless lawsuits and regulatory disputes. Litigation is now one of the most influential tools by which the environmental movement changes society.

Further reading

- Robert Mitchell, *From Conservation to Environmental Movement: The Development of the Modern Environmental Lobbies* (Resources for the Future, 1985)
- Duke University case study, cspcs.sanford.duke.edu/sites/default/files/descriptive/environmental_public_interest_law_centers.pdf

———— **1970** ————
An Explosion of Giving for Gay Advocacy

In 1970, RESIST, a Massachusetts-based funder that had supported draft resistance and opposition to the Vietnam War, awarded what is believed to be the first foundation grant to a gay and lesbian organization. The precise amount given to the Gay Liberation Front, a short-lived political group, is lost to history, but the gift marked the birth of a new field of philanthropy. As recently as 1986, giving to gay and lesbian causes was still tiny ($772,000 that year) but it proceeded to grow explosively—to $11 million in 1998, $49 million in 2004, and $123 million in 2011.

During the 1980s, the overwhelming majority of gay philanthropy involved health services, in response to the spread of HIV and AIDS. First there was donor funding for direct medical care at clinics. Then came a giant advocacy push to expand government spending, which rose from $8 million (1982) to $30 *billion* (2014) at the federal level alone.

With radical groups like ACT UP and Queer Nation using protests to gain political traction, discrimination and "human rights" issues soon moved to the fore. Philanthropic giving became increasingly oriented toward public policy. Groups like the National LGBTQ Task Force (organizing), GLAAD (advocacy), PFLAG (support groups), Lambda Legal (litigation), and Human Rights Campaign (advocacy and lobbying) began to rake in tens of millions of dollars in contributions. During the decade starting in 2004, promotion of gay marriage became a dominant issue, with nonprofits like Freedom to Marry receiving multimillions of donations for action campaigns.

In 2012 more than half of all philanthropic donations to gay causes came either from foundations wholly focused on gay issues (36 percent) or anonymous givers (15 percent). Of the remaining gifts, 42 percent came from multi-issue foundations, and 7 percent from corporations. The top funders that year (after the $20 million given anonymously) were the Ford ($11 million), Gill ($9 million), and Arcus ($8 million) foundations.

The vast portion of this philanthropy is directed toward advocacy, litigation, media campaigns, political organizing, and other policy-related work. Only 11 percent of gay-related giving from 1970 to 2010 went for direct services to gay populations.

In the last decade, about 800 institutions and thousands of individual donors have given more than a billion dollars to gay causes. With more than nine tenths of gay-oriented giving having emerged within the past decade and a half, this new field is likely to continue to mushroom in the future.

Further reading

- 2012 tracking report for gay philanthropy, lgbtfunders.org/files/2012_Tracking_ Report_Lesbian_Gay_Bisexual_Transgender_and_Queer_Grantmaking_by_US_ Foundations.pdf
- *Forty Years of LBGTQ Philanthropy 1970-2010*, lgbtfunders.org/files/40years_ lgbtqphilanthrophy.pdf

--------- **1972** ---------

Joe Coors Brews Up the Heritage Foundation

After backing Ronald Reagan's Presidential bid in 1968, beer magnate Joseph Coors concluded that an intellectual infrastructure for shaping public policies was just as important as good candidates. Liberals already had a policy infrastructure in universities and organizations like the Brookings Institution. Coors decided that conservatives needed think tanks of their own—so in 1972 he wrote a $250,000 check to begin the Heritage Foundation. Other philanthropists like the Samuel Roberts Noble Foundation and Richard Mellon Scaife joined the cause, but the Coors cash was catalytic, and also consistent. Coors continued to invest in the Heritage Foundation over many years, including a $300,000 gift in 1980 that allowed it to move to improved offices.

As Ronald Reagan finally took office in 1981, the Heritage Foundation issued *Mandate for Leadership*, a book of nearly 1,100 pages that became a policy blueprint for his administration. The think tank became active in virtually every area of government action, from welfare transfers to national defense. It eventually grew into the biggest and most influential think tank on the right.

Coors was also a principal backer of the Free Congress Foundation (a D.C. think tank focused on social issues), the Mountain States Legal Foundation (a public-interest law firm), and the Independence Institute (a Colorado-based free-market think tank). Yet Heritage remained his largest legacy. "There wouldn't be a Heritage Foundation without Joe Coors," said longtime Heritage president Edwin Feulner. In 2013, the organization spent $77 million, most of it raised from individual donations.

Further reading

• Nicole Hoplin and Ron Robinson, *Funding Fathers* (Regnery, 2008)

• Lee Edwards, *The Power of Ideas: The Heritage Foundation at 25 Years* (Jameson Books, 1997)

1972

Feminist Flurry From the Ford Foundation

In 1972, Ford Foundation president McGeorge Bundy pledged "to investigate grantmaking possibilities in the area of women's rights and opportunities." Between that moment and the end of the 1970s, dedicated women's programs accounted for more than one out of every 20 dollars the foundation spent.

At first, the Ford Foundation moved to create special programs within organizations it already supported. So the Women's Rights Project was promoted at the American Civil Liberties Union. The Minority Women's Employment Program was funded at the NAACP Legal and Educational Defense Fund, and the Chicana Rights Project got money at the Mexican American Legal Defense and Educational Fund.

The most influential of these was the ACLU project, co-founded in 1972 by Ruth Bader Ginsburg. Ginsburg's strategy was to file lawsuits based on a new reading of the Fourteenth Amendment's equal protection clause, leading the courts to wipe out gender distinctions in everything from employment rules to family law. In 1993, Ginsburg became a justice of the U.S. Supreme Court.

In 1980, Ford's trustees turned up the flow of money even further, committing the foundation to spending more than 10 percent of its resources on explicit women's causes. In addition to paying for various legal challenges, the foundation put money into supporting abortion, research on sex stereotypes, and increasing female leadership at unions. By 1986, Ford had spent $70 million in these areas, and women comprised a majority of its professional staff. "Ford's early funding for women's organizations and women's issues," philanthropic consultant Mary Ellen Capek concluded, "lent credibility" to feminist organizations.

Further reading

• *Washington Post* description of Ginsburg's work, washingtonpost.com/wp-dyn/content/article/2007/08/23/AR2007082300903_pf.html

• Duke University case study, cspcs.sanford.duke.edu/sites/default/files/descriptive/rights_and_opportunities_of_women.pdf

1973

Filer Commission Defends Private Giving

Public debate over the Tax Reform Act of 1969 stirred up some basic questions and criticisms of the role of private philanthropy in America. Several public figures decided it would be a good idea to examine and address some of these controversies with a blue-ribbon commission. It was a suggestion from John Rockefeller III that sparked creation of the panel, and his family provided $200,000 to organize and fund its investigation. More than 700 other individuals and organizations also helped underwrite the Commission on Private Philanthropy and Public Needs.

Rockefeller invited Aetna Insurance chairman John Filer to lead the commission of two dozen prominent Americans, and it became popularly known as the Filer Commission. The group commissioned 85 studies, and convened many meetings over a two-year period. In 1975 it issued a 240-page report full of data and recommendations.

The commission described a "third sector," distinct from government and business, that plays a unique role in American life. "Private support is a fundamental underpinning for hundreds of thousands of institutions and organizations," said the report. "It is the ingredient that keeps private nonprofit organizations alive and private, keeps them from withering away or becoming mere adjuncts of government." The commission defended tax deductibility of contributions made to charity, and suggested self-policing and consistent rules to protect the integrity and positive social effects of independent giving.

At a time of rumblings against independent giving, the Filer Commission's work is credited with heading off possible political intrusions into philanthropy—thus protecting the right of Americans to direct their money into private solutions to public problems.

Further reading

• Report of the Filer Commission, archives.iupui.edu/bitstream/handle/2450/889/giving.pdf?sequence=1

• Eleanor Brilliant, *Private Charity and Public Inquiry: A History of the Filer and Peterson Commissions* (Indiana University Press, 2000)

1974

Launching the Law and Economics Movement

The area where John Olin invested more donated resources than any other—the law and economics movement—was a matter of abiding personal interest for the philanthropist. Olin became persuaded that studying the interplay between laws and economic behavior was an important new academic discipline that could have potent implications for governance and public policy. Hoping to nudge America's dominant lawyer class toward a more sophisticated understanding of markets and economic discipline, Olin's foundation made its first grant for law and economics in 1974—awarding $100,000 to the Law and Economics Center run by Henry Manne at the University of Miami. The center sponsored fellowships allowing students with graduate degrees in economics to receive legal training, and staged educational seminars introducing judges to important economic concepts.

Much more Olin funding would follow during the next two decades. The original Law and Economics Center migrated from Miami to Emory University and finally to George Mason University. And additional centers for the study of law and economics were endowed by the foundation at many top law schools, including Chicago, Harvard, Stanford, Virginia, and Yale. By the time the Olin Foundation closed in 2005, it had spent more than $68 million to root the law and economics movement on campuses and in courthouses.

Olin's efforts began bearing rich fruit as early as the 1980s, as economic understanding and reasoning became much more visible within American law. Judges and legislators paid greater attention to incentive effects, to regulatory costs, to the benefits of competition. Most every year, beginning in 1985, there was at least one Olin Fellow from a law and economics center represented among the clerks selected for the U.S. Supreme Court. Nobel 1991 economics laureate Ronald Coase once said that "without all the work in law and economics, a great part of which has been supported by the John M. Olin Foundation, it is doubtful whether the importance of my work would have been recognized."

Further reading

• John J. Miller, *A Gift of Freedom: How the John M. Olin Foundation Changed America* (Encounter Books, 2006)

--------------------------------- **1976** ---------------------------------

A Donor-advised Fund for Liberal Policy Reform

Campus protestor and student activist Drummond Pike took a position in 1970 at a youth group funded by the Ford Foundation. There he met philanthropists looking for ways to use their money to alter public policy. In 1976, Pike and Jane Bagley Lehman, heir to the Reynolds tobacco fortune, co-created the Tides Foundation to bankroll left-wing groups and causes.

Tides pioneered the use of donor-advised funds for public-policy purposes, allowing wealthy liberals to fund social change. An early coup was helping Hollywood producer Norman Lear create People for the American Way, one of the leading left-activist groups of the 1980s. Tides also helped establish the National Network of Grantmakers to unite "progressive" donors. (Later, Pike went on to serve as treasurer of the Democracy Alliance—see 2005 entry.)

Today the Tides Foundation manages 373 donor-advised funds averaging several hundred thousand dollars each. Through them, the foundation distributes around $100 million every year to promote causes like "global warming, AIDS treatment and prevention, and economic disparity," to quote its website. The San Francisco-based organization also operates the Tides Center, created in 1996, to sponsor nascent "social justice" nonprofits, offering them technical, administrative, financial, human-resources, and public-relations services while guiding their activism, and connecting them with donors willing to fund their projects. This and other Tides subgroups spend about as much again as the foundation, making Tides as a whole an approximately $200 million per year operation.

Further reading

• Tides Foundation history, tides.org/about/history

--------------------------------- **1977** ---------------------------------

Rise of the Cato Institute

When businessman Charles Koch learned that Libertarian Party leader Ed Crane was thinking about leaving politics, he asked what it would take to keep him involved. Crane suggested that libertarianism needed a think tank: a public-policy organization that would join political debates with deep research and a crisp point of view. Koch agreed to fund its launch.

The Cato Institute—named for *Cato's Letters*, a set of eighteenth-century essays on freedom—opened its doors in San Francisco in 1977. It published newsletters and policy reports and provided radio commentaries. In 1981 it moved to Washington, D.C. Over the next three decades Cato grew rapidly into one of the country's prominent policy-forming organizations. It is best known for championing free-market policy reforms like Social Security privatization, school choice, and free trade, along with libertarian causes like open-borders immigration, drug legalization, and a dovish foreign policy.

From their founding days, Charles and David Koch's accumulated gifts to the Cato Institute come to about $30 million. The institute raised a total of $400 million during that period, from tens of thousands of donors. In 2014, Cato had more than 100 staffers, and 2014 donations exceeding $29 million (87 percent of that from individual donors).

Further reading

- Brian Doherty, *Radicals for Capitalism: A Freewheeling History of the Modern American Libertarian Movement* (PublicAffairs, 2007)
- Cato Institute Annual Report, cato.org/sites/cato.org/files/pubs/pdf/annual-report-2013.pdf

---

1977

Expanding Ideological Diversity Among Reporters

Decades of research have shown that the large majority of working journalists define themselves as political liberals. Conservatives who consider this a problem have made efforts, with donor support, to train young journalists who are more open to including conservative perspectives in their stories. The oldest of these programs is the National Journalism Center, which since 1977 has offered budding reporters the chance to intern with media outlets in Washington, D.C., while attending journalism classes taught by experienced professionals, many of them alumni of the program. Now operating under the sponsorship of Young America's Foundation, the NJC has put 2,000 beginning practitioners through its 12-week internship program.

The newest effort to introduce more political balance into journalism is the Student Free Press Association, launched in 2010 to give conservative-leaning campus journalists a national website where they can release their work, as well as paid fellowships with publishers of political journalism. And back in 1994 the Phillips Foundation launched the Robert Novak Journalism Fellowship, awarding more than $6 million over the next two decades to 117 young reporters in the form of $25,000 part-time or $50,000 full-time fellowships giving them a year to produce a deeply researched story. In 2013 the program was transferred to the Fund for American Studies.

A fourth program for nurturing conservative or libertarian journalists is the Buckley Journalism Fellowship. Since 2009 it has installed one or two top young writers per year at *National Review*, the leading conservative politics magazine. The $75,000 cost for each fellow is covered by donations.

Further reading

• *Philanthropy* magazine article, philanthropyroundtable.org/topic/excellence_in_philanthropy/new_balance

---

1978

A Popular Tax Revolt

In a 1978 referendum, nearly two thirds of California voters approved Proposition 13, which lowered and capped the state's property taxes and heralded the coming of a nationwide "tax revolt" that helped sweep Ronald Reagan into office in 1980. Behind the success of Proposition 13 stood thousands of grassroots philanthropists. The sponsor organization, the United Organization of Taxpayers, relied on 50,000 small donors who offered up $440,000 and an estimated one million hours of volunteer time to get the measure on the ballot.

The *New York Times* described the measure's passage as "the beginning of a tax revolt—a modern Boston Tea Party." During the two years following, California property and sales taxes were cut by more than $4 billion. In 1980 the tax revolt moved to Washington. Reagan cut tax rates sharply during his first year in office, and chopped the top income tax rate down to 28 percent in 1986.

Further reading

• Alvin Rabushka and Pauline Ryan, *The Tax Revolt* (Hoover Institution, 1982)

1978

MacArthur's Money Moves Left

Shortly before businessman John MacArthur died, as one of the two or three wealthiest men in America, the insurance and real-estate magnate created a foundation. He was a selfish and misanthropic man, however, and gave little thought to how its board would execute the philanthropy carried out in his name. "You people, after I'm dead, will have to learn how to spend it," he told his lawyer. MacArthur's son from the first of his two marriages, Rod, eventually launched a pitched battle for control of the trust, and won. Ever since, the John D. and Catherine T. MacArthur Foundation has been one of America's largest funders of left-of-center public causes.

The foundation is perhaps best known for its "genius grants," which are no-strings-attached fellowships that pay $500,000 over five years, typically to artists, scientists, and political activists. Yet that makes up only a small portion of MacArthur's overall giving. During the days of the Soviet Union, the foundation was a major financier of the arms-control movement, pouring money into groups such as the Arms Control Association, the Center for Defense Information, the Federation of American Scientists, and the Union of Concerned Scientists. Other prominent recipients of MacArthur support include the American Civil Liberties Union, the Brookings Institution, the Carnegie Endowment for International Peace, the NAACP, and Planned Parenthood. In 2014, the foundation held assets exceeding $6.3 billion.

Further reading
• Nancy Kriplen, *The Eccentric Billionaire: John D. MacArthur* (Amacom, 2008)

1978

Questioning Statism in Manhattan and Elsewhere

While visiting the U.S. after World War II, entrepreneur Antony Fisher was impressed by the work of agriculturalists at Cornell University who were transforming chicken farming from a cottage industry into an efficient modern process. When he went back to Britain he set up similar operations growing chickens on a large scale, which altered Britain's diet and made Fisher a wealthy man. With some of the first profits from this business he set out to feed new thinking as well in his home country.

Discouraged to see centralizing economic policies sweep Britain after a war that had been fought to preserve freedom, Fisher visited free-market thinker Friedrich Hayek and told him he was considering entering politics. Hayek argued that the better course would be help change the intellectual currents running in the direction of socialism. In response, Fisher founded London's Institute of Educational Affairs, one of the world's first think tanks, which produced new ideas and experts that subsequently redirected both British and American politics. In recognition of Fisher's achievement, Nobel economist Milton Friedman wrote that "the U-turn in British policy executed by Margaret Thatcher owes more to him than any other individual."

Though business reversals later cost Fisher his fortune, he kept raising money for additional think tanks—this time in North America. In New York he was the progenitor, in 1978, of today's Manhattan Institute, which quickly shaped national debate by supporting landmark books on supply-side economics (*Wealth and Poverty* by George Gilder) and welfare reform (*Losing Ground* by Charles Murray). In the 1990s, New York City Mayor Rudy Giuliani looked to the Manhattan Institute for crucial ideas on law enforcement and other subjects.

Fisher was also behind the launch of the Pacific Research Institute in San Francisco, the National Center for Policy Analysis in Dallas, and the Fraser Institute in Vancouver. He created the Atlas Economic Research Foundation, which raises capital to launch new free-market groups in parts of the world that have inadequate experience in capitalism. Atlas has seeded more than 400 market-oriented organizations in over 80 countries.

By funding fresh ideas, and thinking of change in terms of decades rather than months, Antony Fisher helped create an international backlash against statism during the second half of the twentieth century.

Further reading

- Gerald Frost, *Antony Fisher: Champion of Liberty* (Profile Books, 2002)
- Tom Wolfe on the birth of the Manhattan Institute, manhattan-institute.org/turningintellect/chapter1.html

---

1980

Starting the Presses for Conservative Student Journalists

In 1980, Irving Kristol encouraged donors to support a new conservative student publication at the University of Chicago. Before long, the John M. Olin Foundation and other donors were building the Collegiate Network, a consortium of conservative and libertarian student publications that voiced an alternative to left-wing political correctness on campus, and trained a generation of writers and editors. Since 1995 the Collegiate Network has been administered by the Intercollegiate Studies Institute.

Thanks to donor support that paid for printing costs, most of the country's top colleges and universities had a conservative student publication by the 1990s. Many prominent writers emerged from these publications, including Pulitzer-winner Joseph Rago (*Dartmouth Review*),

ABC News correspondent Jonathan Karl (*Vassar Spectator*), *New York Times* columnist Ross Douthat (*Harvard Salient)*, commentator Ann Coulter (*Cornell Review*), *National Review* editor Rich Lowry (*Virginia Advocate*), blogger Michelle Malkin (*Oberlin Forum*), author and Silicon Valley investor Peter Thiel (*Stanford Review*), author Dinesh D'Souza and radio host Laura Ingraham (both *Dartmouth Review*), and many others. "If everything we have done since was stripped away, leaving only the Collegiate Network as our legacy," said longtime Olin Foundation head James Piereson in 2004, "we would still proudly say our work yielded enormous success."

Further reading

• The Collegiate Network, collegiatenetwork.org

1980

Mothers Against Drunk Driving

In 1980, the mother of a 13-year-old California girl who was killed by a repeat drunk driver founded a nonprofit to fight back. Mothers Against Drunk Driving helped set the drinking age at 21 in all states, promoted tougher sanctions and the deployment of new technology against impaired driving, and rated states on DUI enforcement. In the first five years of the group's existence annual traffic deaths related to alcohol were reduced by 20 percent—representing 6,000 lives saved. By 2013, alcohol-related deaths had been roughly cut in half, a total saving of about 300,000 lives.

Even still, alcohol-related crashes remain the most frequently committed violent crime in the U.S. On average, one American is killed by a drunk driver every 40 minutes. Economic losses exceed $114 billion per year.

In the 1990s MADD began to receive significant amounts of money from the federal government. The organization grew into a large bureaucracy, spending $20 million on annual staff salaries by 2009.

Further reading

• History of Mothers Against Drunk Driving, madd.org/about-us/mission

1980

Putting Milton Friedman on PBS

After the liberal economist John Kenneth Galbraith filmed *The Age of Uncertainty*, a television series for the BBC, several American philanthropists and corporations looked for a way to even the ideological balance sheet. They turned to Nobel Prize-winning economist Milton Friedman, who guided viewers through economic successes and failures around the globe, including their social effects, in a ten-part television series that appeared on PBS in 1980. The Sarah Scaife Foundation led the way, with a grant of $500,000. The John M. Olin Foundation contributed $250,000, Getty Oil Company $330,000, and the Reader's Digest Association $300,000. Other supporters included the Lilly Endowment, and the National Federation of Independent Business.

The show made a vigorous intellectual case for capitalism, and was a smashing popular success. A book co-authored by Milton's wife, Rose, and published as a companion to the television series hit the bestseller lists in the United States and abroad. In the wake of *Free to Choose*, Friedman was perhaps the most popular and influential economist on the planet.

Further reading

• Video archive, freetochoose.tv/broadcast.php?series=ftc80

• Milton and Rose Friedman, *Free to Choose: A Personal Statement* (Harcourt Brace Jovanovich, 1980)

1980

Human Rights Campaign

The Human Rights Campaign began life in 1980 as a PAC—a mechanism for funneling campaign donations to elect gay-friendly politicians. In 1982 the organization distributed $140,000 to 118 congressional candidates. Four decades later, HRC was the largest gay-advocacy group in the country, and electoral campaigning was still a huge part of its purpose. In the 2012 Presidential campaign year, the HRC raised or contributed more than $20 million to influence referenda on same-sex marriage, elect pro-gay members of Congress, and re-elect Barack Obama.

In 1995, when HRC was a $6 million organization with both 501(c)(3) advocacy and 501(c)(4) political action arms, it reorganized—adding new family projects and work projects, and expanding all research, communications, and public relations efforts. The nonprofit grew rapidly into a $54 million-per-year operation by 2013. Major donors now supply 22 percent of its income; smaller individual contributions total 38 percent; bequests come to 5 percent; and investments, merchandise, and special events provide a quarter of the group's revenue.

The Human Rights Campaign operates a sophisticated and effective lobbying effort in Washington, D.C. It recruits attorneys from major law firms to provide pro bono litigation services. And it has worked hard to make allies among other activist groups on the political left so it can later call in chits for its priorities.

HRC has also assiduously cultivated the entertainment industry. Producers, writers, actors, musicians, and others have been honored at dinners, given awards, and involved in marketing efforts. This has yielded not only many celebrity endorsements and financial contributions, but also television story lines that have brought gay-friendly ideas and characters into the living rooms of everyday Americans over two decades—which the organization has found invaluable to its political and policy advocacy.

Further reading

• Independent Sector case study, independentsector.org/uploads/advocacystudy/IS-BeyondtheCause-HRC.pdf

--- **1980** ---

Austrian Economics Along the Potomac

A center devoted to market-based economics and philosophy, called the Austrian Economics Program, was established at Rutgers University in the late-1970s with a grant from philanthropist Charles Koch. It was promptly squeezed by a hiring freeze. The president of George Mason University, just across the Potomac from Washington, D.C., invited the program to relocate to his campus in 1980. There, it eventually became known as the Mercatus Center (mercatus is Latin for "marketplace"), and with steady donations from the Charles Koch Charitable Foundation it grew into a very active academic hub and economic think tank.

More generally, a stream of Koch support that eventually totaled tens of millions of dollars was crucial in turning the George Mason economics department into one of the best in the nation. Two GMU economists have been awarded Nobel prizes: James Buchanan in 1986 and Vernon Smith in 2002. Public-choice theory and other concepts used to assess government policies today have been honed at the northern Virginia institution.

In 1985, George Mason University also became home to the Institute for Humane Studies, another quietly influential product of long-term Koch support. With online instructional materials, lectures, debates, seminars, and scholarships that help students pursue further studies, IHS now trains hundreds of thousands of students in principles of liberty and economic success. Over 1,700 of its alumni have become professors, and they will teach an estimated 10 million students over their careers. Some will also shape public policy through their research.

The Charles Koch Foundation has greatly expanded its giving to higher education over the last decade. "Currently we're fortunate to support over 350 programs, and over 250 colleges and universities across the country," says John Hardin, director of university relations at the foundation. Grants underwrite everything from guest lectures by leading scholars to special student seminars, from course-development assistance for faculty to student research fellowships.

Further reading

• About the Mercatus Center, mercatus.org/content/about

• Institute for Humane Studies support for professors, supportihs.org/professors

---

1981

New Efforts to Open Minds on Campus

Philanthropists bothered by the conformity of liberal orthodoxy on college campuses have long supported outposts where alternative views could be offered to a new generation of young students. The founding of the Intercollegiate Studies Institute in 1953 was an early effort to reintroduce students to the deep Western values behind America's founding. Many other such efforts followed.

In 1981, the John M. Olin Foundation awarded $50,000 to professor Allan Bloom at the University of Chicago to seed a new center for exploring political philosophy and democracy. In addition to funding a series of lectures, conferences, and fellowships, this support allowed Bloom to write a pathbreaking book warning of the perils of cultural relativism and declining intellectual standards on campus. *The Closing of the American Mind* became an unlikely bestseller in 1987, occupying the top spot on the *New York Times* bestseller list for four months with withering criticisms of modern universities for dismissing great books and timeless truths in favor of trendy ideology.

The bestseller *Illiberal Education* by Dinesh D'Souza, which extended this argument and popularized the term "political correctness," was also produced with support from Olin. Olin likewise funded a series of faculty fellowships that nurtured unconventional young scholars like John DiIulio, Frederick Kagan, and John Yoo. Other donors sponsored similar initiatives to open higher ed to points of view differing from the liberal conventions that dominate campuses. ACTA was founded in 1995 to mobilize trustee and alumni donors.

The James Madison Program in American Ideals and Institutions at Princeton University, for instance, was founded by professor Robert

George in 2000 with startup funding from the Olin and Bradley foundations, then donations from Princeton alumni. And there are other such groups. With financial support from a range of donors, the Intercollegiate Studies Institute, the Fund for American Studies, the Institute for Humane Studies, and similar organizations run summer programs, reading groups, websites, and special networks that aim to round out student educations with ideas, scholars, and philosophical perspectives not otherwise represented on most college campuses. The National Association of Scholars is a similar effort to support dissenting professors; funded by donors since 1987, it has 3,000 members, holds conferences, and publishes a quarterly journal. The Veritas Fund for Higher Education is a more recent creation that allows donors to fund professors who teach America's founding principles and history.

Another venture to improve civics knowledge among American undergraduates is the Jack Miller Center. It has established more than 50 on-campus institutes dedicated to study of our classic national texts, with funding from the entrepreneur who helped create the Staples company. He and other donors have committed over $50 million to the undertaking.

Further reading

- *New York Times* reporting, nytimes.com/2008/09/22/education/22conservative. html?pagewanted=print&_r=0
- *Philanthropy* magazine article, philanthropyroundtable.org/topic/excellence_in_ philanthropy/a_new_birth_of_civic_education_on_campus

———— 1981 ————

Give Peace a Grant

Coincident with the election of President Ronald Reagan, a "nuclear freeze" movement sprang up to oppose research and development of nuclear technology, advocate for disarmament, criticize American "belligerence," resist a general U.S. defense buildup, and vehemently oppose the placement of missiles in Europe to balance a Soviet missile buildup. In 1981 the movement went public with its first rally, and garnered endorsements from pacifist, religious, and union groups. Referenda declaring "nuclear-free zones" were placed on ballots in many cities. The "freeze" agitation peaked in a large 1982 gathering in New York City during a U.N. special session on disarmament, and culminated with inclusion of freeze rhetoric in the Democratic Party platform during the 1984 race for President.

At the heart of these efforts were a handful of major donors, and a new philanthropic entity. From 1974 to 1982 three foundations—Ford, the Rockefeller Brothers Fund, and Rockefeller Family Fund—spent about $7 million to build up anti-nuclear groups. Then in 1981, the Ploughshares Fund was started by an ACLU San Francisco board member who argued that "the threat of nuclear war overshadows everything else." The fund was established specifically to coordinate donations to disarmament and peace groups, and guide creation of their strategies.

Ploughshares has since channeled more than $100 million to peace groups, making it the largest philanthropy on this topic. It still exists today, its $11 million of income in 2014 came from about 2,000 individuals plus foundations like the Carnegie Corporation, the Compton, Ford, MacArthur, Turner, Rockefeller, and Hewlett foundations, and the Open Society Institute. It re-grants roughly half of its revenue to peace groups, and does some of its own programming with the rest.

Joan Kroc, heiress to the McDonald's fortune, also became a passionate nuclear disarmer in the 1980s. In 1985 she spent millions on advocacy, including ads in major publications calling for disarmament. She also reprinted and publicly distributed the book *Missile Envy* by Helen Caldicott. Kroc endowed two major academic centers for "peace studies"—the Kroc Institute for International Peace Studies at the University of Notre Dame, and a similar institute at the University of San Diego.

Further reading

• 2014 annual report of Ploughshares Fund, ploughshares.org/sites/default/files/resources/2014%20Ploughshares%20Annual%20Report.pdf

---

1982

Birth of the Federalist Society

The Institute for Educational Affairs, a group backed by the Olin, Earhart, JM, Scaife, and Smith Richardson foundations, provided a grant of $15,000 in 1982 to underwrite a legal conference on federalism put on by law students with an interest in conservative politics. Speakers at the forum, which took place at Yale, included future Supreme Court Justice Antonin Scalia and federal appeals Judge Robert Bork. Using the successful conference as a springboard, several of the organizers—including future senator and energy secretary Spencer Abraham and future Congressman David McIntosh—decided to form a national group with student-run local chapters, calling it the Federalist Society for Law and Public Policy.

Strong interest among students and additional foundation support allowed the group to grow rapidly. By the 1990s the Federalist Society had become one of the most influential legal groups in the country. On appointments to the federal judiciary, its influence arguably surpassed even the American Bar Association.

In 2014, the Federalist Society had chapters at every accredited law school in the United States, 10,000 student members, 30,000 members of its Lawyers Division, and a budget of more than $11 million. Inspired by its success, several philanthropists have tried to adapt its model to business schools (the Adam Smith Society), medical schools (the Benjamin Rush Society), and schools where students are trained in foreign policy (the Alexander Hamilton Society).

Further reading

• About the Federalist Society, fed-soc.org/aboutus

— 1984 —

A Foundation Behind the Iron Curtain

In 1984, currency speculator George Soros established the first private foundation in a communist country, in his native Hungary. The government in Budapest hoped that by sponsoring Hungarian students to study in Western countries the Soros Foundation-Hungary would improve the regime's scientific knowledge. But the returning students also brought back pro-Western ideas. In addition, the foundation equipped Hungarian libraries with copy machines, making it easier for dissidents to publish underground newspapers and spread samizdat literature.

"The formula was simple," wrote Soros. "Any activity or association that was not under the supervision or control of the authorities created alternatives and thereby weakened the monopoly of dogma." As the Cold War ended, Soros spent $123 million, between 1989 and 1994 to establish similar foundations across Central Europe, aiming to encourage the development of democracy and human rights.

Later, Soros started operations in Africa, Asia, and the Caribbean. Everywhere he went he called for the creation of "open societies," which he defined as threatened by both communism and what he dubbed "market fundamentalism." Critics, as in a 1997 *Forbes* cover story, noted that Soros projects generally "have an exclusively left-wing bias."

Further reading

• George Soros, *Open Society: Reforming Global Capitalism* (PublicAffairs, 2000)

• *Forbes* posting, listserv.buffalo.edu/cgi-bin/wa?A2=ind9911&L=JUST-WATCH-L&D=0&P=512135

1984
Religion in Public Life

A Lutheran minister (later a Catholic priest) who had been an anti-war activist in the 1960s, Richard John Neuhaus, took a look at the rise of the Religious Right in the 1970s and found himself in democratic sympathy. The gatekeepers of culture, he concluded, had largely banished from public discourse any serious expression of religion—the most important element in the life of many Americans. He predicted "a deepening crisis of legitimacy if the courts persist in systematically ruling out of order the moral traditions in which Western law has developed, and which bear for the overwhelming majority of the American people a living sense of right and wrong."

Neuhaus began to formulate these ideas while examining the nonprofit sector with funding from the Lilly Endowment. He received grants from the Bradley and Olin foundations to write the book he ultimately titled *The Naked Public Square*, which came out in 1984. Both his title and his thesis went mainline, and even commentators who "subscribed to exaggerated notions of church-state separation," as Neuhaus put it, began to acknowledge that America is harmed when all moral calculus is stripped from public discussion and policy. With continuing donor support, Neuhaus subsequently published the influential journal *First Things*, which deepened and extended this understanding of religion's healthy role in public life.

Further reading

• *Philanthropy* magazine article, philanthropyroundtable.org/topic/excellence_in_philanthropy/eight_books_that_changed_america

1984
Koch Brothers Take Up Advocacy

From the mid-'70s to mid-'80s, brothers Charles and David Koch contributed to public-policy philanthropy mainly by building the Cato Institute, Mercatus Center, and other research organizations capable of formulating detailed critiques of national problems (see 1977 and 1980 entries). In 1984 the Koch brothers took a step toward more direct advocacy. They provided about a million dollars a year to help launch Citizens for a Sound Economy, which quickly attracted additional funding from other foundation and business donors. The group distributed studies, analysis, polling, and other information to promote a vision of "less government, lower taxes, and less regulation." It attracted prominent staff like former U.S. Office of Management and Budget director James Miller, economist Larry Kudlow, and retired Congressman Dick Armey. The group rescued the Tax Foundation, since 1937 an invaluable collator of tax data.

In 2004, Citizens for a Sound Economy restructured into two new organizations: FreedomWorks (which over the next few years organized several million activists interested in individual liberty and limited government) and Americans for Prosperity (which built a similar following, including 2 million members, 35 state chapters, and financial support from 100,000 contributors) in order to "educate citizens about economic policy and mobilize those citizens as advocates in the public-policy process." Both groups were important in building the organizational and intellectual resources of the so-called Tea Party movement as an alternative channel for activism by libertarians and conservatives frustrated with the Republican party establishment.

Over a period of decades, the Koch brothers contributed more than $200 million to three dozen or so advocacy organizations focused on free-market reforms. (Meanwhile they have been only light contributors to political candidates.) In 2003 the Kochs also started convening semi-annual free-enterprise seminars where other donors interested in public policies were invited to discuss topics like budget control, health care, climate change, tax reduction, and respect for Constitutional limits on government, and then encouraged to contribute to advocacy groups promoting market-oriented solutions to such problems. The first seminars included less than 20 people, but donor participation gradually grew, and over a decade several hundred million dollars were donated by attendees to organizations active in public-policy debates. The last Koch seminar in 2015 was attended by about 450 donors, with the goal of encouraging $889 million in annual donations to groups active in policy and political advocacy.

Further reading

• Brian Doherty, *Radicals for Capitalism* (PublicAffairs, 2008)

• Charles Koch description of his policy philanthropy, online.wsj.com/news/articles/SB1 0001424052702303978304579475860515021286

---------------------------------- **1985** ----------------------------------

Minting New Democrats

Following President Ronald Reagan's landslide re-election in 1984, moderate Democrats sought ways to push their party away from doctrinaire

liberalism and toward the political center. Party loyalist Al From organized wealthy benefactors in a series of private retreats, then tapped them
for donations with which to found the Democratic Leadership Council—dedicated to supporting more moderate so-called "New Democrats."The DLC functioned as an alternative and rival to the Democratic
National Committee, causing controversy within party ranks but also
preparing the way for future victories.

In 1989, the DLC formed a nonprofit research arm, the Progressive
Policy Institute, to operate as a think tank for centrist Democrats. Wall
Street magnate Michael Steinhardt served as PPI's board chairman, pledg-
ing hundreds of thousands of dollars to the organization. By 1992, this
"pint-sized think tank" with a budget of just $700,000 had become the
primary idea-generator for Bill Clinton's campaign for President. Once
in the White House, Clinton staffed his administration with numerous alumni of the Democratic Leadership Council and the Progressive
Policy Institute, looking to them for ideas on trade promotion, welfare
reform, and streamlining government. By 2001, the DLC and PPI had a
combined budget of $7 million.

With the resurgence of liberalism inside the Democratic party during
the first decade of the twenty-first century, the DLC and PPI struggled
to remain relevant. In 2011 the DLC formally dissolved and donated its
archive to the Clinton Foundation. The Progressive Policy Institute continues as a small entity seeking policies it views as centrist and sensible.

Further reading

• Kenneth Baer, *Reinventing Democrats* (University of Kansas Press, 2000)

• Critical review in *American Prospect*, prospect.org/article/how–dlc–does–it

---

1986

Sparking Welfare Reform

In 1986, the Lynde and Harry Bradley Foundation built an intellectual
coalition for welfare reform. Its $300,000 grant assembled top conser-
vative and liberal social scientists to see if agreement could be found on
ways to reduce the destructive effects of welfare programs on family
structure, work rates, crime levels, and other social factors. Members of
the new group on both sides of the political divide made concessions,
and a final report entitled *The New Consensus on Family and Welfare* was
drafted under the leadership of Michael Novak.

The conservatives acknowledged that government has a role to play
in the alleviation of suffering. The liberals admitted that welfare programs

often produce dysfunctional levels of dependency. The report sketched the outlines of new programs with work requirements and supports that would be healthier for U.S. society. This new synthesis proved to be the kernel of the welfare-reform compromise that was eventually debated and passed into law during the Clinton administration.

Another bit of seminal philanthropy was the 1982 funding from the Olin Foundation that helped Charles Murray write his influential critique of the existing welfare state, *Losing Ground*. Olin grants also supported two books by Lawrence Mead that made the case for work requirements in return for cash payments. The Bradley Foundation sped welfare reform as well by paying for the research that led to Marvin Olasky's book *The Tragedy of American Compassion*—which uncovered the forgotten but highly effective religious-based charity of the nineteenth century, inspiring both revisions to government transfer programs and, later, revived interest in faith-based social work.

The most direct way Bradley advanced welfare reform, though, was by helping set a successful template in their home state of Wisconsin. The foundation established the new Wisconsin Policy Research Institute to take some of the fresh theory being generated by national scholars and reformers and translate it into practical new policies that could improve the lot of the poor in Milwaukee and the rest of the state.

This activity emboldened Wisconsin Governor Tommy Thompson to launch demonstration projects overhauling welfare in a couple of Wisconsin counties. Soon these experiments were expanded to the entire state. Instead of handing out welfare checks as automatic entitlements, the state began to require certain constructive behaviors from recipients, such as finding employment or pursuing an education, while offering them help with child care, transportation, and other practical barriers to work. When he needed additional scholarly help in designing these reforms, and encountered resistance from academics at the University of Wisconsin, Thompson turned to the Hudson Institute, also supported by Bradley (and Olin).

These late-1980s experiments resulted in dramatic reductions in welfare dependency across Wisconsin, rising work rates, and improved child welfare. That in turn inspired the federal welfare-reform legislation signed into law by President Clinton in 1996, which quickly cut national welfare caseloads in half, chopped poverty rates, and brought other healthy results. By using its home state of Wisconsin as a "laboratory of democracy," the Bradley Foundation proved that smart local philanthropy could yield powerful national results.

Further reading
- First-hand account on creating the *New Consensus report*, firstthings.com/web-exclusives/2006/08/bill-clinton-and-welfare-refor
- Lawrence Mead, *Government Matters: Welfare Reform in Wisconsin* (Princeton University Press, 2005)

1986

ACLU LGBT Project

Since establishing its LGBT Project in 1986 (to expand lesbian, gay, bisexual, and transgender rights), the American Civil Liberties Union has received about $20 million of earmarked donations to support that work. Lawsuits brought by the organization have upended numerous public policies at both the state and national level. ACLU litigation was crucial, for instance, in undermining voter initiatives passed in California (barring same-sex marriage) and Colorado (barring the granting of protected status to homosexuals), effectively blocking future popular votes on these issues. In 1997 an ACLU suit in New Jersey established the first right of gay couples to adopt children. ACLU lawsuits in scores of states were vital in gradually creating a right to same-sex marriage. And it was an ACLU case that invalidated the Defense of Marriage Act that had been passed by Congress and signed by President Clinton. The organization's LGBT Project continues to have strong effects on law, policy, and public opinion in all of these areas, along with a growing advocacy for individuals who decide to change their sex—helping them in child custody, college housing, military service, health-insurance, public restroom usage, and other disputes.

Further reading
- ACLU LGBT Project, aclu.org/lgbt-rights

1986

Creating State Think Tanks

Thomas Roe, founder of the construction-supply firm Builder Marts, was an active public-policy donor until his death in 2000. When he expressed an interest in the "New Federalism" proposed by Ronald Reagan, which would allow states to solve their own problems as an alternative to standardized programs from Washington, Reagan challenged him to "do something about it." Roe decided that supporting market-oriented think tanks in every state would help. In 1986 he founded the South Carolina Policy Council in his native place.

Simultaneously, activists favoring decentralized and limited government started similar policy centers in other states—like the Independence Institute in Colorado, and the Mackinac Center in Michigan. With Roe's encouragement and financial support these organizations began to collaborate and learn from each other. In 1992, they organized the State Policy Network, a consortium of free-market think tanks focused on improving public policy in state capitals rather than via federal legislation in D.C.

Roe served as SPN's founding chairman and its major financial backer. At its launch, SPN had a dozen think tanks as members; by 2014 it numbered 64 think tanks representing all 50 states, with combined budgets exceeding $80 million. In addition to the traditional think-tank work of policy analysis, they are increasingly becoming involved in new ventures like nonprofit journalism and public-interest litigation.

Further reading

• Thomas Roe history, capitalresearch.org/wp-content/uploads/May-2007-Foundation-Watch.pdf

• Directory of SPN state think tanks, spn.org/docLib/20120501_Map2012.pdf

—— 1986 ——

Bradley Foundation Sparks School Choice

One of the first major initiatives of the Lynde and Harry Bradley Foundation was to bring school choice to its home city of Milwaukee. In so doing, it both revolutionized local schooling and created a powerful demonstration project for the rest of the country. The foundation's early work in this area involved building an intellectual framework. Their 1986 grant to the Brookings Institution for the groundbreaking research of John Chubb and Terry Moe resulted in the book *Politics, Markets, and America's Schools*. Chubb and Moe added convincing empirical data to longstanding theoretical arguments in favor of school choice that had been formulated by scholars like Milton Friedman.

Before long, the Bradley Foundation was involved in even more practical work—laboring with black community activists in Milwaukee and the administration of Republican Governor Tommy Thompson who were developing legislation that would allow low-income children trapped in poor public schools to attend private and parochial schools. A small program was launched and grew steadily in size and strength. During the 1990s it survived repeated legal assaults and political challenges, becoming the country's longest-living and most-watched private school-choice program in the United States. By the 2014-15 academic year, more than 26,000 students were attending 113 schools under the Milwaukee Parental Choice Program.

Milwaukee's successes inspired similar voucher and school-choice programs in Florida, Pennsylvania, Arizona, Ohio, Indiana, and other states. Research on student performance indicates that school choice improves high-school graduation rates, college admittance, and college persistence. While participants typically enter their choice schools one to two years behind grade level, achievement test results at choice schools are equal to or higher than at public schools. Voucher programs save taxpayer dollars (the Milwaukee program reduced state spending by $52 million in 2011) and encourage public schools to improve by applying competitive pressure.

The Milwaukee program came under renewed pressure in 2011 when the ACLU and Disability Rights Wisconsin filed a complaint alleging that the private schools that parents were choosing for their children were not following disability law. In 2013 the Obama administration's Department of Justice Civil Rights Division sent the Wisconsin education superintendent a letter pressing the ACLU's arguments, and threatening that "the United States reserves its right to pursue enforcement through other means." The Wisconsin Institute for Law & Liberty, a public-interest law firm partly funded by the Bradley and Kern foundations, is defending the program.

Further reading

• 2012 comprehensive review of Milwaukee program, uaedreform.org/downloads/2012/02/report-36-the-comprehensive-longitudinal-evaluation-of-the-milwaukee-parental-choice-program.pdf

• Wisconsin Institute for Law & Liberty analysis of U.S. Department of Justice letter, will-law.org/home/WILL-Blog/2013/08/28/WILL-RESPONDS-TO-US-DOJ

————————— **1988** —————————

Pew Warms to Climate Change

In 1988, the Pew Charitable Trusts, whose resources derive from Sun Oil, offered a $120,000 gift to the University of California at Santa Barbara to study "the impact of climate change on northern temperate forest reserves." Since then, climate change has been a major priority of Pew, one of the largest and most powerful philanthropies in the country.

In 1998, for instance, Pew put up $12 million to launch the Pew Center on Global Climate Change. It produced nearly 100 reports, had witnesses testify before Congress 30 times, and worked to influence regional and international talks on setting new climate and energy policies. The organization is now known as the Center for Climate and Energy Solutions, and continues its work with an annual budget of around $4 million and support from the Hewlett, Rockefeller Brothers, Energy, and Alcoa foundations.

In 2002, Pew converted itself from private foundation to public charity, so it could not only provide funds for public-policy causes but also lobby and raise funds from others on their behalf, putting "an emphasis on action." In 2007, for instance, it played a major role in launching the U.S. Climate Action Partnership, a group wholly focused on lobbying for government controls on greenhouse gases. The Pew Charitable Trusts currently spend about $300 million every year, with a strong focus on influencing public policy.

Further reading

• 2004 Capital Research Center analysis, capitalresearch.org/wp-content/uploads/2013/01/FW0113.pdf

• Center for Climate and Energy Solutions public-policy activity, c2es.org/about/history

1988

A Think Tank for Family Reinforcement

When Michigan auto-parts executive Edgar Prince visited Christian radio personality James Dobson in Colorado in 1988, he learned that Dobson was trying to raise $1 million to jumpstart the Family Research Council, a small and languishing think tank. Prince immediately pledged the full amount, a contribution that allowed Gary Bauer to join FRC as its president. This launched a phase of rapid growth for FRC, giving Americans concerned with family breakdown and religious conservatives an institutional voice they previously lacked in Washington public policy circles. By the late 1990s, the FRC had grown into a major organization, with a budget of $14 million, 120 employees, and its own building in the nation's capital. The organization played a role in Supreme Court confirmation battles, passage of child tax credits, the ban on partial-birth abortion, and many other issue debates.

Further reading

• Family Research Council history, frc.org/historymission

1989

New Approach to Race Discrimination

During the 1980s, scholars such as Thomas Sowell developed intellectual arguments against the racial preferences advocated by the civil-rights establishment. By the end of the decade, conservative foundations were ready to translate these new ideas into law and policy. In 1988, attorneys Michael Greve and Michael McDonald persuaded the Bradley, Olin, and Smith Richardson foundations to provide seed money to start the Center for Individual Rights, which filed suit against public universities over their use of racial quotas and preferences to shape their student bodies. The center won *Hopwood v. Texas* in federal court in 1996, marking the first victory against color-coded admissions. In 2003, a pair of CIR-driven cases involving the University of Michigan went to the Supreme Court, which accepted the constitutionality of race-based admissions for particular purposes, establishing a stalemate in use of racial preferences.

A range of donor-backed organizations now argues both in courts of law and in the court of public opinion for limits on race-conscious policies. The California Civil Rights Initiative, approved by California voters in 1996, banned the use of race in that state's public employment, contracting, and college admissions. Ward Connerly of the American Civil Rights Institute led the campaign on its behalf, and later became involved in similarly successful efforts in Arizona, Michigan, Washington, and elsewhere. For other recent philanthropically supported cases see 2013 entry on "Supreme Assistance."

Further reading

• Steven Teles, *The Rise of the Conservative Legal Movement* (Princeton University Press, 2008)

1989

Reinventing Development Economics

In the 1970s, the conventional wisdom in international aid organizations was that the biggest hurdles to the economic development of poor nations were external factors like the legacy of colonialism and ongoing exploitation by rich countries. With the help of the Smith Richardson Foundation and other donors, Peruvian economist Hernando de Soto conducted research that showed actually the most serious impediments to growth in poor nations were self-inflicted government policies that interfere with property ownership and business enterprise.

In 1989's *The Other Path*, de Soto demonstrated that many of the world's poor made most of their income in the black market, and would be dramatically helped if entrepreneurship and private property were protected rather than discriminated against in law. De Soto's Peruvian think tank, the Institute for Liberty and Democracy, pushed for land-title reforms, recognition of underground small businesses, and other market-based reforms. Developing countries in South America and elsewhere that instituted pro-market policies with ILD assistance experienced a brought a burst of prosperity in the two decades following.

In Peru, the war of ideas was also a war of bombs and bullets, and the Maoist rebel group known as the Shining Path targeted de Soto for death. During this tense period, the Smith Richardson Foundation offered protection. "The foundation is an old and loyal friend which, when the ILD was being bombed and shot at during the early 1990s, provided us with a bullet-proof vehicle, thus enabling us to continue with our work," wrote de Soto in the acknowledgments to his 2000 book, *The Mystery of Capital.*

Hernando De Soto is now one of the world's most influential development economists.

Further reading

• PBS interview with Hernando de Soto, pbs.org/wgbh/commandingheights/shared/minitextlo/int_hernandodesoto.html

• The work of the ILD, ild.org.pe/index.php/es/introduction

1991

Campaigning Against Tobacco

The Robert Wood Johnson Foundation began a long-term public crusade against tobacco use in 1991. Moving far beyond traditional medical efforts and using all the levers of public-policy advocacy, the group invested more than $500 million of its own funds, and recruited allies to contribute more. This massive philanthropic investment hastened many changes in law and policy that damped smoking: the Synar Amendment requiring states to prohibit the sale of tobacco to minors, public-health warnings against secondhand smoke, smoking bans on airplanes and in public spaces, bans on tobacco advertising, and agreements with Hollywood to stop glamorizing smoking in movies and TV. Starting in 1998, the Master Settlement Agreement transferred billions of dollars from cigarette companies to state governments, to settle suits over the public costs of treating smoking-related illness.

In 1996 the R. W. Johnson Foundation joined the American Cancer Society, American Heart Association, American Medical Association, and others in launching the National Center for Tobacco-Free Kids. The foundation put $84 million into that effort over the next 11 years.

The foundation pushed hard for higher cigarette taxes to suppress use. "Raising tobacco taxes is our No. 1 strategy," said one collaborating activist. "The tobacco industry...can't repeal the laws of economics." RWJ devoted $99 million to its SmokeLess States program. When the campaign was over, more than 30 states had increased cigarette taxes and six had approved indoor-air laws that proscribed smoking in workplaces and restaurants. The federal government doubled cigarette excise taxes in 2009.

It's not clear what would have happened to tobacco use absent this intervention led by the Robert Wood Johnson Foundation. The decline in smoking in the U.S. has actually been quite steady since the first U.S. Surgeon General report warning of tobacco's dangers appeared in the mid-1960s. In any case, the fraction of active cigarette smokers in America fell from 27 percent in 1994 to 17 percent in 2014, and it is estimated that more than 8 million lives have been saved as a result of reduced tobacco use—which proceeded faster and further in the U.S. than in most other countries.

Further reading

• Anti-tobacco efforts of R. W. Johnson Foundation, rwjf.org/en/research-publications/find-rwjf-research/2011/04/the-tobacco-campaigns-.html

1991

Institute for Justice

In 1991, former Reagan administration lawyer Chip Mellor approached philanthropist Charles Koch with an idea for a "national law firm on liberty" that he would co-found with litigator Clint Bolick. Koch pledged up to $500,000 per year for three years. The Institute for Justice never needed this full amount, though. It quickly raised additional funds from other sources, especially as it began accepting and winning cases.

IJ rapidly became one of the leading firms pursuing "public interest" cases in the courts, usually for no fee, by aggressively litigating in four areas: economic rights, private-property protection, school choice, and free speech. It has taken numerous cases all the way to the U.S. Supreme Court. In *Zelman v. Simmons-Harris* (2002), for instance, the high court endorsed public funding of private-school vouchers. In *Kelo v. City of New London* (2005), the justices rejected IJ's call to forbid use of eminent domain for economic development, but a public backlash stirred up by the case compelled state legislatures around the country to restrict the use of eminent domain via new laws—highlighting the success of IJ's model combining good lawyering with strategic research, media savvy, and political activism.

The organization's second donor, retired investor Robert Wilson, helped fuel it to new heights when, after years of making annual gifts of $35,000 and promising more only "when the time is right," he issued a challenge grant in 2008. Over a period of five years, he donated $15 million on the condition that IJ raise $2 of additional new contributions for every $1 he donated. This $45 million total infusion allowed the organization to expand significantly and become one of the nation's leading litigants for liberty. In 2014, futures trader and longtime IJ supporter William Dunn revived the 1:2 challenge with an offer to give IJ $5 million if the organization would raise $10 million to match it.

In 2010, IJ launched an initiative to challenge civil forfeiture, which allows law-enforcement officials to permanently seize private property including homes, cars, and cash even if the owners haven't been charged or convicted of a crime. Applying its trademark mix of research, cutting-edge litigation, media campaigning, and legislative advocacy, IJ set out to end or limit the practice. Its research report, "Policing for Profit: The Abuse of Civil Asset Forfeiture Laws" graded every state forfeiture law and found that only three states received a B or higher. The institute simultaneously launched litigation in Georgia, Massachusetts, and Philadelphia, and lawsuits challenging currency seizures by the federal government.

Early in 2015, the U.S. Department of Justice announced it was suspending its program for sharing proceeds of civil forfeitures with police departments, and would review how it uses the law. At the same time, legislation was introduced in the House and Senate to rein in civil forfeiture practices.

By 2014, the Institute for Justice had more than 80 employees (about half of them lawyers), five state offices in addition to its headquarters, and a legal clinic on entrepreneurship at the University of Chicago.

Further reading

• *Wall Street Journal* profile of Chip Mellor, online.wsj.com/news/articles/SB10001424052970203513604577144902274972614?mod=ITP_opinion_0&mg=-reno64-wsj

• About the Institute for Justice, ij.org/about-ij-ij-at-a-glance

---

1991

Backscratching Philanthropy Sows Havoc

Charitable donations aimed at influencing policy can occasionally lead to disaster, particularly if they are entangled with taxpayer money. That's the lesson of Fannie Mae and Freddie Mac, so-called government-sponsored enterprises created by Congress to lubricate the housing market. The two agencies were allowed to operate almost like corporations—including in setting up foundation arms and making large donations to nonprofits, even though they were neither real private companies nor real philanthropists.

Fannie Mae had become insolvent during the 1980s, and government officials were exploring ways of ending the government privileges (like loose capital standards) that kept it and Freddie Mac afloat. In 1988, the White House Commission on Privatization called for an end to "all federal benefits and backing for Fannie and Freddie." In the 1990 reconciliation act, the Congressional Budget Office was asked to study the financial risks to taxpayers created by these government-sheltered housing subsidizers.

To fight back, Fannie Mae hired the political operator who had run Walter Mondale's presidential campaign. When Jim Johnson became CEO in 1991, two of his first ventures were to 1) allocate $10 billion for low-income people to borrow money to buy houses, and 2) establish a string of "partnership offices" in congressional districts across the U.S. where Fannie Mae would distribute grants to local nonprofits and win allies. As a Fannie Mae executive told *New York Times* reporter Gretchen Morgenson, "the partnership offices gave us an enormous advantage when Congress was debating further regulations. We were able to call... upon all our partners in the cities where we had these offices and say you have to weigh in. Write to Congress."

Johnson put $350 million into Fannie Mae's foundation and started making hundred-thousand-dollar gifts to scores of advocacy groups and nonprofits. In the words of the *Times* reporter, Fannie's CEO made the foundation "a powerhouse in charitable giving that targeted organizations associated with favored politicians, or located in their areas." For instance, a nonprofit founded by the mother of Barney Frank (who became chairman of the House Financial Services Committee) was twice given an "Award of Excellence" by Fannie Mae.

In addition to myriad local nonprofits, national activist groups like ACORN, the National Council of La Raza, and the National Low Income Housing Coalition were showered with grants and attention. Poverty and minority advocates were charmed when Johnson announced in 1994 that Fannie Mae would spend $1 trillion on "affordable housing" over the next seven years. When the bills aimed at reining in reckless mortgage underwriting finally came up in Congress, Fannie and Freddie literally wrote much of the language, according to the *New York Times*. Not only was privatization of the agencies fended off, but so were stricter operating standards.

Fannie and Freddie's share of the mortgage market soared from 5 percent in 1990 to ten times that much in 2008. And at that point the entire U.S. housing market melted down, made toxic by mortgages pumped into non-creditworthy households. The economic trauma caused by the subprime-mortgage mess damaged family incomes and national prosperity for years thereafter.

Further reading

- Gretchen Morgenson and Joshua Rosner, *Reckless Endangerment* (St. Martin's Press, 2011)
- Heritage Foundation research report, heritage.org/research/reports/2013/11/fannie-and-freddie-what-record-of-success#_ftn25
- *Philanthropy Daily* analysis, philanthropydaily.com/a-public-private-disaster

—————————— **1991** ——————————

Energy Foundation

Three large foundations—Rockefeller, MacArthur, and the Pew Charitable Trusts—pledged a combined $20 million in 1991 to found a new organization devoted to political-campaign-style efforts to change U.S. energy policy: reducing energy use, promoting renewable sources, and (most recently) pushing the U.S. economy away from "yesterday's fossil-fuel technologies" via proposed government caps and taxes. The Energy Foundation is the resulting conduit. It collects money from large givers, then re-grants it to groups scrambling to change policy. The original donors were eventually joined by the Packard, Hewlett, and McKnight foundations, and a few wealthy donors like Jeff Skoll, Tom Steyer, Julian Robertson, and James Simons.

The Energy Foundation was influential in convincing around three dozen states to set controversial regulations requiring utilities to generate a minimum fraction of their electric power from renewable or alternative sources, passing on the increased costs to their customers. The EF also helped convince regulators in California to require that one out of every six cars purchased in the state by 2025 be a zero-emission electric plug-in. The foundation then helped export the California standard to a dozen other states.

The Energy Foundation now funnels approximately $80 million per year from its supporting philanthropists to about 500 different action groups.

Further reading

• Duke University case study, cspcs.sanford.duke.edu/sites/default/files/descriptive/energy_foundation.pdf

1993

Scuttling HillaryCare with Faxed Memos

Shortly after Bill Clinton's election, Republican operative Bill Kristol raised $1.3 million from conservative foundations and New York donors to fund a nonprofit activist organization to resist nationalized health care. Clinton had promised a health-care overhaul as a signature effort, and tasked First Lady Hillary Rodham Clinton and top aides to come up with a proposal. Their solution, critics noted, would have had the government take direction of one seventh of the American economy.

Kristol and a few donor-financed assistants were among the chief organizers of opposition to the plan. They drafted strategy memos and broadcast them to politicians and journalists via fax machines (then a cutting-edge technology). At a time when polls indicated wide support for a new health-care law, the organization insisted that "there is no health-care crisis." Eventually, rising public opposition forced the White House to abandon its massive reform, and set the stage for Republican domination of the 1994 elections—which broke the Democrats' grip on Congress for the first time in decades.

From this success sprouted the Project for the New American Century, which continued the strategy of faxed memos but in the service of a hawkish foreign policy, and then creation of the *Weekly Standard*, a conservative magazine launched in 1995 with Kristol as editor.

Further reading

• Nina Easton, *Gang of Five: Leaders at the Center of the Conservative Crusade* (Simon & Schuster, 2000)

• Haynes Johnson and David Broder, *The System: The American Way of Politics at the Breaking Point* (Little, Brown, 1996)

1994

Dick Weekley Trims Lawsuits in Texas

Houston real-estate developer Dick Weekley worried that runaway litigation costs in trial-lawyer-friendly Texas were imperiling the state's business environment. So in 1994 he and several allies founded a nonprofit called Texans for Lawsuit Reform. The group's mission statement called lawsuit abuse "the No. 1 threat to Texas's economic future."

At first, Weekley contributed his time to the project. Before long, he was contributing his money and raising additional funds from other Texans. Within two years, TLR had convinced the state legislature to put some limits on punitive-damage awards. As the organization pushed for more changes and helped finance the campaigns of like-minded political candidates, it attracted a mass following. In 2014, TLR had more than 16,000 individual supporters, representing 1,266 different trades and professions, from 857 towns across the state. "Membership continues to grow because Texans recognize that a small, powerful group of plaintiff lawyers are abusing the system for financial gain, resulting in harm to consumers and the Texas economy," said Weekley. "Other groups have raised more money," wrote *Texas Monthly* in 2011, "but none have been so single-minded in their pursuit of an ideological goal."

TLR's biggest breakthroughs came in 2003. To supplement its research and educational work, the organization had added a political action arm, TLR PAC, to fund candidates. The PAC's donations played a key role in the 2002 Republican takeover of the Texas House of Representatives (which Democrats had controlled since Reconstruction). A flood of reforms followed in the next legislative year. Lawmakers overhauled the rules on medical-malpractice lawsuits, for example, adopting a cap on non-economic damages.

By 2008, TLR could take credit for almost two dozen important reforms, and Texas had transformed itself from lawsuit mecca to leader in legal moderation. A 2008 economic analysis calculated that 8.5 percent of the state's economic growth since 1995 was due to lawsuit reform. It credited lawsuit reform with bringing 499,000 new jobs, a 21 percent reduction in medical liability insurance costs, and health insurance coverage for 430,000 formerly uninsured Texans. TLR continues to pursue adjustments to the state civil-justice system in each legislative session.

Further reading

- "New group hopes to quell lawsuit abuse," *Houston Chronicle*, August 30, 1994
- The Perryman Group, "Texas Turnaround: The Impact of Lawsuit Reform on Economic Activity in the Lone Star State," April 2008

1994

Tim Gill Puts Big Money Into Gay Rights

In 1994, Tim Gill, founder of the software company Quark, set up his Gill Foundation with a fierce focus on changing public policies and officeholders to advance gay rights. A decade later he established a political-action arm focused directly on influencing elections, and formulated a specific plan to legalize gay marriage within ten years. Gill subsequently devoted more than $300 million of personal and foundation gifts to these causes, to great effect.

Gill's gay-marriage goals were largely achieved within his ten-year time frame. And his donations also helped swell AIDS funding, create new hate-crime categories, defeat a Constitutional amendment to define traditional marriage, repeal the military's prohibitions on overt homosexuality, undo religious-freedom protections in federal and state laws, and promote the Employment Non-Discrimination Act legislation making sexual orientation and gender identity protected categories in labor law. "Normalizing LGBT people in the eyes of the public" has been at the heart of his effort.

Gill made a special push to turn his home state of Colorado into a model. Working with three wealthy colleagues, he set out to establish a cautionary for policymakers in other places by defeating political candidates viewed as hostile to gay causes. The heavily funded effort succeeded at flipping Colorado politics for a period of years (see 2008 entry), a success that public-policy donors in other states subsequently worked to copy.

In 2014 it was reported that Gill will spend at least $25 million over the next few years to remake policies and attitudes in Southern and Western states into forms more friendly to gay rights. This funding will help nonprofit groups like the Human Rights Campaign and the ACLU bring in new staff for major initiatives to shift law and culture in culturally conservative states.

Further reading
• *New York Times* article, nytimes.com/2014/04/28/us/politics/gay-rights-push-shifts-its-focus-south-and-west.html?smid=tw-share&_r=0

--------- **1994** ---------

Tug-of-war Over Campaign Finance

In the decade between 1994 and 2004, philanthropists proclaiming the importance of "taking the money out of politics" spent more than $140 million on politics. Eight liberal foundations supplied 88 percent of this funding that sought to restrict paid speech in political campaigns, with the Pew Charitable Trusts alone spending more than $40 million. Grants went to organizations such as the Center for Responsive Politics, the Center for Public Integrity, Democracy 21, and the League of

Women Voters Education Fund. Large grants also went to liberal media organizations like NPR and the *American Prospect* to pay for stories on campaign-finance reform.

"The idea was to create an impression that a mass movement was afoot—that everywhere [members of Congress] looked, in academic institutions, in the business community, in religious groups, in ethnic groups, everywhere, people were talking about reform," explained former Pew program officer Sean Treglia at an academic conference after campaign-finance reform had already passed Congress. He added that he "always encouraged the grantees never to mention Pew" because the disclosure would clash with an image of grassroots activism.

Whatever the motives and tactics, the results were clear: In 2002, the so-called McCain-Feingold campaign reform act, a sweeping measure that regulated both dollars and words in political campaigns, was passed into law. Almost immediately, however, this legislative victory turned into a legal rout. Judges repeatedly trimmed the law's limits on what campaigns, corporations, and labor unions could do and say. The biggest blow came in 2010, with the *Citizens United* ruling in which the U.S. Supreme Court found that the First Amendment to the Constitution prohibits government from restricting independent political expenditures by nonprofits, corporations, labor unions, and other associations.

The Pew Charitable Trusts halted its philanthropy in this area in 2008, and the philanthropic enthusiasts for throttling campaign spending gradually recognized that they had reached an impasse.

Further reading

• *New York Post* reporting on Treglia presentation, rhsager.com/blog/index.php/buying-reform

--------------------------------- **1994** ---------------------------------

Soros Declares War on the War on Drugs

When Arizona and California became the first states to approve the "medical" use of marijuana in 1996, it was currency speculator George Soros who, as the *New York Times* put it, "almost singlehandedly" made these victories possible. He made million-dollar donations on behalf of ballot referenda and other organizing efforts.

With the door cracked open by "medical marijuana," Soros continued to contribute several million dollars every year to promote wider drug legalizations. He backed organizations like the 501(c)(3) nonprofit Drug Policy Alliance and its political-campaign arm, Drug Policy Action.

These organizations first expanded legalization of medical marijuana to 20 states, then pushed through open-ended sanctionings of recreational use of marijuana products—first in Colorado and Washington state, followed by Alaska, Oregon, and D.C.

From 1994 to 2014, George Soros poured at least $80 million into efforts to undo drug prohibitions, prompting Joseph Califano of Columbia University's National Center on Addiction and Substance Abuse to label him the "Daddy Warbucks of drug legalization." Nearly matching Soros in funding the relaxation of drug laws was Peter Lewis, former chairman of Progressive Insurance and an active pot smoker himself. In the decades before his death in 2013, Lewis donated up to $60 million for the cause of legalization. Between them, Soros and Lewis provided more than two thirds of the funding for the groups that drove the marijuana legalizations in states like Colorado and Washington.

Further reading

• *Philanthropy* magazine article, philanthropyroundtable.org/topic/excellence_in_philanthropy/drug_donors

• 1996 *New York Times* report, nytimes.com/1996/12/17/us/with-big-money-and-brash-ideas-a-billionaire-redefines-charity.html

1994

A New Way to Fight Crime

In 1982, social scientists George Kelling and James Q. Wilson published an article arguing that speedy public reaction to petty disorders like a broken window could head off more serious crimes—which often spike when perpetrators get the sense that no one is paying attention. With support from the Olin Foundation and other donors, this argument was developed further at the Manhattan Institute (where Kelling became a senior fellow), and empirical studies showed the theory to be accurate.

One of those listening was Rudolph Giuliani. When he became New York City mayor in 1994 he and police commissioner William Bratton rolled out a radically different policing style, cracking down on small crimes like subway fare jumping and aggressive panhandling, pushing officers out onto streets, and using detailed crime data to allocate police resources and hold precinct commanders accountable. Within five years, major crimes in New York were cut in half (homicides dropped by two thirds), and those declines continued for years thereafter. The new policing techniques were copied in many other cities, and the safety and savor of urban life in America was dramatically changed for the better.

Further reading

• Manhattan Institute work on "broken windows" policing, manhattan-institute.org/html/critical_acclaim-fixing_broken.htm

---

1997

Nudging Congress By Funding School Choice in D.C.

Investor Theodore Forstmann and Walmart heir John Walton were disappointed by waffling in Congress in the mid-1990s over a school-choice pilot program. There were proposals, enthusiastically backed by local residents, to help Washington, D.C., families trapped in miserable public schools place their children in private or parochial alternatives, but they were going nowhere. The Congressional indecision "was a joke," Forstmann concluded. "So we said, 'Okay, we'll do it. Let's get this program going and see if it works.'"

Forstmann and Walton joined forces in 1997 to donate $6 million to the Washington Scholarship Fund. The fund was a roaring success, with low-income families in the nation's capital lining up several deep for every available scholarship. (This inspired Walton and Forstmann to collaborate in 1998 on a national version of their project: the Children's Scholarship Fund, which they launched with contributions of $50 million each. For more information on this and other private philanthropy advancing school choice, charter schooling, and other innovations in school reform, see The Philanthropy Roundtable's companion list of Achievements in Education giving, and school-reform guidebooks.)

Because all of this happened right in Congress's backyard, the philanthropic effort influenced politics and national opinion. In 2004, legislation finally passed creating the D.C. Opportunity Scholarship Program, the first federally funded school voucher program in the U.S. As of 2015 it provides scholarships of $8,000-$12,000 to low-income families so they can send their children to private or religious schools of their choice, benefiting more than 5,000 children.

Further reading

• *Philanthropy* magazine article, philanthropyroundtable.org/topic/excellence_in_philanthropy/education_reform_goes_private

• 2012 *New York Times* reporting upon renewal of federal program, thecaucus.blogs.nytimes.com/2012/06/18/much-debated-scholarship-program-for-d-c-students-is-renewed

1998

Moving On to Internet Politics

Unhappy at the prospect of Bill Clinton's impeachment, software entrepreneurs Joan Blades and Wes Boyd set up an online petition that soon grew into a major force for mobilizing liberal donors and voters via the Internet. The MoveOn.org website became a hub for communication and fundraising for left-wing causes, including environmental controls, liberal social issues, and opposition to the war on terror. The group has used a 501(c)(4) advocacy arm, a Political Action Committee, a 527 political fund, hundreds of Internet petitions, and other mechanisms to influence policies and politics with its donations. The group's growth was accelerated by multimillion-dollar gifts during the 2004 election cycle from Linda Pritzker, George Soros, Peter Lewis, and other large patrons. It also accumulated many small donors and volunteer activists and claimed 8 million participants as of 2014. In its first decade-and-a-half of existence, MoveOn raised and spent close to $100 million to promote favored policies.

Further reading

• MoveOn website, front.moveon.org/about/#.VH3z_our9UQ

1999

A Donor-advised Fund for Conservative Policy Reform

Twenty-three years after the Tides Foundation invented the funding collective for public-policy causes (see 1976 entry), liberty-minded donors created a counterpart organization. Called DonorsTrust, it helps philanthropists create donor-advised funds that encourage "limited government, personal responsibility, and free enterprise." The entity was founded in 1999, just as donor-advised funds were taking off as funding mechanisms for all sorts of charitable purposes.

Since opening its doors in northern Virginia, DonorsTrust has made over $600 million in grants recommended by its donors. Philanthropists attracted to DonorsTrust run the full spectrum of the Right, from libertarians to conservative traditionalists. The beneficiaries of their grants range widely—economic-research organizations, religious groups, hawkish foreign-policy advocates, outfits working to reduce imprisonment rates, you name it. Grants also go to hospitals, schools, camps, and other causes not related to public policy.

Like the Tides Foundation, notes co-founder Kim Dennis, DonorsTrust was inspired by the creativity of its donors to eventually expand beyond just administering donor-advised funds. The group can now also help incubate new charities and projects. And as with Tides, part of the power of DonorsTrust is that it helps philanthropists magnify the effect of their donations by bundling them together with funds from other like-minded contributors.

To make sure that donations go to the purposes philanthropists actually intend (rather than causes favored by administrators acting after the donor is out of the picture—a problem at many foundations), DonorsTrust recommends that accounts should "sunset" (be fully spent) while givers are still around to help set priorities. As a "fail-safe" to pre-serve donor intent, the organization allows no perpetual trusts. "Only the original donor can name successor advisers, and accounts should be closed 20 years after a donor's death," explains president Whitney Ball.

Further reading

- About DonorsTrust, donorstrust.org/AboutUs/MissionPrinciples.aspx
- *National Review* essay on DonorsTrust and Tides Foundation, nationalreview.com/article/388705/dark-money-bill-zeiser

2000

Open Society Opens Door to Gay Marriage

Among many other public-policy causes, the Open Society Foundations funded by financial speculator George Soros have been leading donors to gay rights. Their Lesbian, Gay, Bisexual, Transgender, and Intersex program gives $5-10 million per year to upwards of 70 advocacy groups. Their most consequential grants in this area may have come between the years of 2000 and 2005, when they invested millions in political and legal efforts to promote gay marriage. They were among the first significant funders of two of the groups that led this campaign: Freedom to Marry, and the Civil Marriage Collaborative. In 2004, Massachusetts became the first state to establish gay marriage, and from then on activist funders piled onto the cause. Open Society, however, was a pioneer.

Further reading

- *Inside Philanthropy* scorecard, insidephilanthropy.com/home/2014/10/7/the-marriage-equality-hall-of-fame-8-funders-who-helped-make.html

2003

Remaking the Think Tank Into Political War Room

As they prepared for the 2004 presidential election and beyond, a small group of liberal donors led by bankers Herb and Marion Sandler

concluded that the Left needed a new kind of think tank that would combine public-policy research with political activism. Joined by real-estate
magnate Steve Bing, insurance mogul Peter Lewis, and investor George
Soros, they bankrolled the Center for American Progress, to be directed
by Clinton-administration operative John Podesta. They were motivated
by a sense among many liberals that Republicans benefitted from an
infrastructure of conservative think tanks, and that Democrats enjoyed
nothing similar. The Brookings Institution, numerous academic centers
at universities, and many liberal advocacy organizations existed, but these
funders did not consider them as effective as groups like the Heritage
Foundation, the Cato Institute, and the American Enterprise Institute. A
series of reports from the left-wing National Committee for Responsive
Philanthropy on how the right-leaning think tanks had been built by
donors was also influential in sparking wealthy liberals to act.

Podesta's idea was to create a nonprofit organization that would
have a traditional think-tank arm (a research group eligible for
tax-deductible donations), as well as a legislative advocacy arm (not
eligible for tax-deductible donations). This combination of 501(c)(3)
and 501(c)(4) was an innovation for large-scale research institutions.
"With the Center for American Progress, Podesta was trying to create something new," wrote journalist Byron York, "a think tank that
doubled as a campaign war room." Podesta himself described CAP as
"a think tank on steroids."

The donors did not achieve their immediate objective of electing a
Democrat to the Presidency in 2004, but CAP became an aggressive part
of the left-wing political machine. Its "communications" department
became its largest office, and dispatching the organization's employees
for "rapid response" media attacks on conservative arguments or proponents became the central function of the group. Its influence on the
political discourse aided Democratic triumphs in the 2006 congressional
elections, and Barack Obama's victories in 2008 and 2012.

By 2014, the group's budget was more than $45 million. Copying
Podesta's model, the Heritage Foundation launched its own 501(c)(4)
group seven years after the launch of CAP.

Further reading

• Byron York, *The Vast Left Wing Conspiracy,* (Crown Forum, 2005)

• *New York Times* analysis, nytimes.com/2008/11/07/us/politics/07podesta.html

• "Devaluing the Think Tank," *National Affairs,* nationalaffairs.com/publications/detail/
devaluing-the-think-tank

2004
Skoll Pioneers "Filmanthropy"

Movies with a political message are hardly a new phenomenon, but never before has a donor made social change via film the focus of his philanthropy. In 2004, eBay co-founder Jeffrey Skoll founded Participant Media, into which he poured "hundreds of millions of dollars...with much more to follow," understanding that "everything I put into Participant, I don't expect to get back." The company began to produce films with a strong liberal-activist tilt, paired with accompanying media campaigns aimed at translating public sentiment stirred up by the films into legislation or other political action.

By the end of 2014 Skoll's venture had produced more than 60 films, convinced stars like Matt Damon, Gwyneth Paltrow, Tom Hanks, Julia Roberts, Benedict Cumberbatch, and George Clooney to take roles for far less than their normal fees, and charmed Hollywood into more than 30 Oscar nominations. The movies included titles like *An Inconvenient Truth* (which won Al Gore his Nobel Peace Prize for climate-change alarmism), *Good Night, and Good Luck* (skewering McCarthyism), *Syriana* (big oil threatens the world), *Charlie Wilson's War* (right-wing Americans planted the seeds of al-Qaeda), *The Help* (on mistreatment of African-American domestic workers), and many others. Corporate abuses, violence against women, gay rights, and environmental and union causes are other favorite topics of the studio. One of the studio's early films, *Waiting for Superman*, drew acclaim from school reformers on all parts of the political spectrum.

Each Participant movie is launched with a companion "social action campaign"(coordinated by a separate division) that prompts consumers to take some political or economic action, promotes the film for use in school, holds special screenings for legislators and journalists, and so forth. Participant has even teamed up with the Gates and Knight foundations to fund work at University of Southern California's Annenberg School for Communication and Journalism that aims to create reliable measures of whether, and how, entertainment can spur citizens to become social activists.

Though none have made a commitment to "filmanthropy" on the scale of Jeff Skoll, other philanthropists have funded movie-making in an attempt to influence cultural and political trends. These have included AOL founder Ted Leonsis, backer of a website for short documentaries known as SnagFilms, and businessman Philip Anschutz, who financed major movies like the Narnia series, and others based on classic children's books, in order to encourage popular entertainment that is more friendly to families raising youngsters.

Further reading

• *Philanthropy* magazine article, philanthropyroundtable.org/topic/excellence_in_ philanthropy/changing_the_world_through_storytelling

2005

Democracy Alliance

Rob Stein had worked for the Democratic National Committee, the Clinton-Gore campaign and administration, and a private-equity firm. Then he set out on a new task: to convince wealthy liberal donors to pay for political infrastructure that would beat conservatives in policy and electoral contests. He put together a PowerPoint cautionary, travelled the country, and in 2005 kicked off a new group: the Democracy Alliance.

The philanthropic and political giving club invites to its closed-door meetings individuals who have donated at least $200,000 to one of its favored activist organizations. It has about 100 members, who have included major donors like George Soros, Tim Gill, Chris Hughes, Patricia Stryker, and Tom Steyer, plus the leaders of unions that command large political funds like NEA, the American Federation of Teachers, and the Service Employees International Union. The alliance doesn't collect money itself but rather encourages and coordinates donations to political groups it selects and endorses—21 "core" groups plus 180 other organizations designated to fill a role on its "Progressive Infrastructure Map." These include operations like the Center for American Progress, Media Matters, the Center on Budget and Policy Priorities, and a variety of electioneering groups (America Votes, Catalist, Emily's List, Organizing for Action, etc.).

Beneficiaries of Democracy Alliance funding include a wide mix of groups: There are 501(c)(3) nonprofits that must mostly steer clear of lobbying and politics (for which donations are tax deductible and public). Also 501(c)(4) social-welfare groups who can lobby and advocate for public policies, and get in involved in modest amounts of electioneering. (Donations to them are not deductible, but are anonymous.) And 527 Political Action Committees and Super PACs, both of which give directly to political candidates (with donations being publicly disclosed and non-tax-deductible).

Donations earmarked through the Democracy Alliance total about $70 million per year. Including funds raised from other sources, just the

21 core groups in the Democracy Alliance portfolio set in motion $374 million of spending to boost liberal policy causes and political candidates in the 2014 midterm election, according to *Politico*. In private meetings held after the 2014 conservative wave, the alliance formulated a giving plan with four goals: Increase funding for liberal groups. Motivate progressives. Persuade independents. Divide the right and reduce its funding.

Further reading

• *New York Times* reporting, nytimes.com/2014/11/14/us/politics/shaking-off-midterm-drubbing-liberal-donors-look-6-years-ahead.html?_r=0

2006

Stryker Roils Michigan Politics

Jon Stryker, the billionaire heir to the Stryker medical-instruments fortune, set up the Arcus Foundation in 2000. It almost immediately became a national force for lawmaking and electioneering on behalf of gay rights, thanks to $78 million of targeted donations to gay groups in just its first ten years.

Stryker also used his giving to change the political calculus in his home state of Michigan. At the same time he and his sister, Pat, were using their inherited billions to help flip Colorado into the political blue column (see 2008 entry), he was carrying out a similar game plan on the Great Lakes. He employed philanthropic donations plus $5 million of PAC spending to help flip the Michigan state House from Republican to Democrat control, and to help Jennifer Granholm defeat Dick DeVos in the governor's race.

Further reading

• *Inside Philanthropy* scorecard, insidephilanthropy.com/home/2014/10/7/the-marriage-equality-hall-of-fame-8-funders-who-helped-make.html

2006

Intelligence Squared Debates

Robert Rosenkranz made a fortune in insurance and investing, and when he began to give money away his first interest was in efforts to improve public policy and governance. He supported the Federalist Society and Manhattan Institute. He funded Rosenkranz Hall to house Yale University's political science department and international relations program.

But Rosenkranz mourned the disappearance of respectful, meaty, intelligent public debate, seemingly squeezed out by the rise of personal, partisan, and emotional political wrangling on Internet and media outlets. Then during a trip to London in 2005 he took in a high-quality Oxford-style debate organized by a new group called Intelligence Squared. His efforts to find partners who could arrange similarly informative and entertaining debates with his funding were disappointed, so Rosenkranz decided to use his foundation to stage them himself.

He purchased the rights for an American version of Intelligence Squared, hired a former *Nightline* producer to orchestrate, and debuted the first debates before live New York City audiences in 2006. Rosenkranz immersed himself in the process—choosing many of the topics, suggesting sparring partners on opposite sides of important public questions, and delivering opening remarks that framed the issues being argued over.

The Intelligence Squared debates quickly became popular, both as live events and as media and Internet phenomena—most of them are aired over NPR, streamed and posted as videos on the Web, and offered as podcasts. Not only the audience but also website visitors are given a chance to vote their own position on the debate topic, both before it takes place and right after. The statistical change in opinion as a result of the back-and-forth on stage is used to judge who won the argument.

As of 2014 there had been about 100 jousts, on hot topics in public policy like "Too many kids go to college," "A booming China spells trouble for America," "Global warming is not a crisis," and "FDA caution is hazardous to our health." Many constructive and enjoyable discussions, along with several awards for best public-affairs programming, have resulted from the mix of top-flight thinkers and lively controversialists arguing within a fair and scrupulously structured discussion format. Rosenkranz remains a central funder of the effort, but other philanthropists like Paul Singer and Gerry Ohrstrom, plus foundations like Rupe, Sackler, and Bradley, have also provided grants to keep the smart arguments flowing.

Further reading

- *Philanthropy* magazine article, philanthropyroundtable.org/topic/excellence_in_ philanthropy/resolved
- Origins of Intelligence Squared, philanthropyroundtable.org/topic/excellence_in_ philanthropy/intelligence_squared

2006

Nudging States Left

A year after a group of liberal donors set up the Democracy Alliance, the same forces joined together to establish the Committee on States in 2006. Just as the Democracy Alliance (see 2005 entry) is a conduit for steering donor money to approved left-wing national political organizations, the Committee on States is a conduit for steering money to left-wing political organizations working on the state level. In every state where it operates, the group recruits major donors and recommends places to send money. The funds pay for political data and analysis, grassroots organizing, opposition research, fundraising, and messaging. The goal is to elect officeholders who will enact liberal policies and be in position to influence the redrawing of election districts in the states after the 2020 census.

The committee is a nonprofit 501(c)(4) advocacy organization. Under IRS rules, such groups can advocate for public policies without limitation, can urge particular votes on issues, and can depict candidates in positive or negative ways, but must not make active electioneering their primary purpose. Donations to a (c)(4) are not tax-deductible, but the Committee on States has set up a parallel 501(c)(3) whose more research-related work does allow supporters to deduct their giving.

During the 2014 election cycle the committee coordinated about $50 million of donations made in 20 different states—including $9 million of spending in Wisconsin, $7 million each in North Carolina and Minnesota, and $6 million each in Colorado and Florida. The group hopes to create donor networks in seven more states for the next election. The intent is to establish durable political machines in each place, and the Committee on States aims to increase spending to $100 million per year by 2020.

Liberal philanthropists are funding not only this electoral organizing but also efforts to link liberal officeholders in affinity groups, and supply them with ideas and legislative ammunition. The Public Leadership Institute has established a Progressive Leaders Network that connects 13,000 left-leaning city, county, and state officials. A new group called the State Innovation Exchange was kicked off in 2014 by the donors of the Democracy Alliance. That organization plans to raise $10 million a year in donations "to boost progressive state lawmakers and their causes—partly by drafting model legislation...while also using bare-knuckle tactics like opposition research and video tracking to derail Republicans and their initiatives," according to *Politico*.

Further reading

- *Mother Jones* reporting, motherjones.com/politics/2014/11/committee-on-states-democracy-alliance-redistricting-2020

- Public Leadership Institute scorecards of legislative results, publicleadershipinstitute. org/tracking
- *Politico* reporting, politico.com/story/2014/11/democrats-create-an-alec-killer-112733.html

2007

ED in '08

A year and a half before the 2008 Presidential election, the foundations of Bill Gates and Eli Broad—which together had already given more than $2 billion to various education-reform causes—announced a $60 million effort to make education a central issue in the political debate. Under the tagline "ED in '08," their campaign launched elaborate communications efforts, celebrity endorsements, fancy campaign paraphernalia, petitions, swing-state advertising, other media efforts, and meetings with candidates and staff.

Despite being what the *New York Times* described as "one of the most expensive single-issue initiatives ever in a Presidential race," this effort produced no significant increase in the political salience of educational issues. Both parties adopted their usual platform planks on schools, and over the course of the Presidential debates 20 education-related questions were posed to the candidates—not significantly different from previous election cycles. By the time they had spent $25 million, the Gates and Broad Foundations announced that no further money would be put into the initiative.

Reflecting on the aborted project shortly after the election, Bill Gates observed that "most of what we were causing people to do was mouth platitudes." Fuzzy, generalized efforts to influence policy while dancing around controversial details may not be worth the effort, many observers and donors concluded.

Further reading

- *New York Times* story on campaign's launch, nytimes.com/2007/04/25/education/ 25schools.html?_r=0
- Bill Gates reflects on ED in '08 in *Education Week*, blogs.edweek.org/edweek/ campaign-k-12/2008/11/bill_gates_on_ed_in_08_mouthin.html

2007

Designed to Win Climate-policy Fights

"Left unattended, human-induced climate change could overshadow all our other efforts to cure diseases, reduce poverty, prevent warfare and preserve biodiversity. Global, collective action is paramount.... How can philanthropists turn the tide against global warming?"

Those were some of the opening sentences of a 2007 report that the Hewlett, Packard, Doris Duke, Energy, Oak, and Joyce foundations commissioned in hopes of finding ways to "*win* in the battle against climate change." These donors had long been activists on the global-warming issue, and the study they paid for, called *Design to Win*, laid out a strategy for blocking coal-fired power plants and other producers of carbon dioxide in the short term, then creating new policies in the longer term to drastically reduce energy use and greenhouse gas emissions. The report called on climate-concerned philanthropists to increase their giving in this area from the existing $177 million per year to $525 million to $660 million per year.

The very next year, an activist organization called ClimateWorks emerged out of this. The Hewlett Foundation pledged $100 million annually over five years to get it launched, and the Packard Foundation has kicked in $40 million to $60 million per year of crucial support. The Packard and Hewlett foundations are the two largest philanthropic funders of global-warming activism in the world, having between them granted more than a billion dollars over the most recent decade just to their two favorite recipients— ClimateWorks and the Energy Foundation.

These two mega-donors were joined in setting up ClimateWorks by the McKnight, Ford, Rockefeller, Kresge, Moore, and other foundations. The organization channels their donated money to affiliated organizations, and presses for strong new government policies and environmental controls. According to the latest-available IRS filings, ClimateWorks collected $170 million from donors in 2012. The group's official goal is to slash emissions of carbon dioxide and other greenhouse gases by 50 percent by the year 2030.

Further reading
• *Design to Win* report on climate-change philanthropy, climateworks.org/imo/media/doc/design_to_win_final_8_31_07.pdf

---

2008

Cause-oriented Journalism

Take one scoop of donors looking for new ways to affect public opinion and government policy, mix with three scoops of mainstream journalism bleeding red ink in the face of new Internet-based competition, and you get a layer-cake of donor-funded reporting operations. The granddaddy of these creations is ProPublica, founded by hyperactive liberal donors Herb and Marion Sandler to be a twenty-first-century muckraker, with a special focus on topics like gun control, civil rights, health care, fracking, campaign finance limits, labor laws, the Gulf oil spill, Guantanamo, and other policy hot buttons. With more than $35 million of checks written by the Sandlers, ProPublica quickly hired a deep stable of reporters and editors and started churning out heavily researched exposés. The organization posts articles on its own website and lets newspapers run them for free. The operation quickly became a favorite of the journalistic establishment, and was awarded the first Pulitzer Prize for investigative reporting given to an online publication. It now receives support from large foundations like Ford, MacArthur, Annie E. Casey, and Hewlett.

Many local variants of ProPublica, and a few national ones, followed with their own angel funders. These range from the Texas Tribune, funded by Democratic Party donors in that state, to the MinnPost, launched by four public-minded families in Minneapolis, to the Honolulu Civil Beat financed by eBay founder Pierre Omidyar. Watchdog.org, a project of the Franklin Center, was established as a miniature version of ProPublica digging from the right in 29 states as of 2015, and the American Media Institute is struggling to launch itself as another investigative reporting operation positioned on the right side of the political spectrum.

All of these are digital-only publications to contain costs, and they all depend on philanthropic support—primarily annual operating grants, supplemented by small donations from readers. All have demonstrated some ability to influence local or national debates on policy and politics.

Further reading

• *Philanthropy* magazine article, philanthropyroundtable.org/topic/excellence_in_philanthropy/investigative_philanthropy

——— **2008** ———

Advocating for Generational Fairness in Fiscal Policy

Pete Peterson became a billionaire as co-founder of the Blackstone investment firm, but he was the son of poor Greek immigrants and never lost his distaste for profligacy and waste. He watched horrified as the federal budget went from a slight surplus in 1960 to a deficit of 2.6 percent of GDP at the end of the 1970s, and 4.1 percent of GDP (that's $680 billion) as of 2013. Since 2008 Peterson has put more than a billion dollars of his own money into educating policymakers and the public on the dangers of that kind of fiscal imbalance. He warns that "on our current course, our children will not do as well as we have. For years, I have been saying that the American government, and America itself, has to change its spending and borrowing policies."

The Peterson Foundation sponsors conferences, reports, debates, films, and television ads on the dangers of massive federal debt. In 2010 it launched a series of annual fiscal summits for national political leaders. The 2014 version included Bill Clinton, Chris Christie, Nancy Pelosi, Alan Greenspan, and others. In 2011, the foundation funded six think tanks, positioned on both the left and the right, to create plans that would eliminate federal deficits. These were then promoted to lawmakers.

This is somewhat unusual territory for philanthropy, but recently one other donor has become active on the same topic. Hedge-fund founder Stanley Druckenmiller began speaking actively to college students in 2013, warning that out-of-control entitlement spending threatened to degrade the standard of living of their generation.

Further reading

• *Philanthropy* magazine article, philanthropyroundtable.org/topic/economic_opportunity/economia

---

2008

Painting Colorado Bluer

In 2004, Colorado was a solidly Republican state: the governor, both U.S. Senators, and five of seven House members belonged to the GOP, and President George W. Bush won the state's nine electoral votes. By the end of the 2008 elections, everything had reversed: the governor, both U.S. Senators, and five of seven House members were Democrats, and Barack Obama carried the state. National political trends explained some of this transformation. The rest was the work of four liberal philanthropists who set out to remake Colorado through a mix of public-policy giving and campaign donations—software entrepreneur Tim Gill, venture capitalist Rutt Bridges, Internet businessman Jared Polis, and heiress Pat Stryker.

In 1999, Bridges founded the Bighorn Center for Public Policy, a think tank that swiftly altered state campaign-finance rules. The liberal Bell Policy Center was established immediately after. Then came a Colorado version of the national MoveOn.org pressure group, called ProgressNowAction.org. Colorado Media Matters was created in 2006 to influence state reporters and editorial writers. A litigation group, Colorado Ethics Watch, was set up the same year, along with an online newspaper called the Colorado Independent and several blogs like ColoradoPols.com and SquareState.net, all oriented to promoting progressive policies and investigating and criticizing opponents. A new academy to train liberal activists, the Center for Progressive Leadership Colorado, was also funded.

The *Denver Post* characterized the mechanics of the nonprofits set up by the "Four Millionaires" and their allies this way:

> A liberal group with a nonpartisan name like Colorado First puts out a list of polluters and demands official action. A Republican running for Colorado office is on the list. Paid liberal bloggers chatter. An online liberal publication with a newspaper-like name writes an article about the candidate and his company polluting Colorado's streams. A liberal advocacy group puts out a news release, citing the group and the pollution, which sound reputable to an ordinary voter. They mass e-mail the release and attach a catchy phrase to it like "Dirty Doug." At some point, the mainstream media checks out the allegations.

In the 2004, 2006, and 2008 elections, the Four Millionaires spent more than $20 million trying to tip Colorado from Republican to Democrat via a mix of political attack ads during election season and long-term funding for what political analyst Fred Barnes described as "a vast infrastructure of liberal organizations that produces an anti-Republican, anti-conservative echo chamber in politics and the media." They were wildly successful: After the 2008 election, Democrats controlled not only both of Colorado's U.S. Senate seats, five out of seven House seats, and the governor's mansion, but also both chambers of the state legislature. In 2012, according to the *Denver Post*, liberal Super PAC contributions exceeded conservative ones at a rate of 150:1.

Observing this triumph—which became known as the Colorado Model—other donors launched or intensified similar efforts in other "purple" swing states. The Coors Foundation also worked to help Colorado conservatives learn from the progressives' success, and in the deep-red 2014 election, Republicans finally reclaimed one of the two U.S. Senate seats in Colorado. But the other Senate seat and three of the seven House seats remained with Democrats. The incumbent Democrat governor won a tight re-election. Republicans narrowly took control of the state Senate, and they narrowed Democrat control of the state

Assembly from 37-28 to 34-31. Colorado was purple again. But the Gill/Bridges/Polis/Stryker nonprofit infrastructure remains in place.

Further reading

- Rob Witwer and Adam Schrager, *The Blueprint: How Democrats Won Colorado* (Speaker's Corner, 2010)
- *Denver Post* analysis, denverpost.com/ci_20148556/spending-by-super-pacs-colorado-is-dominion-democrats
- Fred Barnes analysis, weeklystandard.com/Content/Public/Artcles/000/000/015/316nfdzw.asp

---

2009

Refocusing Governance in Wisconsin

Back in 1987 the Milwaukee-based Lynde and Harry Bradley Foundation provided a $2.8 million startup grant to launch the Wisconsin Policy Research Institute, a think tank focused on the economic and social health of its home state. The institute published a steady stream of research reports on education problems, the business environment, state pension imbalances, and other concerns.

Then in 2009 and 2010, WPRI rang alarms over runaway government-employee costs and a state budget deficit heading past $3.6 billion. At that time, Democrats controlled both houses of the state legislature as well as the governorship. The 2010 election, though, swept in a Republican governor and flipped control of both the Assembly and State Senate.

Anticipating this power shift, the Bradley Foundation had given the Wisconsin Policy Research Institute a million-dollar grant in 2009 (on top of its normal $400,000 in annual support) to produce a special policy document entitled *Refocus Wisconsin*. "We saw how much the Reagan administration relied on the Heritage Foundation and how much Mayor Rudy Giuliani relied on the Manhattan Institute in New York City," said Bradley president Michael Grebe. "We wanted to support a project that provided a similar level of policy assistance to our own governor and lawmakers." The 154-page publication offered information and policy recommendations on budgeting, taxes, public pensions, and education. The Wisconsin Institute for Law and Liberty and the MacIver Institute, also Bradley grant recipients, offered additional ideas for improving governance in their home state.

When Governor Scott Walker and the new legislative class took office in 2011, they enacted a Budget Repair Bill that dramatically reformed state government—requiring public employees to contribute to their pensions for the first time, trimming the power of public-employee unions (whose membership dropped by half after state and local employees including public-school teachers were allowed to opt out), establishing controls on medical costs, and so forth. After protests, work refusals, legislators going fugitive, and a recall vote on the governor (which he won with a larger percentage of the vote than in his initial election), the reforms stuck, and immediately became an influence on other states.

In his capacity as a private citizen, not a foundation CEO, Bradley president Grebe chaired Governor Walker's re-election campaign in 2014. Walker was returned to office, and the GOP majorities in both state houses were enlarged.

Further reading

• *Refocus Wisconsin* report, wpri.org/WPRI-Files/Special-Reports/Reports-Documents/ WPRI_Refocus_Digest_FNL_090710.pdf

—————————————— 2010 ——————————————
Painting North Carolina Redder

While working for the governor of North Carolina in the 1980s, Art Pope became frustrated by a lack of organizations able to supply well-developed ideas for conservative political reform. After leaving government, he decided to do something about it. Over the next three decades he used his family foundation to donate more than $60 million (earned through the family's privately owned chain of discount stores) to build a robust network of think tanks and advocacy groups in North Carolina. In the process, he turned North Carolina into a swing state where conservative ideas and policymakers are able to match liberal ideas and politicians.

First, Pope created the John Locke Foundation in 1990. The Raleigh center has become one of the most influential state-based free-market think tanks in the country. Legislators now routinely look to the group for alternative state budgets and suggestions on changing taxes. In 2007, its work helped voters around the state defeat a series of county-level tax-hike initiatives. In 2010, former Democratic governor Mike Easley was convicted on federal corruption charges, in part due to the investigative work of the *Carolina Journal*, published by JLF.

With an annual budget of about $3.5 million, the think tank now has a variety of donors, but the John William Pope Foundation (named for Art's father) has remained its major underwriter. Art Pope has also funded the Civitas Institute (which promotes grassroots activism), the North Carolina Institute for Constitutional Law (which litigates), and the Pope Center for Higher Education Policy (which monitors colleges and universities in the state). Left-of-center policy groups still outnumber right-of-center groups by two or three to one in North Carolina, but Pope has created a real competition of ideas in the state.

This new public-policy infrastructure gradually helped change the climate for political reform in North Carolina. In the 2010 elections, voters flipped both the state Senate and House from Democrat to Republican control—the first time since 1870 that a Republican majority had existed in both chambers. In the 2012 elections, voters also picked a Republican governor for the first time in 20 years, and elected three new Republicans to Congress, shifting their state's representation in the U.S. House from 7-6 D to 9-4 R.

Art Pope took a leave from the foundation to become the new governor's budget director, and the state government enacted a burst of dramatic reforms over the next two years—flattening and cutting taxes, reducing the growth rate of the state budget, reforming education. In the 2014 elections, this new political alignment was largely ratified by North Carolina voters, and the Democrat U.S. senator was defeated by a Republican.

Further reading
- *Washington Post* 2014 article, washingtonpost.com/politics/in-nc-conservative-donor-art-pope-sits-at-heart-of-government-he-helped-transform/2014/07/19/eece18ec-0d22-11e4-b8e5-d0de80767fc2_story.html
- Profile of Art Pope in Chapter 9

2010

$27 Million to Pass Obamacare

In the summer of 2008, the three largest unions of government employees and a collection of left-wing organizations including ACORN, MoveOn.org, the Center for American Progress, Alliance for a Just Society, and USAction announced the creation of Health Care for America Now—a political pressure group with a single goal: to pass the Affordable Care Act, popularly known as Obamacare. The group had a $40 million budget, primarily to be used for political ads and organizing. At their launch event that July they unveiled their initial $1.5 million ad purchase. "We began the campaign by attacking the insurance industry as the chief villain in the story," the group summarized in its online history. "This message mobilized the progressive base and moved people in the 'middle'."

It was Atlantic Philanthropies, the foundation created by Duty Free Shoppers Group co-founder Chuck Feeney, that made all of this activity possible. Atlantic launched the Health Care for America Now coalition with a 2007 grant, and put a total of $26.5 million into the cause over a two-year period. This direct intervention in political lobbying was made easier by the fact that Atlantic is headquartered in Bermuda, freeing it from the federal prohibition on lobbying by U.S. foundations.

In the end, the Affordable Care Act passed without a single vote to spare in the U.S. Senate. Absent the investment by Atlantic Philanthropies, noted the *Huffington Post* and other observers, it is unlikely the legislation would have taken effect. And the Atlantic-financed campaign didn't end with passage of the legislation.

"Once the bill became law," explains HCAN's online history, the group "fought back hard against the ACA-attacks in a myriad of ways. Working with unions like AFSCME and SEIU and our field partners, HCAN broadened its 'which side are you on' organizing around Obamacare to protecting Medicare and Medicaid and calling for wealthy Americans and big corporations to pay their fair share in taxes." Once it exhausted its funds, HCAN finally closed down as an organization.

Further reading

• HCAN history, healthcareforamericanow.org/about-us/mission-history

• Profile of Atlantic Philanthropies then-director Gara LaMarche in Chapter 3

2010

Exposing Top Students to the Classics

Retired investor Roger Hertog has made it a centerpiece of his philanthropy to create first-rate intellectual seminars that can inspire top students interested in politics (who are likely to be involved in setting national policies in the future). His Hertog Foundation describes itself as "an educational philanthropy whose mission is to bring the very best ideas in defense of Western civilization to a new generation of intellectual and political leaders." It operates a half-dozen different seminars toward this end.

The Hertog Political Studies Program brings college students to Washington for six weeks of classes on political theory and practice. The foundation's Economic Policy Studies Program is a two-week immersion in the politics and finances of the welfare state. The War Studies Program is a similar session on military and foreign policy. Various Advanced Institutes tutor students and young professionals in specialized areas like Lincoln's political thought or the lessons of the Iraq war. An American History Scholars program is designed for high-school students.

Each of these programs is taught by prominent scholars hired by the foundation. The Hertog Foundation also supports special seminars at Macaulay College and Columbia University to inspire talented students to become engaged citizens acquainted with the best of classic political thinking. The ultimate effects of this work will be felt as graduates of Hertog classes enter positions of influence in government, academe, and other fields.

Further reading

• Syllabus for 2014 Hertog Political Studies Program, hertogfoundation.org/wp-content/uploads/2014/11/PSP_2014_Syllabus.pdf

2010

Fracking Gets Drilled

Drilling horizontally into shale and then cracking it by pumping in water under high pressure—a process known as "fracking"—has had stunning effects on U.S. oil and gas production, turning the U.S. into the world's leading producer of natural gas, and cutting our oil imports sufficiently to crash the world price of oil. The contributions of fracking include more than a million jobs, over $110 billion of GDP, and a reduction in pollution and carbon emissions (due to substitution of gas for coal in electricity production) that has actually pushed U.S. emissions well below our level of the previous ten years, despite population and economic growth.

Even with these dramatic benefits, fracking became a controversial process in recent years, and much of that is due to the effort of a foundation in upstate New York that supports left-wing media, activist, and environmental groups. In 2010 the Park Foundation approached a Cornell University marine ecologist about writing an academic article making the case that shale gas is a dangerous, polluting product. They gave him a $35,000 grant, and when his paper came out a year later scientists from across the ideological spectrum with geology and energy expertise were sharply critical. But a *New York Times* reporter leapt on the article and turned its negative view of natural gas into a cause célèbre, spawning hundreds of spinoff stories.

This was just one of hundreds of interventions in the fracking debate by Park over the last few years. The foundation also offered scores of small grants to activist groups and publications to support anti-fracking articles, conferences, rallies, and legislative campaigns. The *Gasland* films attacking fracking were also funded by Park. By carefully targeting about $3 million per year to a mix of sympathetic academics, ideological publications, and pressure groups, this one medium-sized foundation was able to make a large impression on public policy.

Indeed, this effort was sufficient to get fracking banned in Park's methane-rich home state of New York, and to stimulate similar bans or moratoriums in Maryland, Vermont, a number of U.S. cities and towns, and even locations abroad where the energetic advocacy campaign against shale gas and oil managed to alarm public opinion.

Further reading

• *Philanthropy* magazine article, philanthropyroundtable.org/topic/excellence_in_philanthropy/gas_heat

2010
A New Top Dog in Public-policy Funding

Hedge funder Thomas Steyer made lots of money developing new coal mines in Asia. More recently, he decided fossil fuels are evil, and developed a taste for policy fights on this subject. In 2010, Steyer personally launched and funded a $25 million campaign to defeat a voter proposition in California that would have suspended the state's global warming law (which requires a statewide reduction of greenhouse gases to 1990 levels) until the state unemployment rate fell below 5.5 percent (it was then above 12 percent). The year before, Steyer had given $40 million to Stanford to bankroll a climate and energy center, and the year after he pledged $25 million to Yale for a similar environmental center.

By the time the next election rolled around in 2012, Steyer had funded a California voter proposition of his own. This one would raise about a billion dollars of taxes and steer much of the money into "clean energy" spending. Steyer poured tens of milions of dollars into getting the referendum passed. Next, he started funding and appearing in a series of 90-second ads attacking the Keystone XL pipeline; they were instrumental in stalling that project. The philanthropist has recently been a strong supporter of the Energy Foundation (see 1991 entry).

In 2013, Steyer stepped out as America's No. 1 public-policy and politics donor on the Left. He spent $11 million to help elect Terry McAuliffe as governor of Virginia, millions more on the Democrat primaries in Massachusetts, and then invited a couple dozen other top liberal donors to one of his vacation homes to announce his creation of NextGen Climate—his own politics and policy organization focused on global warming activism. He donated $50 million to the group and asked others for matches so they could inject $100 million into the 2014 elections to seat candidates favoring global-warming controls. In the end, Steyer poured more than $73 million into various 2014 political races.

Steyer has become the largest funder not only of climate causes, but also of the Democratic Party and of the left-wing Democracy Alliance (see 2005 entry). According to the Center for Public Integrity, he gave more than any other political donor in the U.S. in 2014. After the election, his chief strategist told the *New York Times* that "Steyer's spending was a down payment on a multiyear strategy aimed at ensuring that climate change stays at the center of the political debate."

Further reading

• *Chronicle of Philanthropy* summary, philanthropy.com/article/How-Thomas-Steyer-Uses-Charity/146595

2011

Koch Programs for Students

The Charles Koch Institute was founded in 2011 by the billionaire industrialist to run educational programs that give students and professionals a deeper understanding of markets and politics. Its main work in influencing future generations is done through four programs.

The yearlong Koch Associate Program places young people in full-time jobs at public-policy organizations in the Washington, D.C., area while providing a full day each week of classroom training. The Koch Internship Program is a similar venture that works with college students for just one semester. The Koch Fellows Program is much the same but places students in organizations across the country. And the Institute's Liberty@Work effort offers Web-based professional training based on a similar economics-and-politics curriculum. More than 2,000 alumni of these programs had graduated into permanent careers as of 2014, and hundreds of additional individuals are trained every year.

Further reading

• Charles Koch Institute, charleskochinstitute.org/educational-programs

2011
Don't Ask, Don't Tell

In 1987, the J. Roderick MacArthur Foundation awarded a group called Alternatives to Militarism the first known grant to challenge military regulations on homosexual behavior. The topic worked its way into politics, and during the 1992 Presidential race Bill Clinton said he would be willing to sign an executive order permitting homosexuality in the armed forces. The compromise that eventually resulted, known as the "don't ask, don't tell" policy, went into effect in 1993.

Almost immediately, gay activists and their philanthropic supporters went to work to overturn all remaining strictures. The Servicemembers Legal Defense Network was created in 1993 and fueled by more than $7 million in foundation grants. It provided counsel to troops who ran afoul of the ban on open homosexual behavior, ran media campaigns against the rule, and organized the first legislative efforts to go beyond it. Similar work was carried out by other nonprofits operating with donations earmarked for this cause. The American Civil Liberties Union, Lambda Legal, the Gay and Lesbian Alliance Against Defamation, the Center for American Progress and others "played a critical role in mobilizing grassroots support, taking on early legal battles, monitoring media debates, and publishing position papers," according to the *Chronicle of Philanthropy*.

The most dogged and focused efforts on this front were carried out by the Center for the Study of Sexual Minorities in the Military, which changed its name to the Palm Center after receiving a $1 million contribution from the Michael Palm Foundation in 2006. The center produced a steady stream of papers criticizing "don't ask, don't tell" and circulated them through academe and the media. Their work was central to the 2011 establishment of a new policy protecting overt homosexuality in the military. Since overturning "don't ask," the Palm Center's main project has been to end strictures on transgender service and sex changes among military personnel.

Grants of more than $12 million were used to undo "don't ask, don't tell," with the Evelyn and Walter Haas Fund and the Wells Fargo, Gill, and Arcus foundations being other lead donors. Three quarters of that money was offered as super-flexible general operating funding. More than 20 donors supported the organizations leading the charge for at least five years in a row, with many of them loyally providing funds every year for over a decade.

Further reading

• *Chronicle of Philanthropy* reporting, philanthropy.com/article/Philanthropys-Military/128431

• Analysis by Palm Center director, *How We Won: Progressive Lessons from the Repeal of "Don't Ask, Don't Tell,"* howwewon.com

——————————— **2011** ———————————

Avoiding Meltdowns of Public Pensions

The public-pension gap—the retiree and health benefits that have been promised to government workers but not funded—is the single gravest economic threat to the U.S. today. That is the position of the Laura and John Arnold Foundation. It's a strong claim, but there are scary numbers behind it: unfunded state and local promises to civil servants now total a breathtaking $2 trillion.

There are ways out of that deep, deep hole—switching from defined-benefit to defined-contribution pensions (as almost all private companies did decades ago), asking public workers to make co-contributions and co-payments. But these are politically difficult reforms. To make them easier, the Arnold Foundation has offered its services around the country as a kind of *pro bono* think tank—helping states and cities calculate exactly how much they've overpromised, and then advising them on ways to stem their flood of red ink. The foundation offered important technical and communications help that allowed Rhode Island to pass the first major pension reform, heading off a Detroit-like disaster from taking place on the state level. Laura and John Arnold complemented that assistance with personal contributions in support of political leaders and groups fighting for pension reform.

Working with the Pew Center on the States, Arnold then offered research and other help to additional locales with runaway pension costs. Kentucky, San Jose, San Diego, Utah, and other jurisdictions acted. Many others are still scrambling, often with Arnold Foundation aid. In its first three years working on this subject, the foundation spent about $11 million to help formulate more sustainable pension policies, with much additional policy assistance to come. Election contributions to officeholders backing reform, from the Arnolds as individuals, came on top of that funding, and protected the project from being undermined by political opposition.

Further reading

• *Philanthropy* magazine article, philanthropyroundtable.org/topic/excellence_in_philanthropy/solving_the_2_trillion_problem

2013

A Bit of Diversity in the Faculty Lounge

The University of Colorado at Boulder is famous as a citadel of "progressivism," for which it is sometimes referred to as the "Berkeley of the Rockies." All faculty members, for instance, are encouraged to put a prepared statement in their initial class materials telling students they are free to choose a different gender pronoun for themselves if that would make them feel more comfortable.

Many universities offer courses on Marxist thought. In the hope of introducing missing perspectives into the university's teaching, and broadening political discussion on campus, a group of Boulder-area donors including local banker Earl Wright and former Boulder mayor Bob Greenlee proposed to fund within the political-science department a new position in Conservative Thought and Policy. After more than 20 area donors raised a million dollars, a three-year pilot-program was set up to bring a series of visiting scholars to campus on annual rotations.

Political scientist Steven Hayward, CU-Boulder's first Visiting Scholar of Conservative Thought and Policy, taught four classes during the 2013-2014 school year: two on Constitutional law, one on free-market environmentalism, and another on American political thought. He also organized more than a dozen debates and guest lectures that brought center-right scholars to campus. In the fall of 2014, the second visiting scholar arrived—Hillsdale College historian Bradley Birzer.

Further reading

• CU-Boulder announcement of Bradley Birzer appointment, colorado.edu/news/releases/2014/06/03/cu-boulder-appoints-bradley-j-birzer-second-visiting-scholar-conservative

2013

Supreme Assistance

The Searle Freedom Trust was founded in 1998 by Dan Searle with proceeds from the sale of the G. D. Searle pharmaceutical company. The foundation has been a major funder of university professors, supporting career development and detailed, esoteric, long-term research with the goal of bolstering academics working outside of reigning liberal orthodoxies. The trust has also been underwriting online higher education as a way to make college instruction less monolithic.

More recently, Searle has influenced public policy via support for important litigation. "Our biggest victories lately have come in the legal arena," says president Kim Dennis. "There have been numerous Supreme Court decisions that we helped to fund. These produced decisions in policy arenas as diverse as voting rights, environmental regulation, education, and health care."

"Of course these things can all be changed by one heart attack on the Supreme Court," notes Dennis. "But there are also state courts. There's a lot you can do in litigation."

Further reading

• *Shelby County v. Holder* opinion, supremecourt.gov/opinions/12pdf/12-96_6k47.pdf

• *Fisher v. University of Texas* opinion, supremecourtreview.com/case/11-345

• *King v. Burwell* docket, supremecourt.gov/search.aspx?filename=/docketfiles/14-114.htm

---

2014
Suing for Reform

Philanthropists have been funding lawsuits as a way to improve public policies for more than a century. Booker T. Washington secretly financed the *Giles v. Harris* case back in 1903, and throughout the rest of his life paid for other litigation aimed at undoing racial disenfranchisement. (See details at 1903 entry in this Annex.)

In this same spirit, Silicon Valley entrepreneur David Welch spent several million dollars between 2011 and 2014 building a court case that California's teacher-tenure laws—which grant permanent employment after just 18 months on the job, make it nearly impossible to fire even the most terrible teachers, and require school districts to lay teachers off based on seniority rather than competence—deprive students of the right to be educated as guaranteed by the state constitution.

Welch and his wife first tried traditional education philanthropy, giving money to bring new teaching methods and technology into schools. They soon realized that in many public schools, incompetent teachers made necessary educational improvements impossible. So in 2011 they founded a group called Students Matter and gathered facts about the forces blocking school reform.

Eventually David Welch found nine students who said their education suffered after they were stuck in classrooms with poor teachers. He hired a top-flight legal team to help them assemble a court case. He was also savvy enough to fund an accompanying public-relations campaign to fend off the massive counterattack by teacher unions that predictably followed.

In 2014 a judge of the Los Angeles Superior Court ruled that "there are a significant number of grossly ineffective teachers currently active in

California classrooms" and that this causes thousands of students to fall years behind in math and reading. "The evidence is compelling. Indeed, it shocks the conscience," wrote Judge Rolf Treu in his *Vergara v. State of California* decision striking down seniority-based job protections for unionized teachers.

The state appealed, a process that could take three years. Almost immediately, however, other philanthropists and education reformers began to consider similar donor-funded lawsuits in states like New York, Connecticut, New Jersey, New Mexico, Oregon, and elsewhere, aiming to eliminate rigid teacher tenure.

Further reading

• *Philanthropy* magazine article, philanthropyroundtable.org/topic/k_12_education/suing_for_reform

--------- **2014** ---------

A $250 Million Media Experiment

Pierre Omidyar, the billionaire founder of eBay, first pursued an interest in media operations that promote "good government" when he funded a digital "newspaper" devoted to investigative reporting, public policy, and politics in his home state of Hawaii. His appetite whetted, Omidyar considered buying the *Washington Post*, before fellow tech-tycoon and donor Jeff Bezos did so for $250 million in 2013. Instead, Omidyar decided to devote the same pile of money—$250 million—to create his own muckraking publications from scratch. In 2014 he unveiled his first venture: the *Intercept*, an online magazine devoted to "adversarial journalism on national security, criminal justice" and related topics. It was formed around a trio of hard-left reporter-commentators: Jeremy Scahill of the *Nation*, filmmaker Laura Poitras, and Glenn Greenwald, who led publication of the Edward Snowden leaks.

Omidyar's next publication was to be a scathing forum called *Racket* that would "attack Wall Street and the corporate world." Before the venture even published its first story, however, the attacker-in-chief hired by Omidyar to run the publication clashed with his bosses and was accused of sexual harassment by an underling. The venture collapsed and it was announced that the staff hired to run it would be let go.

One year after Omidyar's announcement that he was going to loose on the world a whole stable of digital news sites "that will cover topics ranging from entertainment and sports to business and the economy," the only functioning element was the *Intercept*, and the founding donor was at war with many of the journalistic crusaders he hoped to lead into society-altering news coverage. The effectiveness of this investment is thus yet to be seen. Its sheer size, however, and the interest it has sparked among other donors and a press corps obsessed with new media, guarantee that it will be looked back upon as a milestone in public-policy philanthropy, whether of a positive or negative sort.

Further reading

• *Philanthropy* magazine article, philanthropyroundtable.org/topic/excellence_in_ philanthropy/investigative_philanthropy

• Description of the collapse of *Racket* published by the *Intercept,* firstlook.org/ theintercept/2014/10/30/inside-story-matt-taibbis-departure-first-look-media

─────────────── **2014** ───────────────
Boosting Policy Instruction at U. Chicago

The national rankings of top graduate schools in public policy have held pretty steady for some years, centered on Syracuse University's Maxwell School, the Kennedy School at Harvard, Indiana University, University of Georgia, and the Woodrow Wilson School at Princeton. Recent philanthropic gifts aim to move another entity up that list. The University of Chicago's Harris School of Public Policy is a relative newcomer established in 1988 (thanks to leadership and an endowment gift from businessman Irving Harris). It enrolled 410 graduate students in 2014, and is particularly known for its quantitative training. In 2014, DeVry University co-founder Dennis Keller donated $20 million, and the family of Irving Harris gave another $12.5 million, to build a new home for the graduate school. This will allow expansions into leadership training, with the goal of anointing more trailblazers in public policy.

Further reading

• *Chicago Tribune* reporting on gifts, carrollcountytimes.com/news/ct-university-chicago-harris-school-met-20141105,0,5224617.story

─────────────── **2014** ───────────────
$50 Million for Gun Control

Though he is no longer mayor of New York City, Michael Bloomberg continues to nudge public policy—these days as a donor. In 2014 he put up $50 million to create an educational nonprofit (with separate lobbying and campaign-donation arms) to push for stricter gun control. To put that in perspective, $50 million is about two and a half times what the National Rifle Association spent that same year to campaign for gun-owner rights.

In the run-up to the 2014 election, Bloomberg's groups surveyed candidates on gun issues, and bought millions of dollars of TV issue ads. The allied political action committee made campaign donations to selected candidates at the state and federal levels. *Ad Age* calculated that Bloomberg's money allowed gun-control groups to outspend gun-owner groups by 7:1 on television advertising.

Even still, gun controllers didn't do well in the 2014 election. Bloomberg is swimming against some inhospitable policy currents. According to the Pew Research Center, public support for gun control has deteriorated steadily over the last two decades. When asked "Is it more important to control gun ownership or protect the right of Americans to own guns?" the public flipped from favoring gun control 57-34 percent in 1993, to favoring gun-ownership rights 52-46 percent in 2014. A sharp drop in the rate of murder committed with firearms—from 6.6 victims to 3.2 victims per 100,000 population, between 1993 and 2011—corresponds with a large rise in gun ownership during that same period. Americans owned 310 million firearms in 2009, up from 192 million in 1994.

Further reading

• *Washington Post* analysis, washingtonpost.com/blogs/wonkblog/wp/2014/04/16/can-michael-bloomberg-really-build-a-gun-control-lobby-bigger-than-the-nra

• Congressional Research Service study of gun ownership vs. murder rates, fas.org/sgp/crs/misc/RL32842.pdf

---

2014

Keeping the Lights on in Detroit

Detroit may be America's most ill-governed, and saddest, city. That's the public's verdict: The city's population plummeted from 1.9 million in 1950 to just 689,000 in 2013, the year Detroit filed the nation's largest-ever municipal bankruptcy, estimating that it was $20 billion in debt.

Private philanthropies have tried for years to stanch the worst of Detroit's bleeding. The only streetlights that work in Midtown are the ones paid for by the Hudson-Webber Foundation. In 2013, the Kresge Foundation and some partners donated 100 police cars to the city (where the average response time on a 911 call is 58 minutes). These and other donors poured at least $628 million into the city between 2007 and 2011, particularly hoping to soften life for children and other innocent victims of the misgovernance, and to spark a bit of private-sector economic activity.

In late 2014, a coalition of 15 foundations—both local and national—plus some corporate and individual donors pledged $466 million to shore up the city's insolvent pension system and transfer the Detroit Institute of Arts from city to nonprofit ownership, so that its great works and building wouldn't have to be sold for cash. This philanthropic help was the key to negotiation of a grand bargain of concessions, cuts, and contributions that allowed the city to emerge from bankruptcy. Whether Detroit will ever become a healthy community again remains to be seen, but the donors who had been protecting city residents for decades at least gave the city and the state breathing space to create more responsible and sustainable public policies.

Further reading

- *Philanthropy* magazine article, philanthropyroundtable.org/topic/excellence_in_philanthropy/philanthropy_keeps_the_lights_on_in_detroit
- *Detroit News* report on first payments," detroitnews.com/story/news/local/wayne-county/2014/12/11/first-payment-made-toward-detroits-grand-bargain/20240369

INDEX

ABOUT THE PHILANTHROPY ROUNDTABLE

The Philanthropy Roundtable is America's leading network of charitable donors working to strengthen our free society, uphold donor intent, and protect the freedom to give. Our members include individual philanthropists, families, corporations, and private foundations.

Mission

The Philanthropy Roundtable's mission is to foster excellence in philanthropy, to protect philanthropic freedom, to assist donors in achieving their philanthropic intent, and to help donors advance liberty, opportunity, and personal responsibility in America and abroad.

Principles

- Philanthropic freedom is essential to a free society
- A vibrant private sector generates the wealth that makes philanthropy possible
- Voluntary private action offers solutions to many of society's most pressing challenges
- Excellence in philanthropy is measured by results, not by good intentions
- A respect for donor intent is essential to long-term philanthropic success

Services

World-class conferences

The Philanthropy Roundtable connects you with other savvy donors. Held across the nation throughout the year, our meetings assemble grantmakers and experts to develop strategies for excellent local, state, and national giving. You will hear from innovators in K–12 education, economic opportunity, higher education, national security, and other fields. Our Annual Meeting is the Roundtable's flagship event, gathering the nation's most public-spirited and influential philanthropists for debates, how-to sessions, and discussions on the best ways for private individuals to achieve powerful results through their giving. The Annual Meeting is a stimulating and enjoyable way to meet principled donors seeking the breakthroughs that can solve our nation's greatest challenges.

Breakthrough groups

Our Breakthrough groups—focused program areas—build a critical mass of donors around a topic where dramatic results are within reach. Breakthrough groups become a springboard to help donors achieve lasting effects from their philanthropy. Our specialized staff of experts helps grantmakers invest with care. The Roundtable's K–12 education program is our largest and longest-running Breakthrough group. This network helps donors zero in on today's most promising school reforms. We are the industry-leading convener for philanthropists seeking systemic improvements through competition and parental choice, administrative freedom and accountability, student-centered technology, enhanced teaching and school leadership, and high standards and expectations for students of all backgrounds. We foster productive collaboration among donors of varied ideological perspectives who are united by a devotion to educational excellence.

A powerful voice

The Roundtable's public-policy project, the Alliance for Charitable Reform (ACR), works to advance the principles and preserve the rights of private giving. ACR educates legislators and policymakers about the central role of charitable giving in American life and the crucial importance of protecting philanthropic freedom—the ability of individuals and private organizations to determine how and where to direct their charitable assets. Active in Washington, D.C., and in the states, ACR protects charitable giving, defends the diversity of charitable causes, and battles intrusive government regulation. We believe the capacity of private initiative to address national problems must not be burdened with costly or crippling constraints.

Protection of donor interests

The Philanthropy Roundtable is the leading force in American philanthropy to protect donor intent. Generous givers want assurance that their money will be used for the specific charitable aims and purposes they believe in, not redirected to some other agenda. Unfortunately, donor intent is usually violated in increments, as foundation staff and trustees neglect or misconstrue the founder's values and drift into other purposes. Through education, practical guidance, legislative action, and individual consultation, The Philanthropy Roundtable is active in guarding donor intent. We are happy to advise you on steps you can take to ensure that your mission and goals are protected.

Must-read publications
Philanthropy, the Roundtable's quarterly magazine, is packed with useful and beautifully written real-life stories. It offers practical examples, inspiration, detailed information, history, and clear guidance on the differences between giving that is great and giving that disappoints. We also publish a series of guidebooks that provide detailed information on the very best ways to be effective in particular aspects of philanthropy. These guidebooks are compact, brisk, and readable. Most focus on one particular area of giving—for instance, teaching, charter schools, support for veterans, anti-poverty programs, and other topics of interest to grant makers Real-life examples, hard numbers, management experiences of other donors, recent history, and policy guidance are presented to inform and inspire savvy donors.

Join the Roundtable!
When working with The Philanthropy Roundtable, members are better equipped to achieve long-lasting success with their charitable giving. Your membership in the Roundtable will make you part of a potent network that understands philanthropy and strengthens our free society. Philanthropy Roundtable members range from Forbes 400 individual givers and the largest American foundations to small family foundations and donors just beginning their charitable careers. Our members include:

- Individuals and families
- Private foundations
- Community foundations
- Venture philanthropists
- Corporate giving programs
- Large operating foundations and charities that devote more than half of their budget to external grants

Philanthropists who contribute at least $100,000 annually to charitable causes are eligible to become members of the Roundtable and register for most of our programs. Roundtable events provide you with a solicitation-free environment.

For more information on The Philanthropy Roundtable or to learn about our individual program areas, please call (202) 822-8333 or e-mail main@PhilanthropyRoundtable.org.

ABOUT THE AUTHORS

John J. Miller is director of the Dow Journalism Program at Hillsdale College. He is also national correspondent for *National Review* and the author of five books, including *A Gift of Freedom: How the John M. Olin Foundation Changed America* and *The Big Scrum: How Teddy Roosevelt Saved Football*. He is a contributing editor for *Philanthropy* and the author of *Strategic Investment in Ideas: How Two Foundations Reshaped America*, a Philanthropy Roundtable monograph. In 2009, he founded the Student Free Press Association, which promotes campus journalism through its website, TheCollegeFix.com, as well as internship programs.

Karl Zinsmeister is a vice president at The Philanthropy Roundtable and the author of several books and hundreds of articles. From 2006 to 2009 he served in the White House as the President's chief domestic policy adviser. He has had many first-hand experiences in public-policy philanthropy—from working in Africa with Operation Crossroads (see 1958 entry in Annex), to serving as Research Director of the Working Seminar on Family and American Welfare Policy (see Chapter 1), to a current effort to design with philanthropic funding a better system for assisting wounded warriors.

Ashley May is managing editor of *Philanthropy* magazine, where she has written on donor-funded public-policy litigation, anti-poverty philanthropy, philanthropic efforts to encourage entrepreneurship, and other topics. She previously worked at the American Enterprise Institute for Public Policy Research and Calvin College. She is a graduate of Wheaton College.